BRINGING UP DADDY

BRINGING UP DADDY

Fatherhood and Masculinity in Post-War Hollywood

Stella Bruzzi

 Publishing

To my father Stefano and to the memory of my mother Zara.

First published in 2005 by the
BRITISH FILM INSTITUTE
21 Stephen Street, London W1T 1LN

The British Film Institute's purpose is to champion moving image culture in all its
richness and diversity across the UK, for the benefit of as wide an audience as
possible, and to create and encourage debate.

Cover image: *To Kill a Mockingbird* (Robert Mulligan, 1962) Pakula-Mulligan
Productions/Brentwood Productions/Universal Pictures
Cover design: Paul Wright
Set by Fakenham Photosetting Ltd, Fakenham, Norfolk
Printed in the UK by St Edmundsbury Press, Bury St Edmunds, Suffolk

British Library Cataloguing-in-Publication Data
A catalogue record for this book is available from the British Library

ISBN 1–84457–110–6 (pbk)
ISBN 1–84457–109–2 (hbk)

Contents

Acknowledgments

At the BFI I would like to thank above all Sophia Contento for seeing this project through to completion so expertly and with such tremendous patience and dedication. I am also immensely grateful to the Arts and Humanities Research Council for their financial support of the project and to the expertise of the BFI Library staff. Numerous friends and colleagues have also helped over the time it has taken me to finish this book. In particular I would like to extend warmest thanks to Pamela Church Gibson, who read an early draft of the manuscript, and to Mandy Merck for her excellent copy editing of the Introduction (although any errors outstanding are entirely my own). I am also grateful to those who attended research seminars at Royal Holloway and the Universities of Kent, Reading and Roehampton for their thoughtful feedback. My biggest debt is to Michael Walker, who was so generous with his time and offered me such expert advice throughout this project; our many discussions transformed Chapter 1 and made a huge impact on the rest of the book. On a personal note I, once again, could not have got to the end of this without my family: my children Frank and Phyllis (whose birth held up the completion of this book) and their wonderful dad Mick.

Introduction

There is a universal road sign – slightly different in each country, but nevertheless bearing the same significance – that has always intrigued me. It depicts a tall, old-fashioned father holding onto a much tinier girl, presumably a daughter. Although it has been modified over time, this image is unabashedly nostalgic. In most versions, there is a formality to the cut of the father's clothes and he is still sometimes wearing a hat, a custom that went out in the 1950s; his daughter is as quintessentially feminine as he is manly, always in a dress and frequently wearing an oversize ribbon in her hair. In a few versions, one of her legs is bent slightly at the knee, an often seen little girl pose connoting a certain coquettishness, as if she is pleased to have her father to herself or pleased that she is being seen with him. This sign often appears along bigger roads and in slightly hazardous places; there is one I pass on the way to work on the side of a dual carriageway – four lanes of traffic and a central barrier. The image says many things and the interaction of genders and ages in it brings clichéd, traditional scenarios to mind; for example, that the girl looks secure clutching her father's big hand, while he looks confident and in control. They are not rushing; maybe out for a Sunday stroll while mother makes lunch. Why, though, is this father – the person to whom this sweet thing in her dress and patent leather shoes, her hair done just so has been entrusted – contemplating the foolhardy act of crossing four lanes of fifty miles per hour traffic with his daughter in the first place?

The term 'father' can signify many things. As in the different permutations of this road sign, the father can be both awesome and inept, polarities that inform, actually, much of Hollywood's attitude to fathers. 'Father' is a word that signals the actual individual who takes on the paternal role within a family, although even here the meanings are various. 'Father', for instance, is very different in tenor to 'dad': more formal, less comforting. But what is it to be a father? The phrase 'to father a child' refers to merely the act of successful insemination, although to 'be a father' suggests some measure of nurturing and familial involvement. However, 'father' is also a more abstract, nebulous term than 'dad'; the father, but not the dad, can be a symbolic ideal. Robert Bly in *Iron John* distils the troubles of modern masculinity down to the fact that 'There is not enough father' (Bly 1990: 92), for to Bly, modern masculinity has lost its way because the father's role, traditionally the provider of ballast for that masculinity, has been forgotten. Here, the term 'father' starts to denote 'traditional masculinity', a view of the importance of the father compatible with the older psychological and psychoanalytic belief that the father was the font of all neuroses and the main figure in an individual's unconscious. In Bly's usage, the father becomes an archetype and as such comes to resonate with what our expectations of the symbolic father might be; expectations only tenuously linked to any actual person or working reality.

To return to the road sign: the father in it is iconic. The way he looks aligns him with conservative values and traditionalism; he doesn't want us to question gender roles, he is still the protector and head of the household. In the early years of the new millennium, such an image of the father is idealised and hopelessly outmoded; now, one in two American or British marriages end in divorce and the nuclear family to which this traditional father belongs is no longer the undisputed social norm. The connotations of foolishness and ineptitude that the road sign also carries – that the father is a fool to be jeopardising his daughter's life by tackling a busy road in the first place – are more to do with the actual as opposed to the symbolic father. So often, in life as well as in movies, the real father is a disappointment. The road sign contains both the illusion and the reality of the father figure; both what he aspires to be and what he is.

Hollywood has produced a multitude of films that feature important father figures, but they have rarely been discussed as such. As I conceived of this book, this silence surrounding a fertile and common subject within cinema struck me as odd, as conversely, there exist various articles and books that discuss motherhood and cinema (Kaplan 1992) or the family and film (Traube 1992; Harwood 1997). Having now written this book, I consider this silence to be odd but meaningful. Richard Dyer has remarked of male sexuality that it 'is a bit like air – you breathe it in all the time, but you aren't aware of it much' (Dyer 1985: 28). Since the mid-1980s when Dyer wrote this, there has been a burgeoning of writing about male sexuality, masculinity and the male body. Although within Masculinity Studies in general fathers too have been part of these critical discussions, within Film Studies the father is still 'a bit like air' – omnipresent but rarely talked about. The omission of any sustained analysis of the father within Cinema Studies has guided the approach I've taken here, and it is to my rationale that I now turn.

The purposes of this book are twofold: to offer a historical analysis of Hollywood's representation of the father since World War II and to suggest within this chronology particular themes, arguments or motifs that recur and which, though sometimes compatible with social and cultural history, are not necessarily bound by or subservient to it. I have conceived of this book as a starting point for further discussion about the father in cinema; in that it spans several decades, it is intended as an introduction, in that it offers a historical contextualisation and a theorisation of the father figure, it also offers a critical interpretation of the father and many of the films to which he is key. My selection of films is intended to be logical, not arbitrary. Individual films have been singled out for more sustained discussion because they are somehow representative: of either prevailing social/cultural attitudes to fathers and fatherhood or of Hollywood's own attitudes to fathers and fatherhood. This book charts a journey through several decades of mainstream American film-making and, as such, endeavours to point out trends and important nuances that link films and provide an overall picture of the decades under discussion. This does not mean that anomalous, anachronistic or forgotten films are excluded, although I wanted to ensure that this book wasn't made up of idiosyncratic textual readings.

With this in mind, I should also say something about what I consider a relevant 'father film' to be. Thinking about more current films, a distinction exists between those films that offer active discussions of fatherhood and those that merely happen to have fathers in them. This book concludes with films made around the millennium and so does not encompass the most recent films. However, by way of contemporary examples, whereas *Catch Me If You Can* (2002) or *The Day after Tomorrow* (2004) would be considered films that actively discuss the father, the remake of *Cheaper by the Dozen* (2003) is a film that just happens to have a father in it. Although the first two movies do not focus on fathers in the way *Kramer vs. Kramer* (1979) does (very few films do), they both offer an involved discussion of fatherhood as an issue: what it means to be a father, what the absence of the fathers has meant to their sons, how these sons become reconciled with their fathers, to which one could add how their romanticised claims about fatherhood are more generally reflective of Hollywood's patriarchal tendencies. In *Cheaper by the Dozen*, Steve Martin plays a father who is in virtually every scene in the film. Despite this, *Cheaper by the Dozen* is not concerned with issues of fatherhood; it is a comedy intrigued by the comic permutations of having twelve children and generalised issues of parenting. There is one scene (between Martin and his temporarily disaffected eldest son) in which fathering is talked about, and then only fleetingly.

It is what the father comes to mean as well as how he is portrayed that interest me, and as a result of this *Bringing Up Daddy* examines narrative treatments of the father figure, not only in relation to other films but also in relation to social, cultural and political history. Having said this, films are not used as transparent means of accessing or reflecting socio-political context as they are, for example, in a study such as Quart and Auster's *American Film and Society Since 1945* (2002). The relationship between the cinematic fathers and their historical context is complex, often contradictory, as Hollywood at times reflects but at others goes against contemporaneous social trends. Historically it became apparent that, for example, there was an oscillation (though not an overly rigid one) between traditionalism and liberalism in American attitudes to the father that could be charted from decade to decade: the later 1940s espoused relatively radical opinions of the father, while the 1950s championed traditionalism; the 1960s and 1970s saw this traditionalism broken down, while the 1980s sought to reinstate it; and finally in the 1990s and 2000s, there has been a return to more liberal attitudes, with a further relaxation of gender divisions and a considerable broadening and redefinition of the father's image and role. Hollywood's portrayals of the father have both followed and gone against these trends. Thus, alongside the entwining of Hollywood and history, I have also sought to map the history of Hollywood's own configuration of the father, the narrative patterns, themes, parables and archetypes it repeats over the decades. It is nevertheless impossible to view these recurrent images as entirely independent, as so many of them are necessarily informed by outside forces – not just sociology and political history but also psychology and gender theory.

As a means of managing such eclectic material, each chapter centres on roughly a decade, although Chapter 1 focuses more on the post-war (1945–50) years than the wartime films and Chapter 3 spans the two decades of sexual revolution and women's liberation (1960–79). The portrait of fatherhood that emerges over the post-war decades is both predictable and surprising. In the 1940s, only a few films reflect directly the generally acknowledged truism that women (on both sides of the Atlantic) had become more financially and politically independent, leading to a steep rise in the rate of divorce and to more vulnerable, less secure images of masculinity. The fathering models pervasively proposed by psychologists and sociologists at the time were fundamentally compatible with this new gender balance, but despite Hollywood's subsequent interest in the 'new father', only a few films in the 1940s make reference to his immediate post-war incarnation. A similarly ambivalent relationship to background history exists in the films of the 1950s. Throughout its post-war history, Hollywood uses the 1950s as shorthand for conformity and conservatism, its affluence and anti-liberalism conjured up by the breadwinner fathers of *Pleasantville* (1998) and other films exclaiming 'Honey, I'm home' as they stride through the door after a day at the office, placing their trilby on the hat stand in the hall. The brash machismo and the resurgence of the nuclear family during the Eisenhower era, however, come out not through films about confident breadwinner fathers (most of which Hollywood portrays as miserable, confused or depressed) but more tangentially through films (often Westerns, and so set in the past) about larger-than-life fathers – awesome, omnipotent tycoons who rule not just their families but their ranch, town and surrounding countryside.

In general, the 1960s and 1970s reversed the 1950s' trend towards detached, traditional fathers, chiming with and sometimes directly reflecting feminism's call for men and fathers to abandon their patriarchal roles and become more involved nurturers. Alternative family models were proposed (Germaine Greer's notion of the idyllic Tuscan commune in *The Female Eunuch* [1993] being one of the most appealing) and Hollywood, in part, demonstrated and narrativised the problems with the conventional family structure. Three big Hollywood films released as early as 1962–5 (*To Kill a Mockingbird* [1962], *The Courtship of Eddie's Father* [1962] and *The Sound of Music* [1965]) centre on a lone, widowed father and the direct influence of the gender revolution undertaken in the 1960s and 1970s continues to be evident in later films such as *Kramer vs. Kramer*, another lone father movie and probably the most discussed father film of all time. Both historically and in Hollywood the 1980s saw a return to the ideology of the 1950s, sometimes quite consciously, as with Marty McFly's nostalgic time travelling in *Back to the*

Future (1985). Susan Jeffords in *Hard Bodies: Hollywood Masculinity in the Reagan Era* (1994) posits a direct link between the decade's politics and the type of masculinity found in American films of the time: Reagan's policies were macho and 'hard', as were the men in the movies. Although I have also used many other points of reference, this equation holds true for the representation of fathers in the 1980s: the sensitive, 'soft' dads of films such as *Ordinary* People (1980), *Author! Author!* (1982) and *Mr Mom* (1983) stop appearing about 1983, when action films, war films and money films take over. The father has a minimal and often oppositional role in such films, a figure not just of conformity and conservatism but also of safety and compromise. In this, as in so many other ways, *Fatal Attraction* (1987) is the quintessential 1980s' Hollywood product. Against this backdrop, how then does one explain the emergence at the end of the 1980s of the new man? Jeffords sees films such as *Three Men and a Baby* (1987) and *Look Who's Talking* (1989) as charting the termination of masculinity (see Jeffords 1993b and 1994: 166), but this is both premature and sweeping, as the 1990s subsequently attest.

At the century's end, Hollywood does indeed permit the questioning of traditional gender and family roles as well as traditional politics, but the greater plurality of its representations of the father (notably black and gay Dads appear alongside the wildly different forms of traditional masculinity and fatherhood in films as generically diverse as *Legends of the Fall* [1994] and *Gladiator* [2000]) suggest, quite rightly, that the machismo of the 1980s no longer predominates. Instead, the 1970s' dream of alternative, less prescriptive gender definitions has infiltrated films about fathers – would-be authoritative fathers such as the one in *Affliction* (1997) are ostracised, fathers become overtly sexual, they become romantic protagonists, they are often divorced or bringing up children alone. This diversification of the father's image is entirely compatible with what is going on in the 1990s–2000s in terms of gender politics and with the emergence of a significant body of theoretical, psychological and sociological work into masculinity, a hitherto largely ignored field. In both films and theory, traditional masculinity and fathers are in crisis and new, more flexible and radical alternatives are being sought.

I try throughout this book to convey a period's dominant tone, without wanting to impose onto each chapter an overly prescriptive schema. I have striven for cohesion but have deliberately not constructed a false homogeneity for the entire book. Very few father films are overtly political or based on fact and so are not windows on the world; their relationship to history is fluid, often equivocal, even contradictory. So, some films may reflect the mood of a period while remaining historically anachronistic. Take, for example, *A River Runs Through It* (1992), one of three films Robert Redford has directed to date (alongside *Ordinary People* and *Quiz Show* [1994]) directly concerned with fathering. Set in Montana in 1910, its narrative centres on two sons and their relationships with their parents, most importantly their father, Reverend Maclean, a Presbyterian minister. The family's history is narrated by Norman (Aidan Quinn), the more dutiful brother and concludes with the death of his wilder brother Paul (Brad Pitt). Reverend Maclean seldom discusses Paul after his death, although the voice-over confirms that he was always there in his father's sermons. The film concludes with the last of these, during which the old reverend talks to his congregation about being able to love someone completely without fully understanding them. What is the relationship of a film as seemingly tangential as *A River Runs Through It* to a historical study of fathers and Hollywood? Its setting is superficially unconnected to the 1990s, as is its subject; one could make a historical case for the film on the grounds of Redford's interest in the father, adding an auteurist/historical adjunct onto the overall thesis, but the film's real significance lies in what it conveys about Hollywood's own history of representing the father. *A River Runs Through It* adopts and illustrates several Hollywood conventions: it revolves around two very different brothers and is one of numerous Hollywood reworkings of the story of the prodigal son; it makes the dutiful son into the spokesman for an emotionally and psychologically reticent father; and in terms of when it was made, *A River Runs Through It* forms part of a band of otherwise disparate films which represent a desire for a return to the traditional father (see Chapter 5). The film's relevance to this book is that it resonates with Hollywood's own history rather than with what was being said about fathers and families in the 1990s.

Comparing *A River Runs Through It* to *Regarding Henry* (1991), released the year before, highlights the complexity of Hollywood's interrelationship to history. *Regarding Henry* is, on the surface, even more inconsequential, romantic and mawkish. But, whereas *A River Runs Through It* has received scant attention from film scholars, *Regarding Henry* has received a reasonable amount, certainly more than it deserves. The reason for this is that *Regarding Henry*'s saccharine indictment of 1980s' hyper-masculinity and the decade's 'lunch is for wimps' mentality was effortlessly compatible with what was being said about men and fatherhood in the press and literature of the early 1990s, namely that the ambitious, detached father should return to his home and family and learn to be a dad again. In terms of historical development, this is one of the key trajectories adopted both within and outside Hollywood: that to be a good father meant being there, being at home, knowing your kids. While both *A River Runs Through It* and *Regarding Henry* illustrate tendencies within Hollywood's history, in the latter these tendencies further reflect other socio-political and historical concerns.

Sometimes, as with Redford's film here, the role of history is tenuous, although the role of Hollywood history is not. Having said this, there are general historical changes, discernible in the films I discuss, that even *A River Runs Through It* conforms to. For example, while Hollywood never abandoned the traditional father (the breadwinner, the authoritative father, the masculine father) the very fact that the women's liberation movement happened has made it impossible for representations of the father not to in some way signal this – whether it is through the use of irony, self-conscious stereotyping or stressing the traditional father's maladjustment or anguish.

In attempting both to offer a historical contextualisation for father films and to convey through my analyses of such films the mood and tone of the times, I am indebted to the work of many non-film academics for giving me an understanding of that history, particularly Susan Faludi, Stephanie Coontz and Robert Griswold. I have also undertaken considerable primary research, principally the reading of newspapers, magazines and film reviews and the viewing of documentary films and newsreels. The emphasis placed on each of these differs from chapter to chapter. While there are several allusions made to American women's magazines such as *McCall's* in the earlier chapters, there are very few mentions of these publications made from the mid-1960s on. The reason for this is simply that, while *McCall's* especially had a lot to say about men, gender relations and fathers in the 1940s and 1950s, after the publication at the beginning of the 1960s of *The Feminine Mystique* (in which *McCall's* is criticised explicitly), the magazines seemed to retreat into the traditional, hyper-feminine cocoon Friedan (1963) had – not always accurately – accused them of inhabiting. Similarly, although I have made less use of American newspapers in the early chapters, I follow specific debates contained within their pages from the 1960s to the present, when the historical changes in attitudes to fathers and fathering coincided more obviously with specific social and political events.

Alongside a desire to contextualise Hollywood's portrayal of the father within a broader historical framework, there is the issue of how to approach the father theoretically. Perhaps the most contentious aspect of the book is its use of psychoanalysis, particularly Freud, but the idea of writing a book about the father in Hollywood without recourse to Freudian thinking is perverse; the recurring motifs and themes one finds in Hollywood's father films, the repeated stories and scenarios are so often indebted to Freud. For a variety of reasons we are currently still experiencing a backlash against ahistorical, arbitrarily imposed (or so it is argued) psychoanalytic theory. There are nevertheless many reasons to use psychoanalysis in a study such as this, despite the charge (levelled at psychoanalytic film criticism as early as the mid-1970s by Claire Johnston) that psychoanalysis can blur our engagement with political-cultural issues (see Creed 1998: 86). It is true, as Creed, in her introduction to film and psychoanalysis in *The Oxford Guide to Film Studies*, goes on to argue, that the 'grand narratives' of psychoanalysis (she cites the Oedipus complex and castration anxiety) 'dominated critical activity in the 1970s and early 1980s, running the real danger of sacrificing historical issues in favour of those related to the formation of subjectivity and its relation to ideology' (86). But what do you do with a subject that, by its very nature, centres on father–son anxieties and male fears of abandonment and loss? Freud's 'grand narratives' are explicitly identified, narrativised and elucidated by many of the films under scrutiny here. However, I have tried to do two things: to limit the bulk of my use of psychoanalysis to the early portion of this book – the main concentration of psychoanalytic debate is Chapter 2 (the 1950s) – so that Freud's ideas about the father can be developed logically and so that these psychoanalytic frameworks are there as reference points for later chapters, without having to be repeated endlessly; and to use, where possible, writing that is contemporary to the films under discussion. Thus, Lacan's notion of the Name-of-the-Father, which he began articulating in the 1950s, is applied to the father films of that decade, as it is in the movies of that decade that the father's actual name plays a particularly prominent role.

This convenient marriage of history and psychoanalysis is not always possible, especially in the case of Freud. Freud's articulation of the father's significance to the human psyche, however, was a formative element in shaping the theoretical arguments in this book, so his relevance to this study cannot be overstated. The Hollywood father (in the present but most of all in the past) would make little psychological sense – and would be of diminished interest – without recourse to Freud's theories of the primal father, the Oedipus complex, the development of the ego and id, narcissism and masculinity, the uncanny and the development of sexuality. In the late 1940s and 1950s the Freudian father–child relationship is particularly in evidence: films populated by tycoons, fathers obsessed with their name and matters of inheritance and genealogy, fathers who are killed by fearful and ungrateful sons or fathers who destroy familial relationships because they refuse to assume the father's responsibility and relinquish their sexual desires. With the rise of gender politics in the 1960s, Freud came under attack and his views of masculinity were, though formative, superseded. The broader school of psychology, however, remains the crucial foundation for later thinking on masculinity and fatherhood; without Freud, the writing in the 1990s about men and masculinity would remain obscure and unintelligible, because it was initially through him that we have come to understand what constitutes the traditional father.

Before turning to the whole debate of masculinity and cinema, there is something else that is important and has arisen from my reading of Freud, namely the divergence between the actual and the symbolic father. There is within Freud's own writing a noted difference between the weaker and less adept fathers of the case studies and the strong, authoritarian Oedipal father (see Verhaeghe 2000); the former are actual, real fathers while the latter is their symbolic ideal. Hollywood likewise wants to believe, more often than not, in the symbolic father – what a father would like to be – over his actual, working counterpart, although this awesome primal father increasingly comes under attack. It goes without saying that, in order to contain the number of films to be discussed, the films tackled here all feature an actual father, not only a symbolic one. I do not talk about the 'father' in the purely abstract; the closest I get to this is discussing films in which the father, though immensely important, is dead (although these films, such as *A Few Good Men* [1992], are not examined at length). Otherwise, the films have, as one of the central characters, a father who exists – the biological father, the male primary carer who is not the biological father, the surrogate father and so on.

The division of fatherly experience between what men actually do as fathers and what they would like to represent as fathers is acted out in a multitude of ways: from disappointment with men who are ordinary (the painfulness of *The Man in the Gray Flannel Suit* [1956]) to the exaltation of men who acquire a symbolic importance through death or detachment (*Fort Apache* [1948], *Backdraft* [1991] and many in between). Perhaps most importantly, both Freud and Hollywood have, for all the alternatives that have been presented along the way, exhibited an over-attachment to the traditional father. One consideration, usefully supported by reference to Freud, is whether or not a film has the father as its hero or is a film about a father as seen through the eyes of a child, usually a son. The vast majority of Hollywood films – like Freud's case histories and theories – fall into the latter category, and there are surprisingly few films in which the father is the hero or the figure with which we most readily identify. *The Search* (1948), *To Kill a Mockingbird*, *Kramer vs. Kramer*, *Parenthood* (1989), *Boyz n the Hood* (1991), *A Perfect World* (1993) and *Mrs Doubtfire* (1993) offer a motley bunch of such examples. One reason for the relative lack of identificatory father figures is that Hollywood Dads rarely engage in conversations about their feelings or about being a father (in fact emotional inarticulacy is a common trait among Hollywood's traditional fathers). Consequentially, the father is more likely to be the focus of identification when he has been propelled into a situation that necessitates such talking, such as when he becomes the lone or the surrogate father.

This is one example of Hollywood having constructed its own history of the father that is only partially explained through psychoanalysis or historical context. Over the decades, recurrent motifs and tendencies have emerged. Father–son movies vastly outnumber father–daughter movies and it is usually through a turbulent relationship with his son that a father's role is scrutinised and explained. The sons, in turn, manifest extreme responses towards these fathers, wanting to destroy them, become them (sometimes both at once) or wanting to effect a final reconciliation with an alienated father, often as he lies in bed ill or dying. The surrogate father frequently emerges as a more expert parent than his biological counterpart, although convention dictates that he must in the end renounce the child in his care and remain subservient to the biological parent's dominance (there are a few exceptions to this rule, *Three Men and a Little Lady* [1990], for example). In another attempt to restore the traditional family, a widowed or divorced father is frequently helped by his children to choose a suitable replacement mother/wife and, in Hollywood, the good father is idealised in a way the good mother never has been.

There are an almost unmanageable number of films about fathers produced in Hollywood since the war (the most fertile periods were the 1950s and the 1990s/2000s), but the way in which psychoanalysis has been incorporated into film theory (particularly when used to explain masculinity) suggests reasons for the lack of a sustained study of the Hollywood father to date. In the wake of Laura Mulvey and the psychoanalytic criticism of the 1970s came discussions of men and masculinity. Joan Mellen's *Big Bad*

Wolves: Masculinity in the American Film appeared in 1977, but it took a while for this study to be added to, masculinity only really becoming a significant topic for discussion in relation to film after the publication of two articles written in the early 1980s: Steve Neale's 'Masculinity as Spectacle' (1983) and Richard Dyer's 'Male Sexuality in the Media' (1985). These essays have, in different ways, dictated the path taken by the study of masculinity in cinema.

'Masculinity as Spectacle' has been republished repeatedly, cited and critiqued, and rightly so, for it finally initiated the theoretical discussion of masculinity within film studies. But if Neale established the ground rules for how masculinity in cinema was to be examined, he also laid out the reasons for the continuing silence around the role of the father. Because he takes as his template Mulvey's 'Visual Pleasure and Narrative Cinema' (1985), Neale's arguments about men are almost exclusively body-centred, cementing the belief that the theorisation of gender in cinema is inextricably bound to issues of eroticisation and display. So, male stars, like female stars are in Mulvey, are analysed in terms of masochism, vulnerability, image and the deflection of the erotic gaze; Mulvey's theoretical framework for understanding Hollywood's phallocentric representation of women simply being applied by Neale (and later others) to men. Some writers since have criticised the monolithic, inflexible notion of sexual difference set up by Mulvey and Neale (see Lehman 1993), but it has still predominated. Susan Jeffords in *Hard Bodies* (1994) likewise discusses masculinity in Hollywood cinema in terms of the body, muscle and 'hardness', as does Yvonne Tasker in *Spectacular Bodies: Gender, Genre and the Action Cinema* (1993b), an examination of the Hollywood action film.

Neale alludes to a lot of Westerns, gladiatorial combat films and films in which men are put on display (*Saturday Night Fever* [1977], *Le Samouraï* [1967]); Mellen's cover positions drawings of James Dean, Clint Eastwood, Humphrey Bogart, John Wayne and Clark Gable in front of a silhouette of a wolf's head; Tasker's cover man is the 'muscles from Brussels', Jean-Claude van Damme and Jeffords' sits Ronald Reagan's aging but cheerful head on top of an Arnold Schwarzenegger-sized torso. What do these have in common? The vast majority of them are 'men's men' – swaggering images of machismo and physicality. However, the fact that their bodies are on display rather than hidden also brings out the 'homosocialism' of these ostensibly heterosexual images, Eve Sedgwick's term for the sort of male bonding that denies homosexual intent while allowing intimacy and camaraderie. In these examples, the male body becomes the evocation and representation of the phallus, an over-simplified equation between body and male sexuality critiqued by Dyer when he examines the discrepancy between 'what penises are actually like' and the 'hard, tough and dangerous' symbols used to represent them (Dyer 1985: 30) and questioned since by Peter Lehman.

Since this is how masculinity came to be defined in relation to cinema, it becomes apparent why, within these restrictive theoretical parameters, the figure of the father remained problematic and absent (and why, in the films themselves, he is de-eroticised):

he is not defined by and through his body. The exclusion of the father from Film Studies' dominant discussions of masculinity (I say 'dominant' because there are books about the domestic sphere, such as Elizabeth Traube's *Dreaming Identities: Class, Gender and Generation in 1980s Hollywood Movies* [1992] or Sarah Harwood's *Family Fictions: Representations of the Family in 1980s Hollywood Cinema* [1997] in which the father is talked about more extensively) has a complex, intriguing root. It is the particular conjunction of domesticity, traditionalism and a lack of eroticism that forces fathers to exist outside the discursive limits of Film Studies' definitions of masculinity. The father is domestic (this term I use very broadly to mean that he is involved in the nurturing of children) as he is, by virtue of being the most important representative of patriarchy, a pillar of tradition. Of most interest is the father's relationship to eroticism. As I engaged with the films and issues of this book, it became obvious that the father is a figure of renunciation. J. C. Flügel's model of 'the great masculine renunciation' (1930) – for all its own problems and limitations – proved useful and is discussed in relation to the breadwinner fathers in the films of the 1950s. It is not only in the 1950s that the father is de-sexualised, compelled to renounce or repress his desirability if he is to become a good father. This abdication comes out in a number of ways: the father's body is very rarely on display, and when it is, as in *Bonjour Tristesse* (1957), it commonly becomes a mark of his and his family's dysfunctionality. He is very rarely the object of sexual desire although, as in the comedies of the 1990s, he is frequently the chaste romantic hero. The sexual father is commonly either bad or a pervert (most extremely in *Happiness* [1998]) and for the majority of Hollywood fathers being a moral, symbolic guide is of greater importance than sex.

An interesting enactment of this comes in Hollywood's various widowed or divorced father movies in which the father goes in pursuit of a replacement wife and mother. Here, the potentially disruptive conjunction of fatherhood and sex is managed by the father having been left in charge of either a lone son or an unmanageable brood of children, both of which function as mechanisms for diffusing the father's potential eroticism. In the first scenario (having a lone son) the potentially uncomfortable eroticism created by the father–daughter–maternal substitute triangle (as found in *Bonjour Tristesse*) is repressed in favour of a buddy relationship between a father and his son who desire, for very different reasons, the same woman. The lone father and single son is the family unit at the centre of *Gentleman's Agreement* (1947), *The Courtship of Eddie's Father*, *Kramer vs. Kramer* and *Sleepless in Seattle* (1993) and is repeatedly used elsewhere, as in *Arlington Road* (1999), in which a widower father (Jeff Bridges) has entered into a sexual relationship with a grad student. In the second scenario (the father with multiple children), the possible eroticisation of the father is comparably obscured by the sheer number of children the father has, as in *Houseboat* (1958) or *The Sound of Music*. Although there are intimations in Freud that the man's eroticisation is diminished upon becoming a father, this hysterical need to strip the father of eroticism is

1

Since You Went Away: Masculinity and Change after World War II

Hollywood's handling of World War II constructed a particular relationship between combat, masculinity and the role of the father. Norman Mailer remarked, 'nobody was born a man; you earned manhood provided you were good enough, bold enough' (Gilmore 1990: 19). So the myth goes, that while it was boys who went to war, it was men who came back. Hollywood's tendency in the late 1940s, however, was to focus on boys coming back from the war, fathers and older men proving more marginal and less significant narrative figures. The impact of World War II on mature masculinity was complex. Although it all too soon narrowed its scope, an excellent place to find, in the late 1940s, discussions of war's role in the definition of American masculinity was the women's monthly, *McCall's*, in which writers such as influential psychologist Marynia Farnham explored topical ideas about gender and society. An article from February 1946 adopted the sentiment (without its irony) of Mailer's comment above, as it told its readers 'Now you have a man: a man who has lived in a man's world has come to live with you. Can you live up to him?' World War II changed many aspects of masculinity, including fatherhood; notions of manhood on the battlefield were markedly different from the ideals of masculinity that emerged in peacetime. Following a pronounced but temporary surge in divorces in 1946–7, marriages and births increased and the role of the father, having been less important during the war, became once more, a significant component of masculinity. But, 'fatherhood' is not, as observed in the Introduction to this book, comfortably assimilated into 'masculinity', and what the contemporary images of fatherhood in immediate post-war America demonstrate, both within and outside of Hollywood, is that becoming a father often compromised traditional concepts of what constituted being a man.

Despite the emergence of more enlightened attitudes to fathering in the first half of the twentieth century, the most significant event of the 1940s – the war – heightened the desire for a return to a more traditional patriarchal image. One compelling reason for this was the Depression of the 1930s, when many fathers found themselves unemployed and so confined to a more domestic role. As fatherhood became less defined by work and more identified with childcare so, some psychologists and sociologists have argued, men felt increasingly emasculated. According to Elizabeth and Joseph Pleck, it became clear that 'the central lesson of the Depression was that paternal involvement was never the main goal of fathers or their children: money was' (Pleck and Pleck

1997: 43). At times (such as wartime) when women's earning potential greatly increased, men felt their masculinity to be threatened.

This gender imbalance lies at the heart of *Mildred Pierce* (1945), which, while made at the end of the war, does not make any direct reference to it. By principally feminist film theorists and historians, Mildred's hunger for financial success is not only noted as an underlying reason for the failure of her marriage to Bert but also viewed as representative of the experience of multitudes of American women who found fulfilment in employment during the war. In *Women's Film and Female Experience, 1940–1950*, Andrea S. Walsh comments, '*Like most real-life women in her situation*, Mildred was left with little money and few skills to support her family' (1984: 125; my italics). Walsh then argues that the film's ideological function was to legitimate the pressures on women to leave the workplace and return to the home, while also maintaining that the film manages to be a celebration of female bonding, an equivocal reading that exasperated Linda Williams in 'Feminist Film Theory: *Mildred Pierce* and the Second World War' (1988: 15). Pam Cook, but less overtly than Walsh, located *Mildred Pierce* within its broad sociopolitical context as she interpreted the end (Mildred's reunion with Bert) as 'a reminder of what women must give up for the sake of the patriarchal order' (1998: 80).

Susan Faludi in *Stiffed: The Betrayal of the Modern Man* (1999) expands upon these ideas when arguing that the war proved to be 'the last gasp' as opposed to the crowning moment of a generous, meek and altruistic masculinity. The moment of transition from one kind of masculinity to another is echoed in *Mildred Pierce*, although the common interpretation of Bert as the film's embodiment of traditional patriarchy is hugely problematic, as he is a dull, spineless man. The gentler masculinity that, Faludi suggests, was eventually ousted after the war is, for her, exemplified by war journalist Ernie Pyle's lyrical depictions of 'GI Joe', the 'common man' of war. This humane, anonymous figure is further eulogised in William Wellman's 1945 film about Pyle's time following US troops in the war, *The Story of GI Joe* (Faludi 1999: 17–20). Faludi believes however, that, while the veterans of World War II 'were actually inclined toward a continuation of the common-man ethic', the general public was less keen on sensitive masculinity. The men might have been 'eager to embrace a masculine ideal that revolved around providing rather than dominating' (23), but American society as a whole came out of the war 'with a sense of itself as a *masculine* nation, our "boys" ready to assume the mantle of national authority and international leadership' (16).

This chapter will concern itself with a few films made during the World War II (notably *Since You Went Away* and *Meet Me in St. Louis*) but principally with films made in its immediate aftermath. In the father films of the period, the ambivalence detected by Faludi is also in evidence. Hollywood's attitude to war and fatherhood is unexpected. I am indebted to Michael Walker for the crucial observation that men very rarely return from war as fathers in Hollywood films; soldiers are either without dependents or they die in combat before they can return to their families. There were fewer fathers on active duty during the war than might have been expected, due to the US army's resistance to sending family men; however, this is one of those instances when Hollywood constructs its own independent myth about fatherhood.[1] In the movies, sons come back and fathers die in battle. Those fathers who return are both exceptional and problematic. In *Since You Went Away* or its darker counterpart, Ophuls' *The Reckless Moment* (1949), the fathers are alive at the end of the war, but we never see them. Al in *The Best Years of Our Lives* (1946) is a returning father, but his adjustment to civilian life is fraught, while in *Tomorrow Is Forever* (1946) everyone thinks the father is dead although he has not in fact been killed (this time in World War I) and returns in disguise. In accordance with Mailer's sentiments, Hollywood in the 1940s portrayed combat as a young hero's business, fathers frequently being the men who stayed at home. In *It's a Wonderful Life* (1947), George Bailey, who is unable to enlist due to his partial deafness, is contrasted with his dashing bachelor war hero brother Harry, while in *Gentleman's Agreement* the inference is that widowed father Phil Green did not serve in the war, he, like Bailey, being sharply differentiated from another character who obviously did fight – his best friend, who spends the entire film in full uniform.

Thomas Schatz identifies an immediate post-war trend in Hollywood 'toward serious drama with a strong male focus' (1997: 369), citing *The Best Years of Our Lives* and *It's a Wonderful Life* as important examples; he also detected a rapid phasing out of combat and war movies at the war's end, only to be started up again in the late 1940s with films such as *I Was a Male War Bride* (1949) (368). Schatz writes that 'male melodramas' of 1946–7 centred 'on the efforts of a vaguely despondent male beset by post-war angst to "find himself"' (369), although there were surprisingly few of these films focused on GIs' 'trauma of readjustment', the one example Schatz offers being *Till the End of Time* (1946). Arguably, Hollywood is here reflecting the desire identified by Faludi to repress caring, sensitive masculinity in favour of hyper-masculine toughness. As Schatz suggests, the late 1940s saw an increase in the number of Westerns, particularly military Westerns such as John Ford's cavalry trilogy (Schatz 1997: 372). Alongside these, comedy dramas such as *The Egg and I* (1947), *Life with Father* (1947) and *Ma and Pa Kettle* (1949) in which domestic tribulations become the source of comedy and sentimentality proved extremely popular; these Schatz then links with the 'seemingly endless procession of films celebrating the American hearth and home', which he links to the contemporary social and political desire to persuade women back into the home (373).

Various films released in the late 1940s feature father figures, although conspicuously few of them enter into a discussion of fatherhood as such. Among the different kinds of fathers these films depict, there are very few young fathers, despite a pervasive cultural emphasis on youthful masculinity at the end of the war. In *Movies: A Psychological Study* (1950), which examines films released in the latter half of the 1940s in America, France and Britain, Wolfenstein and Leites differentiate between the 'Older Generation' father – the father who is not the hero but the hero's parent – and the 'The Hero as

Father'. They persistently demonstrate that the majority of fathers in late 1940s' films are older and the father of the hero/heroine rather than the protagonists themselves. Of these fathers they comment:

> The hero's father is usually a sympathetic character, and almost always ineffectual. His relation with the hero is friendly, but he can give him little more than good will. In most cases, it would make no difference to the course of events if the father were eliminated from the story. His is a non-essential background figure (1950: 110).

This generalisation holds for many post-war films: the kindly, ineffectual fathers in *Till the End of Time* or *Teresa* (1951), and the good, upright father in Orson Welles' *The Stranger* (1946). It might be ungenerous to call these fathers 'colourless' (103), but they are all characterised by their marginality to the plot. Wolfenstein and Leites, however, omit to mention films of the late 1940s that significantly fail to conform to their model such as *Fort Apache*, *The Heiress* (1949) and *House of Strangers* (1949), all of which revolve around strong, even abhorrently authoritarian patriarchs or *The Furies*, released in 1950, in which T. C. Jeffords is a cantankerous, volatile cattle baron with barely disguised incestuous yearnings for his daughter.

The rare younger father/hero conventionally becomes a father after the war has ended. Two important examples are Fred Zinnemann's films *The Search* and *Teresa*. In *The Search*, a GI stationed in 1945 Germany takes care of a Czech boy who has lost his mother; in *Teresa*, the youthful returning son/soldier becomes a father after he has returned to America with his Italian bride. Fatherhood in these two films is defined as being *post*-war, suggesting a new beginning and a curing or forgetting of the traumas of war.

As Michael Walker has again identified, a narrative motif persists in Hollywood whereby news of a pregnancy or imminent fatherhood immediately precipitates a soldier's death, so the father-to-be dies in action before he can see his child.[2] Before World War II, this melodramatic conjunction of birth and death is found in films such as *Pilgrimage* (1933) in which the father is killed on the battlefield at the time his (illegitimate) child is born or *The Old Maid* (1939) in which George Brent gets Bette Davis pregnant and is promptly killed in the Civil War. 1940s' examples include *My Foolish Heart* (1949) and *Tomorrow Is Forever* (although in the latter the father turns out not to have died). This central motif is also used to overtly propagandistic effect; in films such as *Tomorrow Is Forever*, *The White Cliffs of Dover* (1944) and *To Each His Own* (1946), the father's sacrifice in World War I is linked specifically to the son's desire to fight in World War II. The incompatibility of soldiering and fatherhood is used to more humorous effect in *The Story of GI Joe*, in which a new father (a secondary character) provides the film's comic relief as, between battles in war-torn Italy, he repeatedly tries to find a gramophone on which to play a recording of his daughter saying 'Hello, Daddy'. Whether or not the father, Private Warnicki, survives the war is left ambiguous. During the sustained bombardment of a hilltop monastery (presumably Monte Cassino), he stumbles back to camp suffering from shell shock and is taken off babbling to the medics. We do not see Warnicki again and his collapse (a sort of death) conforms to Walker's pattern in that it comes at just the point when he manages, finally, to hear his child's voice. This motif of the soldier dying as he is about to become or has just become a father continues to *Pearl Harbor* (2001), a film that echoes another 1940s' concern: who, when the father is dead, is going to father the child about to be born? Establishing another convention about Hollywood fathers, in *Pearl Harbor*, as in *Tomorrow Is Forever* and *My Foolish Heart*, the widow (or presumed widow in *Tomorrow Is Forever*) marries a man who will be a suitable father, but who, crucially, she does not love.

Films that deal with the role of the father in the troubled aftermath of the war reflect the image of America as a nation in transition. Central to the question of the father's role in the late 1940s is the issue of change: how much had war changed the men who fought in it? How much had that same war changed the women and families on the home front? How resolvable would be the differences between the needs and desires of men and women once the men returned home? An article in *McCall's* 'Now You Have a Man' was written relatively soon after the end of the war in February 1946 by Marynia Farnham who, a year later, co-wrote (with Ferdinand Lundberg) the hugely influential *Modern Woman: The Lost Sex*. The article (like the book) painted a narrow, anti-feminist picture of life. Opening with a soldier saying 'I found that I was a man and could act and feel like a man. I am not going to give that up', Farnham continues by suggesting that the wives left at home (whether or not they wanted to give up work) should 'accept' their husbands had changed and 'must be prepared to do the adjusting themselves and learn to live up to the challenge of their men' (*McCall's* 1946a: 18). 'Now You Have a Man' established various fundamental incompatibilities between the man's war experience and the contemporaneous experience on the home front, again intimating that somehow fatherhood – the domestic masculine ideal – was likewise incompatible with being a 'man'. In Farnham's estimation, war was a uniquely, intensely male experience during which men discovered 'that they have this great capacity for identification and common cause, for putting aside the small and the stupid, the cruel and the painful in human emotions' (126).

Women were viewed as largely detrimental to the returning man's well-being; either they kept their sons 'weakened' and 'immature' (126) by practising what Philip Wylie in *Generation of Vipers* (1942) dubbed 'Momism', or they are comically caricatured as a predatory regiment who 'smoke on the street, stand at bars and mingle in male society entirely unrestricted' (*McCall's* 1946a: 126), having usurped the male breadwinning role. Farnham advocates the return to patriarchal order: women should be 'prepared to abdicate in favor of their husbands' (130) and fathers should be demurred to in the home and beyond it must establish themselves as 'the core of the citizenry' (130). In fact, reintegration and yet more shifts in gender roles after the war caused many more problems away fighting in the war. The absent father, because he is not there to be compared unfavourably to his symbolic like, retains his power by remaining (much like Lacan's elusive phallus) constitutively veiled. The absent father can all too easily be misrecognised as the perfect, powerful father whose presence will eventually stabilise and complete the family unit. The problem with the glorified absent father is that he all too uncritically becomes an imaginary evocation, a fantasy figure who fills an emotional and psychological lack. In 'The Significance of the Father in the Destiny of the Individual', which he revised in 1949, Jung wrote: 'behind the father stands the archetype of the father, and in this pre-existent archetype lies the secret of the father's power' (69). The modern father, predominantly because he is traditionally not present as much as the mother, has acquired symbolic significance almost by default, as if psychology has needed to rationalise this absence into something important. The absent or past father models come to represent the mysterious 'power' the real fathers lack.

Cromwell's *Since You Went Away*, scripted by its producer David Selznick, exemplifies this tendency and is frequently cited as illustrative of Hollywood's residual traditionalism, compared often with the more troubled contemporaneous films, *The Reckless Moment* or *Mildred Pierce*. Mary Ann Doane remarks that it is specifically the war that, 'quite predictably, mobilizes the ultraconservative aspects of the cultural construction of motherhood' that *Since You Went Away* embodies and that as a film it is fervently intent upon simply maintaining things '"as they are"' (1987: 78–9). *Since You Went Away* was a wartime production; it was immensely successful (the fourth highest grossing movie of the year) and, as Michael Walker comments, 'the film's propaganda credentials are impeccable' (1982: 54). At the time, James Agee, in his review for *Time* of *Since You Went Away*, noted authenticity alongside idealisation in Selznick's portrayal of the American home, concluding: 'Now and then the idealization runs too far ahead of normal reality. But by and large the blend of flesh and fantasy is pretty close to Hiltonesque life in the U.S. home' (1958: 351).

Selznick's intention with *Since You Went Away* was to tell the story of the American family in wartime. For source material he turned to an original story in *Ladies' Home Journal*, making 'the family somewhat more average middle class' (Behlmer 1972: 326) than in the original and their problems 'as representative of those of the average family as possible' (326). The film tells the story of the Hiltons, mother Ann (Claudette Colbert), two daughters, Jane (Jennifer Jones) and Bridget (Shirley Temple), an old bulldog and a black maid. The Hiltons, like many wartime families, take in a lodger to make ends meet, and both Ann and elder daughter Jane take paid work. Ann receives news that Tim, her husband, is missing in action, but at the end of the film – and just in time for Christmas – a telegram arrives announcing his imminent return. As Doane posits, the film's title implies directly that the narrative occupies the 'meanwhile' between the father's departure and return (1987: 78), as if the women's life has no meaning except when defined in relation to his. In the opening sequence, Ann returns from having

waved her husband off. To the strains of 'There's No Place Like Home', a voice-over tells us 'This is the story of the unconquerable fortress – the American home, 1943' while the camera scans a series of objects that first connote father's recent vacation of that home (his empty chair, his trusty dog, the date and telegram signalling his call-up) and then the life he has left behind (mementoes of his wedding trip, bronze replicas of his children's first shoes, a desk photograph of his wife and daughters). Remembering the father is presented as the essential element that will give the Hilton household a seamless sense of completeness, despite his absence.

While sharing several narrative elements with *The Reckless Moment* (father away due to the war; family left at home), *Since You Went Away* differs markedly from Ophuls' film in tone. The films' attitudes to the American family are quite distinct; whereas in *Since You Went Away*, 'there is no genuine question about the institution's ultimate survival' (Baker 1980: 97), in *The Reckless Moment* the solidity of that same institution is brought into question. Similarly, father Tom Harper's absence in *The Reckless Moment* is viewed far more ambivalently than Tim Hilton's (see Walker 1982: 54), in large measure because, the war having ended, Tom is not performing soldierly heroics but has been despatched as part of the post-war mission to rebuild Germany. Not knowing how traumatic the father's re-entry into society and the home might be, *Since You Went Away* is far more optimistic. The ideological and psychoanalytical conflicts generated in both films (Walker 1982: 54) are suppressed in *Since You Went Away*, which appears explicitly to affirm the dominant ideology that *The Reckless Moment* resolutely subverts. In *Since You Went Away*, Tim's absence is (at least on the surface) the *most* significant element that sustains the Hilton's family morale and Ann conforms to the stereotype of the dutiful wartime wife who 'should be smiling about sending her men off to fight', who does not 'disturb them with gloomy reports of the home front' and who takes a job in wartime production that she is 'ready at the drop of a hatpin to give up to a returning soldier' (Lundberg and Farnham 1947: 9). For a later audience imbued with greater cynicism than the audiences of the 1940s, *Since You Went Away* offers an uneasily hysterical affirmation of the patriotic fatherless home, hinging on this uncomfortable dualism between the idealised absent father and a saccharine picture of the female-only home he has left behind. While it is unlikely that Selznick was trying to be subversive, *Since You Went Away*, seen from a later historical and critical perspective (of reading films 'against the grain') does not seem to so definitively lack the troubledness of *The Reckless Moment* or *Mildred Pierce*.

Because we never see him, Tim, the 'perfect father', functions in a comparable way to the physical manifestation in cases of hysteria, as the tangible evocation of a psychological need, in this case Ann Hilton's need to believe in the father and the resultant

The Hilton family await the return of father Tim

stability of her family. He is as much a symptom of his wife's imagination as he is a cause of her distress (in *Rebecca* – both du Maurier's book and Hitchcock's film – the titular first wife remains the omniscient, defining presence in much the same way). This ambivalence is expressed in a sequence such as Ann and her daughters' trip to the cinema, where, after the main film, there is a newsreel showing American troops in jeeps 'on maneuvers'. Among the troops is Tim Hilton, but whereas his daughters exclaim 'Pop!' at this sighting of their father, Ann, who has snoozed off, misses him. *Since You Went Away* is peppered with such missed sightings of Tim. Not only does the film begin just as he has left and end just before he is due to return, but in between there is the family's abortive trip to New York to see him one last time before he is posted overseas. Ann and her daughters arrive at the designated hotel only to find no Captain Hilton, only a perfunctory note telling them 'orders wouldn't permit me to wait'.

The precariousness of Tim's presence-through-absence is compounded by the abundance of father-substitutes who pass through the family's house while he is away. At the time, it was deemed important to locate male relatives 'who can act as father substitutes' in the father's absence (Hill 1945: 31), but in *Since You Went Away*, such substitutes are not always flattering. Several surrogates are used to consolidate Tim's position as patriarch – Tim's bulldog, Colonel Smollett the wartime lodger, and the Colonel's grandson Bill, a GI who becomes Jane's fiancé and later dies in action. These figures (a canine, an old man and a vulnerable youth) share the crucial attribute of not being found instantly attractive by any of the film's many man-less heterosexual women. Jane grows to love Bill, but when they first meet, she clearly considers him to be unerotic by comparison with 'Uncle Tony' – Tony, the Hiltons' best friend, being the one father substitute who threatens Tim's supremacy. Played by Joseph Cotten, he is an unreformed bachelor, a naval officer who, unlike the other paternal-substitutes, is immediately adored by all the women (anonymous or not) in the film. While it is the graceless, panting bulldog who heaves himself onto his master's favourite armchair or who struggles to mount his bed in order to snuggle up to his dressing gown that functions as Tim's ostensible alter ego, Tony is granted considerably more sexual freedom, a matinée idol filmed in soft-focus close-up or daubed in sensuous chiaroscuro lighting. This binary opposition is intriguing in a film that, in a Foucauldian manner, proclaims sex and the potential for sexual activity just as it advocates its repression. The promulgation of the repression of sex emerges through the many laborious activities revolving around sleeping arrangements and beds after the arrivals, in quick succession, of the Colonel and Tony. At one such juncture, Tony – with plenty of accompanying comic business – pointedly transfers Tim's mattress from the master to the guest bedroom.

'Uncle' Tony exemplifies *Since You Went Away*'s resistance to the sexual male, as such a conjunction between sex and paternalism threatens the absent father. Tony's eroticisation resonates with post-war fears that the returning father would prove incompatible with the home and domestic situation he had left behind. While the 'problem' of gender competition (so often cited in contemporary articles as a potential obstacle to a happy resumption of a marriage) is absent in *Since You Went Away*, the other major cause of marital break-up in the late 1940s (infidelity or falling out of love) is not. Tony's covertly sexual presence inflects the film with doubt over the father's continued desirability. He arrives, portentously, just after Tim has left and is greeted by Ann quite explicitly as the next best thing to Tim being home, making the proximity to the father uncomfortable and unmistakeable. Although there ensues later that same evening one of many revisions of sleeping arrangements, such hysterical enactments of 'innocence' fail to mask convincingly how much of a strain it is to sustain the 'happy family' myth. The sexualised father is not permissible and, to underscore this, *Since You Went Away* confirms Tony's unsuitability to that role as, on the first night of his stay, the cabbie who has brought him to the Hiltons', does indeed assume Tony to be the family's father, a mistake that makes Ann and her daughters laugh so heartily as to imply: 'as if this hunk of a man could be Dad!'

Tony performs the function of what Juliet Mitchell terms (after Lévi-Strauss) the 'maternal brother', the archetypal avuncular figure best equipped to break the familial Oedipal chain and usher the children into society and adulthood (1974: 375) because he is not the father but nevertheless approximates him. Joseph Cotten plays two such roles in the 1940s, as before Tony he played the criminal Uncle Charlie in Hitchcock's *Shadow of a Doubt* (1942), in which his besotted sister's family learn about the potential criminality and violence of adulthood through the intrusion of the glamorous 'maternal brother'. Mitchell focuses on the closeness of the relationship between the 'maternal brother' and his sister, desire for whom is sublimated into such actions as giving her away at her wedding. She argues that the 'distinction between them is minimal and the prohibition on their union (the incest taboo) establishes that smallest of differences which is necessary to inaugurate society' (375–6). Tony enacts this ambivalence and, as a result, serves to clarify the role of the traditional father. As he leaves to go back to his ship, he predicts that, next time they meet, Jane will have forgotten him and fallen in love properly. His prediction (though later complicated by Bill's death in battle) comes true and the connotations of Tony's words and role are clear: the father is the mature love object and neither the father nor the mature love object can be sexual, so a 'maternal uncle' is inserted into the family narrative as the figure onto whom are siphoned off the repressed and unresolved desires for the father.

The Hollywood narrative motif of killing off the soldier as he hears he is about to become a father is imbued with a similar ethos to this de-sexualisation of the soldier–father. The few examples of the eroticised, sexually available father that do exist in the late 1940s are to be found in films in which the father is not directly associated with the army or the war, as it is the specific conjunction of fathering and fighting that is traumatic. In *Margie* (Henry King, 1946), the need to differentiate between sex and the father is emphasised by the narrative's distinction between past and present via the use of extended flashback. The man (French teacher Ralph Fontaine) who becomes the father is thus only an object of his future wife Margie's desire in the past – when she was a susceptible schoolgirl with a crush on him. Despite its date, *Margie* circumvents the war, as does Otto Preminger's *Daisy Kenyon* (1947), in which Dana Andrews plays a young civilian father who has an affair with Daisy Kenyon (Joan Crawford) and divorces his wife. Fitting with Schatz's late 1940s' subgenre of the 'male melodrama', the father's departure from the family in *Daisy Kenyon* is traumatic. A custody battle ensues and, despite his infidelity, the father is portrayed as the better parent because his ex-wife is seen slapping their daughter. The aftermath of war is only dimly acknowledged through a controversial law case involving a Japanese defendant.

Gentleman's Agreement likewise discusses the father's sexual availability (here Gregory Peck's character Phil Green is widowed) within the context of a narrative that distances him from the war. *Gentleman's Agreement* and *Boomerang!* (1947) released the same year, were two important 'social problem' films directed by Elia Kazan for 20th Century-Fox. As a journalist commissioned to write a series of articles on anti-Semitism, Phil Green is linked tangibly to post-war socio-political issues, but (significantly, considering he is a widower–father) not to combat. His civilian status and his domestic arrangements (his mother does the majority of the childcare) subsequently ease the way for Phil to find another partner, Kathy Lacey (Dorothy McGuire), as paternity, sexuality and the war are effectively segregated. *Gentleman's Agreement* exemplifies the manner in which 1940s' Hollywood treated fatherhood: men were fathers, but their fathering was incidental to the narrative and their characterisation. This is not always the case, as later discussions of films such as *Teresa* indicate but, in *Gentleman's Agreement*, Phil's strength and moral rectitude is complemented rather than informed by his role as lone parent. His fight against anti-Semitism and his love affair take precedence over his fathering of Tommy, and there are only a handful of domestic scenes which show father and son together (one involves them making breakfast together, thereby abiding by that Hollywood convention that dictates that this is the meal fathers 'do'). This is the first of Peck's notable father roles, and in later films – *The Man in the Gray Flannel Suit*, *Cape Fear* (1961) and *To Kill a Mockingbird* – fathering becomes a much more prominent issue.

The Returning Father: *The Best Years of Our Lives*; *It's a Wonderful Life*; *Tomorrow Is Forever*

Such neat delineations between sex and war, fathering and social role are absent in the few Hollywood films that do confront specifically the problem of the father's return from the war. To return to the recurring motif of the father-to-be dying during the war, convention dictates virtually that either (as is the case with *The Best Years of Our Lives*) the surviving father's children will have been born before the war or that the father (as occurs in *Gentleman's Agreement* and *It's a Wonderful Life*) remained at home during it and did not fight. *Tomorrow Is Forever* breaks this rule and will be discussed in a moment. Problems of readjustment for the returning father are at the heart of William Wyler's *The Best Years of Our Lives*, a film that contrasts directly with *Since You Went Away*, in which the father's imminent return is heralded as joyful and unproblematic. In response to the obvious trauma of the man's social reintegration, one journal article, written in May 1945, called for the setting up of 'mental hygiene clinics in the home community to make the transition [from active service to home] easier' (Hill 1945: 33): desperate measures for coping with desperate men 'plagued with anxieties' (33). The anticipated neediness and vulnerability of the returning soldier was exacerbated, it has frequently been argued, by the extent to which the American state, immediately after the war, sought to offer the veteran federal support. Many soldiers, like the subject of the *McCall's* piece 'Marriage Is Like This', felt that the legislation implemented to help them and their families – such as the GI Bill of Rights that subsidised the return to education of roughly 50 per cent of the young male population, or the subsidising of veterans' small businesses – symbolically served to undermine their masculinity and independence. In Russell Lynes' 1953 book *A Surfeit of Honey*, the father created by the GI Bill is dubbed the 'servant-father' who, 'left with his books and his babies and his broom', no longer 'laid down the law' (57–8). Although other experts at the time advocated the democratic family model and welcomed the assistance and support of the community (see Reeves 1945), a worry persisted that such 'democracy' signalled the corrosion of the father's authority.

A loss of authority marks Al's return in *The Best Years of Our Lives*, and he is in no way the 'dashing hero in shining uniform, capable of great deeds' (Hill 1945: 32) that the American housewife was thought to desire and anticipate. Significantly, Wyler's intensely realistic film is the only late 1940s' film to contain such a father, confirming Hollywood's flight from these awkward realities. The US government had delayed the draft of fathers until as late as possible, fearful of the effect their absence might have on the family;[3] upon their return from combat they found that things had changed and 'untraditional' women-led families were commonplace. Historian William Tuttle quotes many wives, children and siblings recounting the soldiers' return; fathers were frequently not recognised or viewed as imposters and their manliness appeared diminished. This perceived diminution was variously manifested: some fathers had aged markedly, others were badly injured, many returned psychologically scarred (1993: 212–30).[4]

Whereas Tim Hilton's authority in *Since You Went Away* is preserved by his absence, in *The Best Years of Our Lives*, Al's is 'diminished' by his survival and presence. *The Best Years of Our Lives* (the top picture at the American box office in 1946) focuses on three veterans, Fred, Homer and Al, who meet aboard a plane taking them home to 'Boone City'. The re-entry is traumatic for all three: Fred returns to find his marriage in tatters, Homer has lost both arms in the war and is fearful of what his sweetheart Wilma's reaction will be and Al turns to drink. The film concludes with Homer and Wilma's wedding, the cementing of Fred's relationship with Al's daughter Peggy and Al's renunciation of the bottle, but the film's tone until then has been tense and melancholic. Al's return home, for instance, is a moment of bathos and unease. He enters his apartment, and although pleased to see him, his wife remains awkward and detached, an estrangement then echoed in Al's reunion with his children, Peggy and Rob. He greets them with a jocular 'I don't recognise you, what happened?', to which the quick-tongued Peggy replies: 'Just a few years of normal growth'. The family laugh off this mismatch, but a further exchange between Al and Rob accentuates the schism. Al, who was involved in the aftermath of the attack on Hiroshima, has brought his son a samurai sword, much to Rob's bewilderment. Rob then pointedly remarks that 'The Japanese attach a lot of importance to their family relationships', to which Al, underscoring how out of step he is with both his more knowledgeable children and the times, replies 'Yeah. They're entirely different to us'. The Stevensons have left Al behind and Al represents the returning fathers who 'simply did not measure up' (Griswold 1993: 177). Peggy's assurance that it is 'Nice to have you around Dad, you'll get us back to normal', immediately precedes Al's decision to hit the town and get drunk. The reality, dramatised in *The Best Years of Our Lives*, was that families hardly knew their returning fathers and often begrudged their intrusive presence.

Al returns home and presents his son Rob with a samurai sword

Al's confusion and vulnerability are marked by two narrative devices: his alcohol dependency (a common crutch among veterans) and his inability to marry the values (camaraderie, altruism, classlessness) acquired in the army with his role as middle-class breadwinning father. After advocating 'mental hygiene clinics' to ease the soldier's transition to civilian life, contemporary psychologist Reuben Hill listed the returning soldier's anxieties, from craving excitement, not feeling able to talk freely of his wartime experiences and finding that his wife and children had become 'strange to him' (Hill 1945: 33). Al manifests very similar insecurities. Despite resuming his position in the bank where he had worked prior to being drafted, his anxiety and depression mitigate against him reassuming his role as head of the household unchanged. A manifestation of this is that Al finds it much easier to bond with Fred and Homer (identified with his life independent of his family) than with his wife and children. In *Till the End of Time*, the returning soldier's preference for the company of his wartime buddies over his family causes similar tensions, the hero only feeling able to 'settle down' when he knows that his wartime buddy, who has undergone emergency surgery, is going to be alright (see Wolfenstein and Leites 1950: 55).

As *The Best Years of Our Lives* ends with Homer's wedding, it concludes with the restoration of a particularly potent traditional institution. Among contemporary Hollywood films there are many such tacked-on happy endings, there, in desperation, to paper over troublesome fissures. Often – because, as has been demonstrated, the return of the father was an atypical narrative motif and so a trauma in itself – this masquerade revolved around the father. *It's a Wonderful Life* was made a year after *The Best Years of Our Lives*. Here, the schism is represented by the differentiation between George and Harry Bailey: the depressed older brother who did not fight in the war and Harry, who returns from the war a dashing, unencumbered hero. *It's a Wonderful Life* exemplifies the ambivalence at the core of Hollywood's representation of the post-war father. George Bailey becomes a 'happily married man' with three children, but this contentment is tempered and threatened by his life having been structured around disappointment. As breadwinner and patriarchal protector to the whole town of Bedford Falls, George assumes the dual role of actual and symbolic father, but where does his dutifulness get him? He never pursues his own ambitions to travel the world and, after contemplating suicide, his salvation is at the hands of second-rate angel Clarence. These are the trembling foundations for the film's supposedly joyous ending.

George is neurotically ambivalent about what sort of a man he would like to be; he dreams perpetually of leaving Bedford Falls, but is easily persuaded back by duty, marriage and fatherhood. The path his life takes is dictated by self-sacrifice, and he ultimately sacrifices his masculinity to becoming 'a family man'. Illustrative of his neurotic split, the junctures at which George fantasises about escape are, of course, deeply significant, and one such moment occurs when his wife Mary tells him she is pregnant with their first child. Not unlike the soldiers who die when they learn they are to become fathers, the moment Mary delivers the same news to George is the point at which George renounces all hope of escape from Bedford Falls and his traditional existence. Robert Ray argues that George, in the nightmare vision Clarence conjures up of what Bedford Falls would have become had it lacked his guiding presence, is shown to be the 'centre of the world on whom everything depends' (1985: 200). Such an interpretation is severely undercut by both the representation of George's domesticity and the very presence of Clarence, a classic Hollywood *deus ex machina* – the emergency measure, brought in to impose a fragile sense of order on an imploding situation.

Although the implication is clearly that George is a loving, responsible father, through-out *It's a Wonderful Life* we do not see this. Instead, the longest fathering sequence (immediately prior to George fleeing his home to get drunk and jump off the bridge) shows him as irritable, cruel and angry towards his children. When finally George comes home to discover that his family and friends have saved him by putting together the money his absent-minded uncle has lost, he stands before the Christmas tree and embraces his wife and children. Although this is the clinching image from *It's a Wonderful Life*, in this final scene George looks defeated and desperate – and appears to have aged visibly, in the manner of shell-shocked veterans returning from combat. Here, being a father is what you do when you fail. George may be the figure on whom 'every-thing depends', but who would prefer to be the greying, tweedy, stay-at-home dad rather than his glamorous, youthful, war hero brother Harry?

In *Tomorrow Is Forever*, the mythic father who dies in battle and the demystified father who survives the war are amalgamated. The film was made during the war (shooting took place between March and June 1945) but its release was delayed until after the war had ended, indicating perhaps that the film had having missed its target audience. Although conforming in many ways to the cycle of films in which pregnancy triggers death, *Tomorrow Is Forever* departs from this narrative convention by virtue of the father, John McDonald, not actually dying, but surviving horrific injuries during World War I and returning as 'Eric Kestler'. The motif of a soldier dying just as he is to become a father appears in its purest form in *My Foolish Heart*, illustrating clearly that, as far as Holly-wood was concerned, 'wartime heroes were not suitable to be fathers and hence were killed in action, fatherhood subsequently being passed to the more domesticated men left behind'.[5] Directed by Mark Robson and based on a story in the *New Yorker* by J. D. Salinger, the film takes place largely in flashback. In the present, the marriage of Eloise and Lou is on the brink of collapse. Before the war, Eloise had dated Lou unenthusias-tically, but had fallen in love with Walt. After the attack on Pearl Harbor, Walt is drafted into the air force, and during a period of leave from training, Eloise becomes pregnant. She decides not to tell Walt as, having just listened to her father telling her how he, upon returning from the 1914–18 war, felt trapped in the marriage he had rushed into in 1917, she feels this is a bad way to secure a husband. Likewise Walt does not pro-pose to Eloise, as he is not sure he will return. Just before he is due to leave for active duty, Walt writes Eloise a letter, which he has left to be posted immediately before boarding his plane, which crashes. In traditional melodramatic fashion (see Lisa's last words in *Letter from an Unknown Woman* [1948]), Walt had asked for Eloise shortly before dying and in the letter he has asked her to marry him. Eloise, now needing a father for her child, returns to Lou and they get married. *My Foolish Heart* is relatively risqué in that Lou never realises that his daughter Ramona is not his.

The schematic scenario in *Tomorrow Is Forever* is relatively similar, although its heroine Elizabeth McDonald (Claudette Colbert) unwittingly becomes a bigamist. *Tomorrow Is Forever* begins with the end of the Great War. On returning home from work, Elizabeth receives a telegram informing her that her husband John (Orson Welles) died in action on the eve of the Armistice. She is pregnant and, after having fainted at work, Larry Hamilton (George Brent), her secret admirer and son of her boss, takes her to his aunt's house to recuperate, where she stays until the baby is born. After the birth, Elizabeth stays on with Larry, but at just the moment she voices her concerns that she should return to her own home, he proposes and she accepts. The action then moves on twenty years, to the eve of World War II. Elizabeth and Larry have two sons now and Elizabeth is worried that Drew, her eldest (by John), will be drafted. An Austrian scientist, Eric Kestler, arrives in Baltimore with a girl, Margaret. Kestler is John McDonald under an assumed name and the girl is the daughter of the doctor who saved his life. McDonald had chosen not to return to Elizabeth because of the injuries he had sustained – the first we see of him after this war is in a hospital bed, his face swaddled in bandages. 'Kestler' comes to work for Hamilton and is soon invited to the family home where he immediately recognises Elizabeth. She does not recognise him until much later, although he continues to deny that he is John McDonald. Kestler dies and Elizabeth and Larry are set to look after Margaret as well.

The mechanics of the plot of *Tomorrow Is Forever* serve to signal the film's equivocal relationship to the Hollywood convention that calls for the death of the soldier father-to-be, although the convention is, to an extent, upheld by the dual identity of John McDonald. McDonald, like Tim Hilton in *Since You Went Away*, is presented as the bereft wife's idealised fantasy figure; he is also, as Kestler, the embodiment of Hollywood's discomfort with the traumatised returning father. John McDonald as a youthful soldier only appears in flashback, condemned perpetually to a time that has already passed and to being filtered through Elizabeth's consciousness. McDonald is a cipher while Kestler, who exists only in the film's 'present', is not bound by the parameters of someone else's imagination. Desire for the father is therefore siphoned off onto a figure who, as the convention dictates, is presumed dead, a detachment that renders Elizabeth's enduring love for John chaste and melodramatic. That McDonald represents desirability is endorsed in a scene during Elizabeth's pregnancy. While napping, a sensuous white Persian cat tiptoes across her sleek satin bedspread. As this scene follows on from the exchange between the mutilated McDonald (also in bed) and his doctor, the presence of the cat as a symbolic representation of Elizabeth's desire for her lost husband is unmistakeable. A corpulent but sexy feline seems a peculiarly apposite symbolic alter ego for Orson Welles who plays McDonald, and is certainly a more erotic symbol than the wheezing bulldog used to signal Tim Hilton's enduring presence in *Since You Went Away*.

It is because she thinks her first child's father is dead that Elizabeth can be an innocent bigamist and can conform to that other rigid Hollywood convention of ensuring that the second husband can never match his predecessor's manliness. She even tells Larry that she will 'never love anyone the way I loved John'. That Larry subsequently proposes marriage, demonstrates how essential Hollywood deemed it to negotiate a separation between sex and the father. Elizabeth grows to love Larry but he is always the make-do husband, much as the second husband or partner is in countless women's pictures, *Letter from an Unknown Woman* being one 1940s' example. Wolfenstein and Leites ask 'Can you love twice?', arguing that such a problem is 'peculiarly American' and concluding that yes, in 1940s' Hollywood you could love twice, so long as the second love/husband is not as loved or lovable as the first (1950: 47 ff.). About *Tomorrow Is Forever*, they remark that Elizabeth compensates for her unwitting bigamy by 'never really loving her second husband' (56). The rival remains second best to the dead husband/lover and, as in countless examples from *My Foolish Heart* to *Pearl Harbor*, he was the woman's admirer before she married. The child resulting from these wartime preg-

Drew talks to both his fathers: Larry and McDonald/Kestler (right)

nancies is often the result of an illicit, fleeting love; the nurturing role of carer and provider is passed onto a non-eroticised substitute.

Elizabeth's contentment with Larry is ruptured when, as Kestler, John McDonald returns to Baltimore. Her dormant desire for her first husband remains repressed and is manifested only unconsciously as, unlike Lisa with Stefan in *Letter from an Unknown Woman*, she does not consciously recognise her first husband, although his arrival does prompt her to leaf through the photographs of her first wedding. It is upon Kestler's return that the narrative's rumination on desire and fatherhood becomes intricately convoluted. Because he is presumed dead, McDonald can never be his son's 'real' father, although it does not take him long to gather that Drew is his son, at which point he establishes a close relationship with him as a surrogate almost-parent with whom the young man can talk freely in a way he cannot with Larry, the man he thinks is his father. Through concealing his true identity, McDonald, ironically, is free to become an idealised father figure: the son's confidant, his sage buddy. Just as he is, by chance, granted access to his 'real' child, so he is also kept apart from him, finding he has to enjoy fatherhood vicariously through Larry. During his first evening at the Hamiltons, Kestler exclaims to Larry what 'a tremendous thing it is to have a son', proclaiming his time at his house 'a dream'. The fantasy is being compelled to observe another man leading the domestic 'dream' that is rightfully his. However, Larry too is making do, as Elizabeth rather cruelly emphasises when, distraught at the prospect of Drew enlisting with the Canadian RAF,[6] she blurts out in front of Kestler that Larry is not her son's father.

Tomorrow Is Forever deflects the potential trauma of its narrative complications onto its overly schematic plot. So, as Kestler is bonding with his son, Elizabeth is bonding with Margaret, the disguised McDonald and Elizabeth being implicitly invoked as the film's perfect parental partnership, but one that, like the return from the war of the sexual father, must be repressed. The painful duality of McDonald's position (unable, somewhat like the Little Mermaid, to speak his name) is expressed fully at the film's close. First, on their wedding anniversary, John and Elizabeth meet outside the house they shared while married and she realises finally who he is, although he denies his identity and walks off. Then, having turned his back on 'John McDonald' as it were, he stumbles, as 'Kestler', into a situation that propels him into acting as if he were Drew's father after all. He finds a note addressed to 'Father' on Larry's desk, opens it and discovers that Drew intends to join the RAF without his parents' approval. Kestler tracks down Drew and, as his father's 'friend', persuades him to come home. This act is both the act of the 'real' and of the surrogate father. Lastly, in McDonald/Kestler's final exchange with Elizabeth, he advises her (without explicitly acknowledging who he is) to forget him and the past he represents. Elizabeth asks why he did not return from World War I, to which he replies 'You'll never get back what you lost, you'll only lose what you have, and you have so much more to lose than you had twenty years ago'. McDonald/Kestler effects Elizabeth's final severance from her obligations to the past, a liberating gesture performed, in a film so packed with parallel characters and scenes, in front of a mirror in which both are reflected. The mirror is an apt symbol for introversion and for a morbid obsession with looking back and here it is a direct reference to the scene in which Elizabeth, likewise looking in the mirror, has her first flashback to the night John declared he was joining the army in 1917. So what purpose is served by these multiple plot pirouettes? As *Tomorrow Is Forever* was a wartime production, McDonald's success in persuading his wife to forget him is used as the device to then enable her to forget her misgivings about Drew joining the RAF. So the father's release of his wife enables the latter to, belatedly, perform her patriotic duty and permit her eldest son to go to war. Released from the miseries of the past, Elizabeth then does so quite emphatically by joyously helping Drew to pack his things. McDonald is paying a sort of penance for having survived the war and for having seen his son, so predictably *Tomorrow Is Forever* ends with his death after all.

The End of the Decade Patriarchal Model: *Fort Apache*; *House of Strangers*; *The Heiress*

Much of World War II's emotional, psychological impact on masculinity was, in late 1940s' Hollywood, disavowed. This chapter concludes with analyses of *The Search* and *Teresa*, both of which, more in keeping with contemporary thinking in psychology and sociology, centre on a gentle, co-operative paternal model. As an indication that Hollywood certainly does not always reflect the dominant thinking of the times, the kindly 'new father' image was a rarity in the 1940s. *Fort Apache*, *House of Strangers* and *The Heiress* form a potent trio of movies (all released between 1948 and 1949) which exemplify Hollywood's bias towards strong, authoritarian fathers. The style of fathering exemplified here is not exclusive to these films, although their virtually simultaneous release is an important barometer of what types of father and masculinity Hollywood wanted to promote. The wild, bullying father is a staple of Westerns at the time: Senator in *Duel in the Sun* (1946) or T. C. Jeffries in *The Furies*, in which the father's authority is further complicated by his quasi-incestuous desires for his daughter. The fathers in *Fort Apache*, *House of Strangers* and *The Heiress* share several traits: they are two-dimensional and characterised by a counter-productive inflexibility; they all remain set in their ways and rooted to the past – a nostalgia emphasised by the pre-war settings of all three films.

Such portraits are reflective of certain contemporary attitudes, for example the type of masculinity Susan Faludi claims would have been compatible with the US's expansionist, Cold War aims by 1948–9; the trio of fathers also embody a key paternal archetype (the authoritarian father) to which Hollywood returns continually. Owen Thursday in *Fort Apache*, Gino Monetti in *House of Strangers* and Austin Sloper in *The Heiress* conform to Freud's characterisation of the 'primal father'. Freud returned several times to the myth of the 'primal father', most expansively in 'Totem and Taboo'.

The mythic story is simple: a 'mob of brothers . . . filled with contradictory feelings' kill the father they loathe and fear, only to find themselves filled with remorse and intent upon resuscitating their primal father's image through constructing a substitute totem they subsequently worship (Freud 1913: 204–5). Thus, the sons' hatred is transmuted into admiration. This filial ambivalence, though, is not as striking an insight as what Freud goes on to identify occurs once they have killed him:

> After they had got rid of him, had satisfied their hatred and had put into effect their wish to identify themselves with him, the affection which had all this time been pushed under was bound to make itself felt. . . . The dead father became stronger than the living one had been (1913: 204).

Based on disavowal, the act of hatred and murder is prompted by repressed love, a love that makes the father a stronger and so more enduring image or point of identification than he had been while alive. Through death the real father can become the symbolic father. This ultimately impossible ideal is what prompts the sons to murder, as it is in them that the real–ideal fusion would, if it were possible, take place. Maybe Freud's notion of disavowal can be applied to the presence, throughout Hollywood's history, of certain films which seek to restore the primal father in defiance of the dominant social or psychological conventions of the time.

Symbolic portraits: Gino Monetti looks down at his widow and his son Max as they talk standing beside his coffin in *House of Strangers*

Myth is dependent upon repetition for survival, and it is significant that Hollywood's version of the 'primal father' myth is exemplified by the recurrence of certain narrative motifs. One such recurrent motif is the posse of sons with contradictory feelings towards their father. This motif is present in *House of Strangers* and in the 1950s became a staple element of otherwise quite distinct Westerns such as *The Halliday Brand* (1956), *The Big Country* (1958), *Broken Lance* (1954) – a remake of *House of Strangers*. Another recurrent motif is the patriarch's portrait, used as a symbol of both his power and his defunctness in several films of the time, including *The Furies*, *House of Strangers*, *Broken Lance* and *Fort Apache*. In all these, the father's portrait bears down upon the children and those who survive him; the children refer to it, talk to it and acknowledge its ambivalence. The way in which the father's portrait functions in Hollywood at this time is richly repetitive and demonstrates a crucially stable attitude to the moribund patriarch. The father's portrait prompts both inactivity and activity in his children (more often sons); it reminds them of how they will never equal the father or be as powerful as him, while functioning as the spur to rejecting him and the servility he has imposed. The portrait fixes the father in a moment in time and shows his omnipotence at its height; it is also, paradoxically, indicative of his vulnerability, precisely because it cannot change or answer back. And so, an important moment is when the child (or the successor, as is the case with Sgt Yorke talking about the portrait of Lt Col Thursday at the end of *Fort Apache*) eventually turns his back on the patriarch's image and what it represents.

Mankiewicz's *House of Strangers* is a virtual re-enactment of 'Totem and Taboo' and Max's interaction with Gino's portrait is a quintessential part of this. Gino Monetti (Edward G. Robinson) is a self-made, self-styled banker with four sons: Max, his favourite, and three others (Joe, Pietro and Tony) for whom he has little time and who, in turn, wish him dead. Having been chaotic but generous with his money – he has offered loans to other Italian-Americans without having sufficient collateral to offset them – Gino is put on trial. It is Max, acting as Gino's lawyer, who takes the blame, Joe having tipped off the police that he had tried (unsuccessfully, as it turns out) to bribe a juror. Max goes to prison for seven years. While there, his brothers wrest the bank from Gino, who seeks revenge through Max, sending him furious letters in jail in which he makes him swear that he will 'make them pay'. Gino dies and, after his release from prison, it does indeed seem as if Max is going to avenge his father's death, only to change his mind while contemplating his father's portrait. *House of Strangers* obsessively returns to this picture, most frequently in relation to Max. Most of the film takes place in flashback, a return to the past framed by Max's contemplation of the image of Gino presiding over the sitting room fireplace. However, it is his contemplation of the portrait and concomitantly what Gino stood for, that persuades Max to change his mind and forgive rather than kill his brothers, a symbolic gesture of atonement also seen in Sgt Yorke's actions at the end of *Fort Apache*. It is then Max's brothers who (much like Joseph's jealous siblings in the Bible) try to kill Max, before turning on each other as

Max leaves his feuding family behind and heads off (released from his mutually destructive filial bonds) for a new life.

The feud at the heart of *House of Strangers* enacts primal and perennial struggles between father and sons, reconfiguring the tortured sibling rivalries of the Old Testament (Joseph and his brothers, Cain and Abel, the Prodigal Son) as brothers vie bitterly for their father's affection. Gino is an unsubtle caricature of an unreconstructed immigrant male but, as with Freud's primal father, he is ambivalent. Gino is autocratic, even despotic (he refuses, early in the flashback, to get to the bank at opening time because 'the bank opens when I get there') and one view of him, voiced by Max's girlfriend Irene, is that he is 'an evil man, a bad man' who is better off dead. However, Gino's hubris is tempered by financial and personal naivety and his tyranny is endearingly idiosyncratic, often exploited for comedic effect. *House of Strangers* has one important family dinner scene. Seated around the table are Gino, Joe and his wife, Pietro, Tony, Max's fiancée Maria and her battle-axe mother. Gino has turned up *The Marriage of Figaro* to such a volume that it prohibits familial interaction as the restless family await Max. On a figurative level, the loudness of Gino's music is overwhelming and suggests how impossible it is for other members of his family to exist independently of him. Gino's love of opera though (because it so manifestly overwhelms Gino too), also resonates in its lushness with the munificence he displays towards the clients who come to him for small loans. Gino is misguidedly generous. Then, divested of his power as a banker, he becomes an amiable buffoon who provokes laughter during his trial as he explains that he charged such high interest at source on his loans because he never expected such loans to be repaid.

However, like the primal father, Gino has established a destructive father–son cycle which, as in Freud's paradigmatic narrative, must be broken if the next generation is successfully to negotiate its transition to independence. The Monetti cycle is not broken when Joe, Pietro and Tony divest Gino of his authority by taking over the bank, rather it occurs when Max decides not to carry out Gino's vengeful wishes. As with the myth in 'Totem and Taboo', the price of Max's extrication from the Monetti tribe is the violence needed to effect change and both Max and Joe are nearly killed by Pietro. The break with the primal father is necessarily violent and tumultuous, as it is here and later in Westerns such as *The Furies*, *The Big Country* and *The Halliday Brand*. The basis for this traumatic break is (as occurs in *House of Strangers)* an acknowledgment not only that the father was wrong but also that the perpetrator of the break was wrong for being too like the father. Max is temperamentally similar to Gino, essentially good and capable of love but vengeful and guided by a slippery morality. Following the Oedipal trajectory, the struggle with the primal father is here resolved as Max defies Gino (while talking to his portrait) and then feels free to go off with Irene. The mature sexual bond replaces the bond with the father. As Max says to Pietro when the latter is on the verge of killing Joe, 'You kill Joe, you do it for pa'. Breaking the cycle means no longer acting for and in the shadow of the father.

A similar severance of the father–child bond is effected, with contrasting results, at the end of both *Fort Apache* and *The Heiress*. In the former, for all Thursday's short-comings, the father's legacy is a positive one as he lives on into the next generation through his daughter Philadelphia and her newborn son Michael. In *The Heiress*, Sloper's legacy is characterised by sterility as Catherine, his daughter, is left alone, unwed and as vindictive as her hated father. Thursday (Henry Fonda), who treats his fathering responsibilities as an adjunct to his role as commanding officer of Fort Apache, at least has a quasi-Shakespearean ambivalence to him; Sloper is the most loathsome father in classical Hollywood. Like Othello, Thursday has had a glorious army career, although he finds himself out of tune with the times and customs of his present post. Like Macbeth, he goes into his final battle wounded and facing certain death, with only a sabre to defend himself against the marauding Apaches. Thursday's fatal flaw is his intransi-gence, demonstrated as a stubborn adherence to decorum and rank. Just as he will not countenance the advice of Sgt Yorke about how to confront the Apaches, so he will not contemplate Philadelphia's betrothal to a non-commissioned officer, Michael O'Rourke because, as he reminds both O'Rourke and O'Rourke's father, there is 'a barrier between your class and mine'. O'Rourke senior offers a more kindly, flexible paternal role model and in the end it is this alternative order that takes over in the form of Sgt Yorke, now the Fort's commanding officer. In death Thursday, like the primal father, assumed the role of mythic hero, for although Yorke offers his predecessor a cryptic eulogy (looking away from Thursday's portrait as he comments, 'No man died more gallantly or won more honour for his regiment'), the gathered admirers and members of the press still want to believe in Thursday's 'heroic charge'.

As Faludi believes, post-war American society was more interested in strong, mascu-line archetypes than perhaps the veterans were. (It is significant in this respect that it is Yorke, the soldier, who eulogises the common grunts who died alongside Thursday, and that it is the non-soldiers listening to him who steadfastly admire Thursday, their indi-vidualist hero.) In films of the time this social schism is echoed through the dramatisation of a dialectical opposition between tyranny and autocracy on the one hand and democ-racy and liberalism on the other: Al Stevenson's unease at being restored to his previously lofty social position in the bank in *The Best Years of Our Lives*, Phil's fight against anti-Semitism in *Gentlemen's Agreement*, the relative unimportance of her suitor's impecunious state to Catherine in *The Heiress* or the negative way in which Cliff's parents' snobbery towards their son's army buddy is portrayed in *Till the End of Time*. Sloper's dismissal of Morris Townsend in *The Heiress* is emblematic of this funda-mental generational struggle and of the primal father's destructive need to stop his child from gaining independence. That Sloper is proved right about Townsend's gold-digging intentions is the bitterest touch. Here, there is no symbolic portrait although there is symbolic *mise en scène*, as Wyler constantly emphasises Sloper's aggressive smothering of his daughter's individuality by having him also engulf and dominate the film frame.

Repeatedly, the framing in *The Heiress* has Sloper in close-up, dominating the fore-ground while the other characters hover in his wake. With additional use of wide-angle lenses and deep focus, Wyler renders Sloper authoritative but distorted; at one point – during an argument with Catherine, after he has assured her that he will not sanction her marriage to Townsend – he sidles off left of frame, passing so close to the camera as to virtually touch it. We too become the victims of Sloper's oppressiveness.

The father figures of *Fort Apache*, *House of Strangers* and *The Heiress* (or within a lighter comic context, *Meet Me in St. Louis*) are cinematic configurations of a compen-satory desire to re-establish the old patriarch and, apart from in *The Heiress*, imagine that he could be good. Being set in the past (although *House of Strangers* not by very much) also suggests the films are symbolically eliding the war and its effects, con-structing an image of the father which resuscitated older values and family paradigms, presaging the deeply conservative fathers of a multitude of films made in the 1950s. The past is familiar and so low risk. One notable recurring feature of the post-war films is their shared emphasis upon the unknowability of the future and the element of risk an investment in that future would necessarily entail. A tentativeness characterises many of the new personal relationships in the post-war films, for instance: in *Best Years*, Fred and Peggy only get together properly right at the end as do Cliff and Pat in *Till the End of Time*. In both cases, the lovers are 'star-crossed' in that there is considerable opposi-tion, from within themselves as well as from outside, to their unions.

A more specific narrativisation of risk and investment in the future is offered by the intriguing existence in three films (*The Best Years of Our Lives*, *It's a Wonderful Life*, *House of Strangers*) of the issue of speculative loans. In *Best Years*, Al's new position in the bank is to deal with loans to ex-servicemen, part of the government's programme to reintegrate GIs. A veteran (Novak) comes to see him, requesting a loan to buy a farm. At first, Al is reticent, as the bank's policy is to extend such loans only if there is suffi-cient collateral to secure them. He interrupts the interview with Novak upon seeing Homer getting his monthly $200 disability pay. This encounter prompts Al to agree Novak's loan, assuring Novak 'You look like a good risk to me'. A couple of scenes later Al, having drunk too much, makes an undiplomatic speech at a formal bank dinner dur-ing which he publicly advocates the issuing of such personal loans, concluding that this gamble 'on the future of this country' is the right thing to do. He compares the risk ver-sus collateral dilemma to the battle for Okinawa, positing a hypothetical scenario in which he refused to attack the hill because of insufficient collateral. This hypothetical story concludes with America losing both Okinawa and the war, the significance being, to Al's mind, that the war was won by taking such necessary worthwhile risks.

In *It's a Wonderful Life*, it is again the father, George Bailey, who grants personal loans – and is duly considered to lack business acumen. Once again, in the nightmarish 'Pot-tersville' sequence, a negative fantasy is conjured up as proof of the need to take risks in people. Potter is a rival banker whose business thrives not on risk-taking but on extorting punitive interest and rents from powerless clients. The philosophy of the Bailey family's savings and loans company is to help these same clients by loaning them the money to buy their own homes and so invest in their own futures rather than Potter's. More than once, however, Bailey's idealism brings him to the brink of personal and financial ruin, most importantly when there is a run on his bank. Here, the just-married George uses his own $2,000, put aside for his and Mary's honeymoon, to pay his clammering customers what they need to tide them over and to ensure that the bank does not close. *It's a Wonderful Life* vindicates George's altruism as the citizens of Bedford Falls reciprocate George's generosity by pooling together cash to help tide *him* over at the end after Billy mislays $8,000.

In *House of Strangers* too it is implied, as Gino personally hands out small loans to friends and clients, that such a philosophy of assisting others and investing in the future is naive but good. This ambivalence is indirectly expressive of a certain attitude in all three films to the position of the father – traditionally (and here ironically) a figure commensurate with security and stability. The generosity of Al, George and Gino is commonly endorsed; however, as fathers all three men are pulled two ways. All are able to see the benefits of taking risks – except when it comes to their own respective personal lives. Al initially stands in the way of Fred and Peggy; George's altruism stands in the way of his own desires for travel; and Gino hands out money to friends, but treats his own sons meanly. There was considerable uncertainty about the future in the late 1940s and arguably traditional patriarchs such as Alfonso and Lt Col Thursday offered ballast in an uncertain world more than idealists such as George Bailey might have done.

The Post-war 'New Father': *The Search*, *Teresa*

Needing the future to seem and be assured is maybe one underlying motivation for it being sons rather than fathers who commonly in Hollywood come back from the war, for it is the son and the next generation who will secure that future. As with both *Till the End of Time* and *Teresa*, however, such security is often dependent upon a final reconciliation between father and son. *The Search* and *Teresa* (both directed by Fred Zinnemann) are somewhat anomalous within the framework of Hollywood at the time. In both, fathering functions as a positive symbol for risk-taking and a new beginning. Schatz maintains that, by 1950, 'Hollywood went into a full-scale retreat from message pictures and prestige-level social problem dramas' (1997: 386), citing as reasons events from 1949 such as the establishment of HUAC, the trial of Alger Hiss, the Soviet atom-bomb tests and the fall of China to the Communists. Just as these destabilising events suggest reasons for the creation of primal fathers and for the negative attitude towards risk-taking, so they serve to indicate the extent to which Zinnemann's work at the end of the 1940s and beginning of the 1950s countered such trends.

In *The Search*, Sgt Stevenson (known as Steve), a GI stationed in 1946 Germany, becomes the surrogate father to a Czech boy, Karel, whom he finds amid the rubble of the ruined city and assumes to be an orphan. Steve (played by Montgomery Clift) makes arrangements for Karel to follow him to the US, a plan thwarted by the surprise discovery of the boy's mother. The film concludes with Karel and his mother being reunited and Steve looking on, satisfied that he has done his duty. *Teresa* is a more conventional father–son movie in which the son Philip Cass (John Ericson) returns from fighting in Italy to his family's cramped New York apartment. Scared of his mother (the film offers one of Hollywood's most extreme portrayals of 'Momism'), Philip regresses into flashbacks of the war and hides from his parents the fact that in Italy he got married to an Italian girl, Teresa. Teresa then follows him to New York and gets pregnant, although she leaves Philip because she considers him too immature to be a father. Philip goes in search of Teresa and finds her and their newborn son Filippo in hospital, at which point he becomes ready to face his responsibilities and the future.

Such images of fathering run counter to the patriarchal archetype in other films of the time and exemplify a problem for (if not indeed a threat to) Hollywood's image of hegemonic masculinity. Both Steve and Philip are overtly feminised – the latter is psychologically traumatised (he is seeing a psychiatrist and his flashbacks to the war are imbued with a homosocial attachment to his commanding officer) while the former is androgynous and sexually ambiguous. Both figures are also characterised by a tendency to voice their concerns and feelings about becoming fathers, a level of introspection rarely seen in Hollywood's butcher dads. This, in turn, is reflected in the films' persistent return to the twinned acts of running away and searching, acts that indicate a personal, psychological need and which function as metaphors for the embattled state of post-war masculinity. Feelings of loss, bewilderment and searching are present in many of the more troubled post-war films – the three veterans' vexed wanderings through the alien bars and streets of their hometown in *The Best Years of Our Lives*, McDonald's voyage back to Baltimore to find his wife in *Tomorrow Is Forever*, Philip Cass running away from responsibilities through the streets of New York in *Teresa*. In all these, the search is an actual as well as a figurative one, a search for stability and identity that signifies the search for the father, historically and psychologically the figure who most readily symbolises such qualities. It is historically proven that it has been predominantly women who have called for men to become more involved fathers, and examining these films in conjunction with alternative contemporary films that expunge such complex images of manliness, it is permissible to speculate that men might find it harder to identify with these more ambiguous father figures. These men who cry, run away and form deep attachments to children, bear a greater resemblance to conventional cinematic mothers than to traditionally masculine fathers.

Whether or not *The Search* and *Teresa* more closely resemble contemporary views on fathering than the strong patriarch films released at about the same time is debatable. Offering a surprisingly uniform historical trajectory of fatherhood in the modern age, psychologists and sociologists since the 1940s have argued that generally the 'degree of involvement that a father should have in a family' (Rotundo 1987: 70) has increased with time and that the modern American father abandoned in the early twentieth century his hitherto expected role as distant 'moral overseer' (Pleck 1988: 84). Despite the general trend towards the more involved 'new father' over the centuries, the more modern involved father was not so fulsomely endorsed in the late 1940s. Lundberg and Farnham (1947) again provided a negative view of the 'new father' when they posited that the male archetype 'most fully approved by society' is the 'aggressive, ambitious, energetic . . . go-getter' (346). They also suggest that a father should not venture beyond being a 'spectator' during the 'early months of a child's life' and they dismiss the tendency to 'outline a role for [the father] as baby tender and baby nurse' as 'well intentioned no doubt but mistaken' (348). Such conservative sentiments were further echoed throughout a 1949 collection of essays entitled *The Family: Its Function and Destiny*. The editor Ruth Nanda Anshen refuted in the introduction assumptions made by Marx, Engels and others that ' "progress" consists of the abandonment of the basic family structure and the perpetual creation of novel types of families', asserting instead that the modern 'disintegration' of the family took place alongside a negative decline in philosophy, morality and religion (1949: 4). In the same volume, influential sociologist Talcott Parsons advocated a return to clearly delineated gender roles within the home (Parsons 1949: 193), but it is Therese Benedek who, in the book's last essay, most eloquently elucidated the problem confronting the 1940s' American family when she observed that the father was unable to renounce 'the responsibilities and illusions of the patriarchal husband–father' while at the same time being 'expected to recognise' the need for 'equality' within the home (Benedek 1949: 211).

The late 1940s was a time of retrenchment and regression for the American father. Whereas, prior to World War II, there were noted 'dwindling demands for patriarchal formality' as men 'abandoned the central position in the family to their wives' (although they were not yet entirely comfortable with their roles as 'newly involved' fathers) (Rotundo 1987: 72), just after the war, the 'distant father–breadwinner still prevailed' (Pleck 1988: 90). In 1931, psychoanalyst Alfred Adler conceived of 'the role of the father' as 'every bit as important as the mother's' (1931: 114), suggesting that 'Every father should be aware of the fact that our culture has overemphasized the privileged position of the man' (116) and compensate for such inequality by forging a partnership with his wife, asserting with a resounding, democratic flourish that 'Authority is unnecessary in the family but there must be real co-operation' (120). This nurturing 'new father' had become rarer, but he was still being represented in films such as *The Search* and *Teresa*.

The Search, the first of Zinnemann's three 'social document'[7] World War II films (the others being *The Men* [1950] and *Teresa*), features complex and modern issues of paternity. Steve is one of many Hollywood surrogate fathers. His narrative function, like that of most of his successors, is to be a temporary parent to a parentless child and eventually to restore the child he has taken care of to its mother. As with all of Zinnemann's 'social document' films, *The Search* (filmed on location in Germany in 1947, principally in Munich and Nuremberg) is extremely careful to signal its veracity, thereby countering the melodrama of its plot. Factual details abound: location filming in the real ruins of Berlin, highlighting the United Nations Relief and Rehabilitation Administration from which Karel escapes and using camp survivors rather than actors to play his fellow refugees.[8] In his autobiography, Zinnemann records that he and his producer, Lazar Wechsler, wanted to use realism as a means of explaining to the Americans 'the depth of human suffering in Europe', although he also comments: 'It was most important to make the innocent American audience aware of what had happened in Europe, and for this reason we were obliged to soften the truth' (1992: 57; 61). The convergence of realism and melodrama was noted by many of the (UK) critics. Dylis Powell remarked that 'Looked at coldly, perhaps, it is an exercise in sentimental coincidence. But you can't look at it coldly' (*Sunday Times* 1949). Another British critic, however, found the film 'almost intolerably saccharine and coy' (*Herald* 1949).

 The Search's fraught utopianism is encapsulated in its idealised central relationship between Steve and Karel (whom Steve calls Jim because the boy refuses to reveal his

Surrogate father Steve plays with Karel/Jim

name). Steve finds 'Jim' scavenging a living in the mounds of Berlin rubble, frightened, mute and suffering from amnesia. As Steve learns more about him, so he learns the process of parenting, becoming the boy's tutor, guide and almost father. His role as surrogate father is problematic because it effects the displacement of the biological parents (which is no doubt why we are told early on that Karel's mother is still alive and so likely to be reunited with her only surviving child). This displacement forms the basis for *The Search*, which proves a rare example of the soldier embracing (or being allowed to embrace) the opportunity to become a father. Fatherhood in cinema is too often about denial – the burden of responsibility, the need to provide for the family and be authoritative. Surrogate fathering rarely conforms to this pattern, the most important reason being that surrogacy is commonly a temporary state, the substitute father being classically the finder of lost souls who, through friendship, helps the (usually male) child to develop and flourish so that he can be restored to the biological family happier and better than he was before. The transient nature of cinema surrogacy in turn liberates the surrogate father and permits him to be more adventurous and radical in his attitudes to parenthood than the conventional biological father, as one finds in *The Search* and, much later, in Clint Eastwood's *A Perfect World* (1993).[9] The conventional surrogate father of Hollywood war films is the commanding officer, as in such a context the lack of a parental guide is felt by the inexperienced 'grunts' all the more keenly. Thus, in *Teresa*, Philip Cass over-glorifies his immediate superior, Sgt Dobbs and likewise, in *The Story of GI Joe*, made just at the end of the war, Robert Mitchum as Capt Walker fathers his weary, scared platoon as they battle their way through southern Italy to Rome. Just as Stevenson in *The Search* has finally to give up 'Jim', so another convention surrounding the surrogate father – because of the manner in which such a figure blurs the boundaries between parenting and sexual attraction – is that he must die in order for his 'sons' to be freed from their dubious dependency. This severance is effected most frequently by the convenient death of the commanding officer: in *The Story of GI Joe*, Capt Walker dies before his platoon reach Rome and in *Teresa*, Dobbs is killed in battle. It is another oddity of *The Search* that the surrogate survives.

Confusions surrounding sexuality and gender identity characterise Hollywood's surrogate father. *The Search* came out the year after *Red River* (1948), Montgomery Clift's first film. Both focus on a relationship between a 'man' and a 'boy' (in the former it is the quasi father–son attachment of Tom Dunson to Matthew Garth) and both contain oblique references to homosexual and homosocial desire, centring on Clift. In *The Search*, these allusions serve to demonstrate Steve's ultimate unsuitability to the parental role. When Steve first returns to his digs with Karel, for instance, his fellow GI, Jerry Fisher (Wendell Corey) quips 'who picked up who?'; later Jerry calls Steve 'a sentimental sucker [for] the first kid who comes along and looks at you with his big blue eyes'. Another dubious feature of the conventionalised surrogate father is his configuration as a maternal as opposed to paternal substitute (a cinematic convention not a social one).

Again, *The Search* is similar in this respect to *A Perfect World* as both surrogates more or less explicitly fill in for the mother. Steve himself displays considerable awkwardness at his maternal role. When Jerry's family arrives in Germany, 'Jim' observes a 'complete' family for the first time since his rescue and asks Steve what a mother is; Steve looks implausibly panicked, stammering 'well, a mother is a mother ...' and gropes around for ways of explaining who she is, finally alighting on a picture on his wall that he can use – of two dogs, one big, one small. That the surrogate father is the substitute *mother* and not father is crucial in de-eroticising the bond between 'man' and 'boy'. After this exchange about what a mother is, *The Search* accentuates this need by changing the tone and dynamics of the relationship between Steve and 'Jim' so that Steve progresses from being the potential parent to becoming instead the boy's buddy and guide.

The surrogate father's role is limited and self-sacrificing, an attribute shared with maternal melodramas. Steve can never be 'Jim's' mother, but the fantasy that he still might be is dispelled only by melodramatic coincidence: discovering, at the children's hostel, that Mrs Malik is still alive. In a painfully brief sequence reminiscent of the similarly sacrificial finale to *Stella Dallas*, Steve is instructed by the woman officer in charge to release Karel/'Jim' so that the boy and his mother can be reunited. Like Stella, Steve must be satisfied with delivering Karel to his future happiness and abandoning his own plans. The fairytale potential for the surrogate father to have a long-term relationship with the child (as occurs, rather conveniently, through the biological father's death at the end of *Pearl Harbor*) is never a possibility. *The Search's* power and authenticity lie in its reconfiguring of the monolithic figure of the father. For all its clunkiness (Steve, for instance, builds bridges), it acknowledges, through its central relationship, the extent to which World War II changed everything, that it was never going to be a simple question of going back to the way things were as wartime films such as *Since You Went Away* vouched.

Teresa opens in a similarly documentary-esque manner with a woman at a social security desk looking straight to camera and asking the veterans standing in line if they have found work. After one man is seen running away from the queue, Zinnemann, as in *The Search*, deploys an anonymous voice-over to introduce the man as if he were the subject of a documentary: 'His name is Philip Cass, his occupation is running away'. Cass is literally running: past a movie house (a dream factory) and into a 'Veterans Administration' building for an appointment with his psychiatrist. As we learn at the end of the film, Cass is running away from his own impending fatherhood, although in a fraught monologue he indicates that his conscious anxieties relate to his feelings about his own father:

CASS: My father – he's nowhere that guy. Sometimes I look at him, you know, and think: that's my father. I don't know what's the matter with him. He never knew how to handle me. I mean, he never knew how to make me feel safe, I mean I never felt safe. I wish Dobbs had been my old man . . .

PSYCHIATRIST: A friend in the army?

CASS: Yeah. If Dobbs were here, I could do anything, I wouldn't be in this mess, I'd be out of here. I gotta headache. I don't want to think any more and I don't want to talk. [Cass leaves].

In this diatribe, Cass touches upon three fundamental issues of fathering: rejection and hatred of the weak father, the need for strong substitutes and the worry that the lack of a strong father has in turn affected him. When he returns home to the family apartment, Cass turns his back on his father, a bumbling but kindly man lying on his bed in a vest listening to the radio, closing the door on him in disgust when he proposes they 'listen to the game together'. Philip retreats to bed himself, where begins the flashback that occupies the majority of the film and explicates Cass's fears about fatherhood.

As one contemporary British review of *Teresa* commented wryly, 'Even psychiatry has its modes in Hollywood. At the moment, the Oedipus complex seems to be the most fashionable breakdown of the year' (*Evening Star* 1951). Philip's troubled relationship with his father arguably detracts from the intended subject of the film – the issue of war brides, 'a serious problem which arose all over America' (Zinnemann 1992: 87). This was the subject of the novel by Arthur Hayes, *The Girl on the Via Flaminia*, on which *Teresa* is loosely based. Philip's problems are twofold, as his own 'weakness' is seen implicitly as being the result of his father's perceived 'weakness' and his compensatory Oedipal desire to identify with a strong paternal archetype (as one reviewer remarked, 'Its hero is an insecure weakling with whom no red-blooded American moviegoer will care to identify himself' [*Saturday Review* 1951]). The 1930s and 1940s were overly preoccupied with the weak father. In 'Moses and Monotheism', which he revised in 1939, Freud identified the 'great man' to be the model the child would like the real father to conform to. This 'great man' of legend and childhood is a figure who is admired, trusted and feared, equipped with paternal characteristics identified as 'decisiveness of thought . . . strength of will . . . energy of action' and 'above all . . . autonomy and independence' (356). Max Horkheimer offered a riposte to Freud when he suggested (ten years later) that the child, upon discovering 'that the father is by no means the powerful figure . . . he is pictured to be', goes in search of 'a stronger, more powerful father, for a super-father, as it is furnished by fascist imagery' (1949: 365). In different ways, both Horkheimer and Freud argue that the male child cannot satisfactorily identify with a weak father, leading the needy child to seek out authoritarian substitutes, an action exacerbated during wartime, when the young soldiers' need for a leader becomes tangible. Acknowledging this, Freud, in his discussion of identification in 'Group

Psychology', remarks that it is 'obvious that a soldier takes his superior, that is, in fact leader of the army, as his ideal, while he identifies himself with his equals', adding that 'he becomes ridiculous if he tries to identify himself with the general' (1921: 167). The commanding officer was therefore an ideal role model.

When Cass 'runs away' from the realities of his home life he takes refuge in his wartime memories and it is predictably the figure evoked to the psychiatrist, Sgt Dobbs – legs purposefully astride, hands on manly hips, filmed from below and silhouetted against the parched Italian terrain – who opens the flashback, an exemplary Hollywood superior officer, a figure of longing and need. Philip is prone to swooning, which he does prior to this flashback and, within the flashback, just before Dobbs is killed during a night-time battle, as if without Dobbs he is physically as well as psychologically debilitated. Through his acquisition of Dobbs as his positive paternal role model, Cass is released into at least temporary adulthood (here replacing his fixation on Dobbs with his attraction to Teresa), only to regress when he returns home. This surrogate father–son relationship also remains ambivalent, its unresolved eroticism being suggested by Dobbs' symbolic act of giving Philip his scarf, which he does during the battle in which he dies. This scarf replaces the watch the father bequeaths his son and in *Teresa*, the traditional watch is a gift from Philip's mother not his father and is one that Philip willingly trades for food for Teresa's family. Conversely he covets Dobbs' scarf, a fetish he clings to even as he goes to see his newborn son.

Philip's initial psychological trauma is that he cannot live up to or be Dobbs. As *Teresa* offers one of Hollywood's clearest portraits of 'Momism', this issue of (mis)identification is linked to Mrs Cass, a mother whose unhealthy adoration of her son leads her at one point to complain to Philip (who is again in bed) that 'A woman needs someone . . . not a jellyfish, somebody strong like you'. The term 'jellyfish' stands out as uncomfortably literal and Philip's fear is that he too is a 'jellyfish' like his father and not the virile man Dobbs is and his mother imagines him to be. 'Momism' was an influential, vitriolic notion, born during the war and thus at a time when fathers were often absent, which hinged upon the idea that 'Moms' were permitted to rule because the 1940s' father was so unfailingly flaccid and ineffectual. 'Mom' was fashioned first by journalist Philip Wylie in *Generation of Vipers* in which he described her as 'a jerk', a chain-smoking, drunk, overweight 'middle-aged puffin' who emasculated her sons and who refused to release them from her 'apron strings' (186–204). Psychiatrist Edward Strecker later worried that 'Momism is the product of a social system veering towards a matriarchy' (1946: 30), while psychoanalyst Erik Erikson maintained that 'Mom' was wrongly blamed for 'all that is rotten in the state of the nation' because psychiatry wanted a scapegoat (1950: 280–1). Historian Christopher Lasch maintained that, in the late 1940s when 'Momism' was at its height, psychologists popularly believed that the fateful combination of an overbearing mother and a passive father could cause mental instability in the child, even schizophrenia (1977: 152), a view borne out by Wolfenstein and Leites

Philip Cass on the point of running away from family and responsibility

(writing in 1950) who speculated that psychic disturbances in the children would be frequently traced to this parental mismatch (122). The weak father and the domineering mother was seen at the time as a fateful dyad (and one which Hollywood returns to several times, notably in *Rebel Without a Cause*).

Philip Cass's instability is thereby dramatised as being a symptom of his parents' incompatibility. However, despite its portrayal of Philip's mother as a 'Mom' who spurns her son's wife, who jokes that Philip is her 'boyfriend' and who undermines his attempts to get a job in order to keep him tied to the home, *Teresa* goes against the views of Wylie and Strecker inasmuch as the 'jellyfish' father, 'Mom's' hapless mate, is not seen to be a cause of the son's weakness and immaturity, but rather the figure who finally enables him to mature and leave home. *Teresa* thereby intimates, in contrast to many of the voices quoted above, that the son's genuine, underlying need is to identify with the real and *flawed* father rather than to see himself in the idealised and perfect archetype he adores. Philip (atypically) reaches contentment when he comes to realise that not only is he like his father, but that being like his father is not so bad. The son's need to identify with the real as opposed to the fantasy father is echoed in *Teresa*, ironically in one of its more histrionic sequences. Philip, Teresa and his family are at the beach. Teresa has just learnt that she is pregnant but has not told Philip. Philip gets increasingly agitated as an oppressive montage of voices engulf him – officers taunting him during the war, his mother's voice repeating 'not a jellyfish' and 'not like him'. In a final trau-matised panic he blurts out 'I'm like him', looking with fear and recognition, at his father grimacing as he (once again) twiddles the knobs on his radio to get a better reception. To be like his father is initially presented as nightmarish and although Philip is not 'like' his father inasmuch as he is youthful, the staging of his dramatic recognition of himself in his clumsy, affable 'old man' suggests the inevitability of his own change at the point of becoming a father. As if in a final defiant fling against his 'jellyfish' dad, Philip here towers over him in a pose reminiscent of Dobbs. Clad only in swimming trunks, Philip's young body is resonant of the virility he is about to relinquish.

Emasculation, the last portion of the film implies, is a symptom of fatherhood: Dobbs, like Steve, was a father ideal but not a father, and so his physicality and desirability could remain intact. By *Teresa*'s conclusion, Philip, who has admitted to his psychiatrist that 'Maybe I'm beginning to grow up', is reconciled to responsibility and to renouncing sexu-ality and desire. In direct contrast to the beach scene, for his jubilant visit to the hospital ward to see Teresa and their son Filippo, Philip is shrouded in a regulation white cas-sock, an armless garment that imprisons his body and arms. As Jung would have maintained,[10] Philip Cass finds that the 'father complex' – when an individual's relation-ship with their father stands in the way of their own development – is an obstacle that can be overcome. Part of this 'overcoming' is due to the realisation that the state of fatherhood is one of compromise, even feminisation and weakness, not of hefty masculinity.

Throughout the immediate post-war period, Hollywood's portrayal of the father remained deeply ambivalent. Despite the interest of *Teresa* and *The Search* – and their greater relevance to what later audiences might construe as better paternal role models – such 'sensitive young father' movies were, at the time, anomalous, and would remain so (with a few exceptions) until as late as the 1970s. Although it is father figures such as Philip Cass or Stevenson who might be deemed to reflect the uncertainty dominat-ing images of masculinity at the end of the war, Hollywood was less interested in such compromised, vulnerable images of fatherhood. In tandem with this, several things started to change in terms of its narrative use of the father. The autocratic patriarch became the dominant archetype of 1950s' Hollywood, for example becoming the self-made tycoon, but whereas in the 1950s such narratives revolved almost exclusively around the relationship between father and son, in the 1940s, the coupling of father and daughter was far more common. As in *Teresa* and *The Search*, the representation of the father became almost inseparable from Hollywood's obsession with defining and redefining masculinity, and within such a framework the father–son dynamic was far more important. In the 1940s, the majority of Hollywood's fathers were also the pro-tagonists/heroes of their films; this also changes in the 1950s, suggesting again that the father is the Oedipal father to be feared and revered.

Notes

1. Cf. 'Soldier Boys' chapter in Paul Fussell, *Wartime* (Oxford: Oxford University Press, 1989).

2. A rare exception to this rule from the 1940s is *Pitfall* (1948) in which the protagonist was a father during the war and survives (see Cohan 1997: 39–49 for discussion).

3. Pre-Pearl Harbor fathers remained exempt from the draft in America until 1 October 1943 when a decree abolished Class III-A, which had until that point protected men with dependents from induction. Cf. Tuttle 1993: 30–2.

4. One daughter interviewed by Reuben Hill in 1945, Doris F., is quoted as saying: 'You have no idea how much I dread my dad coming home ... It's been heavenly at home without him around' (Hill 1945: 34).

5. This is taken from an email Michael Walker sent to me during our discussions of these paradigmatic wartime films.

6. Thereby enabling him to enlist pre-Pearl Harbor and the US draft.

7. The term 'social document' films comes from Dorothy Jones who, in 1956, identified the late 1940s in Hollywood as a period in which films were 'beginning to devote themselves seriously to an exploration of some of the social, economic and political problems of the time' (quoted in Neve 1992: 84–5). These films have often been critically dismissed (see Ray 1985: 155).

8. For a discussion of these elements in *The Search*, see Sternberg 1994: 109–12.

9. *A Perfect World* follows a very similar story to the British film, *Hunted* (Charles Crichton, 1952), in which Dirk Bogarde plays a runaway murderer who kidnaps and befriends a boy who has run away from home. Bogarde stars again as a surrogate father to a lonely boy in *The Spanish Gardener* (Philip Leacock, 1956). Bogarde's homosexuality and the concomitant sexualisation of the older man's relationship with a boy echo the dynamics of *The Search*.

10. See 'The Personal and the Collective Unconscious', reprinted in Beebe 1989.

2

The Return of the Patriarch: Generation and Traditionalism in the 1950s

The 1950s furnished the imaginations of future generations with the most enduring image of the traditional family. However, as historian Stephanie Coontz has since observed, the ideal of the nuclear family was, in the 1950s, 'a qualitatively new phenomenon' (2000: 25) and one that reversed as opposed to continued trends established in previous decades.[1] For the first time in a hundred years, women were marrying and having children earlier, the birth rate increased, divorce rates declined and women's 'educational parity with men dropped sharply' (25). Alongside a reaffirmation of traditional gender distinctions within the family came the resurgence of the patriarchal father. This return to traditionalism had much to do with America's growing affluence; as John Demos notes in his social history of the American father, a more affluent peacetime meant the reinforcement of 'traditional domestic arrangements' (1986: 63). With irony and resentment, early feminist Simone de Beauvoir (whose seminal text *The Second Sex* was translated into English in 1953) characterised the traditional father thus:

> The life of the father has a mysterious prestige: the hours he spends at home, the room where he works, the objects he has around him, his pursuits, his hobbies, have a sacred character. He supports the family, and he is the responsible head of the family. As a rule his work takes him outside, and so it is through him that the family communicates with the rest of the world: he incarnates the immense, difficult, and marvellous world of adventure; he personifies transcendence, he is God (1949: 314).

Freud's writings were particularly influential in America at the time and, because of the prevalence in the public consciousness of this 'mysterious' and omnipotent archetype, representations of the father in the 1950s recall, almost instinctively, Freud's fearful Oedipal father. Founding American feminist Betty Friedan argued that, in the 1950s, Freudian psychology 'became an all-embracing American ideology', 'a new religion' that 'provided a convenient escape' from the big political issues of the time (1963: 110), while women's historian Marilyn Yalom points to the 1950s as the 'golden age of Freudians in America' (2001: 361). Freud's belief in the importance of sexuality to the formation of the ego found a populist spokesman in Alfred Kinsey and, specifically in terms of the myths of fatherhood that the films of the time embellished and constructed, Freudian archetypes are peculiarly apt – the son's need to identify with his father, the daughter's repressed attraction towards him, the smothering, successful patriarch, the brutish primitive father. The father's not entirely explicable omnipotence is evident in a film such as *All that Heaven Allows* (1956). In a classic Sirkian moment that exemplifies this ambiguity, Ned, the Oedipal son of his widowed mother Cary, refuses to countenance the idea of her marrying the family's gardener, Ron Kirby. Ron tells Cary that such a marriage would go against 'everything that father stood for'. As always with Sirk, where actors and objects are placed is as important as dialogue in conveying meaning, and in this sequence Ned's focus is the spot on the mantelpiece where a sports cup won by his father used to sit, but which Cary has recently cleared away. Ned thumps the spot where the trophy used to be, admonishing Cary for having abandoned father's sense of 'tradition' and for having renounced all 'sense of obligation to father's memory'. Ned's is a circular argument, however. The father 'stood for' tradition, but what that 'tradition' is, he never defines.

The 1950s offered an ambivalent image of the father. A yearning for the strong authoritarian patriarch synchronous with the Freudian model was manifested in the films of the 1950s as a fascination with the domineering father who is frequently out of control. Alongside this father resided the paternal image most readily associated with the 1950s – the nine-to-five 'man in the grey flannel suit'. This is the father evoked repeatedly in the pages of *Ladies' Home Journal* or *McCall's* in regular columns such as *LHJ*'s DIY roundup 'There's a Man in the House', sandwiched between other regular 1950s' columns such as 'Making Marriage Work' and worried discussions (in the wake of the Kinsey reports) of sexual 'abnormality'.[2] Despite the social prevalence of the breadwinner, one significant anomaly is the extent to which Hollywood undermined the traditional family man during the 1950s. There are fewer such dads than one might expect, making Steve Cohan's assertion that the breadwinner father of films such as *The Man in the Gray Flannel Suit* (1956) represented 1950s' hegemonic masculinity (1997: Chapter 2) a contentious one. The 1950s' domesticated male tended to appear either in melodramas (*Bigger than Life*, *There's Always Tomorrow*, *Rebel Without a Cause* [all 1956], *The Wrong Man* [1957]) or comedies (*Father of the Bride* [1950] and *Father's Little Dividend* [1951], the Jerry Lewis films *Rock-a-Bye Baby* [1957] or *The Geisha Boy* [1958], *The Seven Year Itch* [1955], *Pillow Talk* [1959]). Neither genre is particularly masculine, and so the father's presence here problematised his supposed hegemony.

Far more prevalent within Hollywood, were images of the strong, autocratic, even despotic father. In these films, the father is the distant parent observed from the child's point of view. As a result of this detachment, he is more likely to retain his symbolic power, a power that the films regularly reconfigure as extraordinary jobs or social roles. The tycoon, the self-made man, the pillar of the community figures prominently in *A Place in the Sun* (1951), *Giant* (1956), *Written on the Wind* (1956), *While the City Sleeps* (1956), *The Long, Hot Summer* (1958). The patriarchal name in such films literally dominates the narrative space – flashing in neon over a cityscape the patriarch presides over or owns, inscribed over the entrance to a vast family ranch, a street or a town. In keeping with the prevailing masculinism of 1950s' America, such films revolve around a fraught central relationship between father and son. According to Susan Faludi, the prioritisation of the father–son bond at the time was perniciously pervasive and 'To grow up a girl in this era was to look on in envy, and to see the boy as being automatically entitled and powerful' (1999: 24–5). Supporting this understanding of the symbolic importance of male familial relationships, Dr Spock commented at the time that 'The rivalrous antagonism of son to father shows on the surface less frequently because sons seem to be, on the average, more in awe of their fathers than girls are of their mothers' (*Ladies' Home Journal*, 1958a: 48). Such 'awe' is not, in the films, represented exclusively as positive. The domineering father is particularly negatively portrayed in Westerns in which he rules over a posse of sons: *Broken Lance*, *The Halliday Brand* and *The Big Country*. Characterised by ancient feuds and extreme violence (as is *The Furies*), the father's law (so strong as to have hitherto seemed unassailable) must be overturned if the younger generation is to survive. The rites of succession are never smooth. In Westerns and other father films of the 1950s there is an obsession with progeny and the family name living on after the father's death, the latter often represented as impotence or problems with fertility, as in *Written on the Wind*, *Cat on a Hot Tin Roof* (1958) and *The Long, Hot Summer*. These tensions are compounded by the sons of these films being so dominated by their fathers that they are either incapable of or unwilling to fill their shoes.

The overriding preoccupation with generation (Spock's remarks above were made in an article focused on the aggressive child) found its echo in a series of self-consciously Oedipal films. The father–son movies often couched the Oedipal dilemma in the son's traumatic response to the father's rule as in *Rebel Without a Cause* and *East of Eden* (1955) or centred on the issue of the son's sexuality as in *Tea and Sympathy* (1956), *Written on the Wind*, *Cat on a Hot Tin Roof* and *The Long, Hot Summer* all of which twin issues of sex and sexuality to another more acceptable 'problem'. In *Tea and Sympathy*, the father's despair at his son's feminisation (which most critics interpret as a metonym for homosexuality) is displaced onto an absurd anxiety that his son wants to become a folksinger, while in the latter three, impotence and homosexuality are insinuated via alcoholism. The power–sex correlation of the Oedipus complex comes out in the few father–daughter films of the decade as unresolved, quasi-incestuous sexual tension. Displaced incestuous desire between father and daughter is central to *Angel Face* (1953), *Bonjour Tristesse* and *The Big Country* and features overtly in *Peyton Place* (1957). Hollywood fathers of the 1950s are extreme – either obscenely dominant or awkwardly weak, the compromise father figures (both played by Robert Mitchum) of *River of No Return* (1954) or *Home from the Hill* (1959) (part hunter–hero, part nurturing dad) proving isolated examples. More typical of the time is the nightmarish sinful father (Mitchum again) in *The Night of the Hunter* (1955) or the 'ordinary' father of *Violent Saturday* (1955), whose son is teased because he did not fight in the war. Although there are discernible trends in Hollywood's representation of the father in the 1950s, its films both go with and against social trends. Hollywood's most distinctive departure was its portrayal of the breadwinner as troubled, repressive and ineffectual.

Breadwinner Fathers: *Father of the Bride, There's Always Tomorrow, The Man in the Gray Flannel Suit, Bigger than Life*

In *Masked Men: Masculinity and the Movies in the Fifties*, Cohan argues that the 'standard biography of hegemonic masculinity that all American men were assumed to have shared' was to have first fought in the war and then become head of the household (1997: 36). However, as demonstrated by Hollywood's output in the 1940s, heroism – and by implication manliness – did not reside comfortably within the figure of the father and breadwinner and neither, in cinema, is the latter unproblematically hegemonic. Cohan concludes his analysis of *The Man in the Gray Flannel Suit* with the observation: 'this film shows that, if you take away the suit, you will have trouble finding the man' (78). This is a neat summary, but the 1950s' Hollywood breadwinner is less straightforward than this. In the series of films to be discussed, the eponymous 'man in grey' is neither simply dull nor hegemonic but a site of conflict, irresolution and painful compromise. He is neither the aspirational model nor the empty signifier Cohan suggests. He is a contradictory figure in whom several ideals of post-war American masculinity collide but ultimately fail to homogenise. The man returned to his dual role of provider and head of the household, but with his increasingly domestic role came fear, lack and loss.

The breadwinner's disempowerment is exemplified by comedies such as Minnelli's *Father of the Bride* and *Father's Little Dividend*. In the first, the Banks family are preparing for daughter Kay's wedding, while in the latter, they welcome the subsequent arrival of a grandchild. More acutely than Minnelli's earlier *Meet Me in St. Louis*, the comedy of *Father of the Bride* revolves around the father's inherent duality, between patriarchal success (and the economic indispensability of the upper-middle-class father–provider) and endearing buffoonery. The paradox of Stanley Bank's position is presumed to be that, for all the comedy at his expense (in the run up to Kay's wedding Stanley is the butt of most of the film's jokes), his centrality within the family remains unquestioned. As James Naremore comments, 'the father might be a clown, but he remains the embodiment of paternalistic values' (1993: 94).[3] This position seems to be only just tenable. If *Since You Went Away* made clear from its very title the importance of the absent father to the wartime family, so '*Father of the Bride*' likewise underscores the relative anonymity and marginality of the father at the ritualised moment of his daughter's flight from the family home.

Interesting sociological research sustains the view that it is precisely Stanley's incompetence (the manifestation, it would appear, of his loss of power) that is crucial to his recuperation. Ineptitude is often the trait associated with Hollywood's comic father: the

Troubled breadwinners: Cliff distraught after Norma's departure and Ed bearing down on his son Richie

jokes at the expense of Bick Benedict's dignity in *Giant* or the father-to-be (again played by Rock Hudson) being dragged off by two figures in white coats at the end of *Pillow Talk*. In the Jerry Lewis comedy *Rock-a-Bye Baby*, Clayton's surrogate fatherhood is constructed around incompetence as he feeds milk to his triplets through the distended fingers of a pair of rubber gloves or takes them for a stroll in three cots tied together. However, glorification of the paternal role is never far away. For all Clayton's ineptitude, his childishness is both the reason that glamorous movie star Carla decided to leave her babies with him while she goes off to shoot a movie in the first place and the reason why he eventually proves to be a good father. Infantilisation and buffoonery are recurring characteristics of Hollywood's good, often surrogate, fathers as in the later examples, *Three Men and a Baby* and *Big Daddy*. Clayton, like these other ostensibly inept fathers, is finally endorsed as an effective parent. Once the triplets have been returned to Carla, Clayton, at the end of *Rock-a-Bye Baby*, is rewarded for his pains with a solid relationship and quintuplets of his own.

Certain sociologists have argued that from the end of the nineteenth to the mid-twentieth century, many images of the father in popular culture were merely 'well-known variants' of the 'incompetent' type (Demos quoted in LaRossa *et al.* 1991: 988). Citing examples from cartoon strips, radio and television comedies and popular Broadway productions, they observe that father figures 'burbled and bumbled, and occasionally made fools of themselves' and were pitted against 'long-suffering wives and clever children' who patronised them (988) – precisely the dichotomy of *Father of the Bride*. A study by Randal Day and Wade Mackay of 'incompetent' father images in *Saturday Evening Post* family cartoons from the 1920s to the 1970s suggests that father figures are more likely than mothers to be depicted as incompetent in times of relative male supremacy (LaRossa *et al.* 1991: 988–90). In subsequent research by LaRossa *et al.*, there emerges a similar pattern, that, after a period of relative gender equality, 'the period from 1945 to 1968 witnessed a return to a 1920s-like portrayal of sharp gender differences in parental incompetence, with fathers much more likely than mothers to be depicted as incompetent' (LaRossa *et al.* 1991: 992).

The comedy of *Father of the Bride* takes place in flashback and begins with a monologue to camera by Stanley Banks (Spencer Tracy) the evening after Kay's wedding. Stanley bemoans the loss of his supremacy and the loss of Kay's adoration of him. *Father of the Bride* conforms loosely to a three-act structure through which Stanley's demotion is charted. The first 'act' closes with the Banks' engagement party, at which Stanley is relegated to the kitchen to mix the drinks. He never manages to deliver the speech he has planned and a friend warns him 'From now on the gals take over. Your function is to pay the bills'. The father's incompetence is here transmuted into servility. The central act of the film is Stanley's nadir; he has now little function except to manifest incompetence, exemplified by the glorious mime of Stanley squeezing himself into the dress coat he has preserved from his own wedding and hopes to wear to Kay's. With trepidation but irrepressible confidence, Stanley gingerly inserts himself into the suit, suck-ing in his stomach in order to do up his waistcoat buttons. Triumphant, he turns to admire his reflection, his stomach folded and his arms splayed because the suit is too tight. Drastic recuperation or denial is needed if Naremore's view that Stanley, even when clowning, 'remains the embodiment of paternalistic values' (1993: 94) is to be sustained, and salvation comes in the form of Kay, who is soon made to look even more silly than Stanley as she temporarily calls off the wedding because her fiancé Buckley has chosen Nova Scotia for their honeymoon.

The third 'act' builds up to Kay's wedding and should be the paterfamilias's crown-ing moment. Patriarchal equilibrium, however, is only equivocally restored. On the eve of the ceremony, Stanley has a nightmare in which all paternal credibility is lost as his unconscious summons forth a buffoonish image of himself in frayed clothes arriving late at the church and unable to walk up the aisle, as the church floor has become the spongy consistency of a cheap mattress. Stanley is roused from his nightmare by Kay scream-ing in horror at the spectacle of her father's humiliation. Cohan, like Naremore, argues that the jokes aimed at Stanley do not detract from the 'breadwinner's masculinity' and that 'the family cannot function without him as its psychological leader' (1997: 52). Stan-ley's position as patriarch is not, however, altogether recuperated by the actual ceremony going without a hitch as through the film he is increasingly marginalised by the women.

The 1950s' domestic father was, at the very least, an ambivalent archetype and the image of the father generated by American women's magazines resonates with these conflicting ideals. The returning husband is undoubtedly the unnamed beneficiary of all the cooking, housework, self-adornment and emotional outpourings in their columns. However, when named, he is portrayed as boringly functional (the DIY expert who would make use of 'There's a Man in the House') or he is gently mocked. In George Starbuck Galbraith's double-edged 'Hold Your Man and Stay Human' (*McCall's* 1961), the wife is urged to

> Above all, be sure to make home a haven he can come to, a retreat from the fret and
> tension of his work. If you have not had the good sense to deliver and rear flawless,
> quiet children, you will have to see to it that your normal brats are not a strain on your
> husband's nerves. The youngsters may be fed cornflakes and locked in their bedroom
> before Daddy gets home. ... Don't depress your man with a recital of your petty
> domestic woes. Listen to a recital of his petty office woes; then call up a female friend,
> and recite *your* woes loudly and in detail, so he can hear you (168).

Daddy-O is likewise patronised in Dr Spock's *Baby and Child Care*. In the 1958 edition (*Baby and Child Care* was first published in 1955), Spock speculated that one reaction to his wife's pregnancy might be 'pride in his virility' (1958: 27); then he assured his male readers (or was he really assuring attentive mothers?) that 'a man can be a warm father and a real man at the same time' (29), although this only means he has to do routine tasks occasionally – 'He might make the formula on Sunday' (30). The 1950s' father, despite his importance to the home, occupied only a marginal role when it came to nurturing, and it is significant that the incompetence of the comedic father more often than not revolves around domestic chores and childcare.

British psychologist John Bowlby's 'attachment theory' was deeply influential during the 1950s and 60s and worked in parallel to Spock's more practical manual. Both focused on the centrality of the mother to the child's upbringing and so implied the con-comitant redundancy of the father within the domestic sphere. In November 1958 (the year Bowlby first wrote up his theories), *Ladies' Home Journal* ran the article 'Should Mothers of Young Children Work?',[4] in which Bowlby argues that a child needs '*one* person whom they know and trust to mother them' (*Ladies' Home Journal* 1958b: 154). The child is drawn by 'instinctive behaviour' to the mother who most likely fulfils this role.[5] In his writings, however, while his language presupposes that to look after is 'to *mother*', Bowlby never definitively stated that the child's significant adult had to be the mother; that the carer was the mother was 1950s' social convention. What is beginning to emerge is that the father's incompetence in part stems, therefore, from his ignorance of domestic affairs and child-rearing resulting from being the family breadwinner, detached from the home.

The archetypal routine of the 1950s' breadwinner is illustrated perfectly in *The Man in the Gray Flannel Suit*: the first time we see Tom Rath, he is travelling home to Con-necticut on the commuter train from New York, doing a crossword and talking to his regular middle-aged travelling buddy; he is met at the station by his wife Betsy who recites her 'petty domestic woes' as she drives him home. This is an archetypal 1950s' scene: the father's daily commute, his distance from domestic life, the proliferation (par-ticularly in the US and the UK) of suburbia and the commuter belt. In the affluent, conservative post-war period this lifestyle pattern re-enforced gender divisions which had become blurred during the 1940s, when more women worked.

The majority of studies of fatherhood see this ritualised distancing of the father from the domestic domain as rooted in the changes brought about to family life by the Indus-trial Revolution. Psychologists Lundberg and Farnham melodramatically argued in the late 1940s that the 'hammer blows of the Industrial Revolution' destroyed the home and bred 'deep unhappiness – not only in women but in society as a whole' (1947: 93) because it changed work patterns and compelled fathers to cease working at home (95). Industri-alisation is also blamed for reducing that home to a 'household' which did not 'fulfil the general conditions psychically required of a home' (93). Later sociologists and psycholo-gists likewise link the father's breadwinning role to the changes brought about by the Industrial Revolution (see Lamb 1986; Rotundo 1987; LaRossa *et al.* 1991; Pleck and Pleck 1997) and they too view the transition equivocally. Pleck and Pleck signal that the father's

to the fore in Todd Haynes' *Far from Heaven* [2003] a remake of *All that Heaven Allows*). To borrow Foucault's notion of the 'repressive hypothesis', although the implied intention of Kinsey's exhaustive research, his graphs and tables is to dampen desire and de-eroticise sex, the laborious naming of male sexual activity has the effect of bringing to light what had hitherto been repressed: the eroticism of the average American male.

These multiplying ambiguities and repressions can be located within the troubled father figures in *The Man in the Gray Flannel Suit*, *There's Always Tomorrow* and *Bigger than Life*, which, alongside *The Wrong Man*, constitute a significant group of 1950s' breadwinner films. Sexuality is at the heart of all these depictions of the father. It is most central to the plot of *The Man in the Gray Flannel Suit*, in which Tom Rath (Gregory Peck), who has a family of three children in America, discovers that, as the result of an affair with an Italian girl Maria while serving in the Allied campaign of 1943–4, he also has a son in Italy.[7] In *There's Always Tomorrow*, Cliff (Fred McMurray) contemplates leaving his family for old acquaintance, Norma (Barbara Stanwyck), before deciding to stay with his wife and children. In *Bigger than Life*, Lou presumes her husband Ed (James Mason) is having an affair when in fact he is moonlighting at a cab firm in order to earn extra money.

Denial and renunciation are here expressed in narrative terms. Tom's memories of the war are colourful and erotic, but their intensity is relegated to three flashbacks: two while on the train and the other while he is filling out an application for a new job. The stability of his family and his role within it are expressly dependent upon maintaining a separation between these sexual memories and his home life. The act of giving up is most clearly articulated in *There's Always Tomorrow*. In the film's second scene, Cliff arrives home with a bunch of flowers for his wife Marion whose birthday it is. In a scene imbued with unbearable poignancy, Cliff is all but ignored by both Marion and their three children; they all hurry past, greeting Cliff cursorily as they go about doing something else. Cliff's offer to Marion of theatre tickets then is rejected without hesitation, as that evening is also their youngest daughter's first ballet performance, which automatically takes precedence over spending an evening with her husband. Although, like Stanley Banks, Cliff is of little interest to his children except as a gracious benefactor and of almost as little interest to his wife, what comes through more than anything in this scene is Cliff's desire – his desire to love and to be found desirable; he looks with longing at a wife who all too readily turns away the moment a child needs her.

That evening, when Cliff is alone, Norma arrives unexpectedly and rekindles his repressed desire to desire, only for Cliff later to renounce her in favour of paternal duty. Within Douglas Sirk's highly wrought visual style, the home is used symbolically to mimic and express Cliff's conscious repression. When Cliff returns home at the end of the film, having just parted for the last time from Norma, Sirk intercuts Cliff opening a window and gazing up at a plane in the sky with a tearful Norma aboard her plane bound for New York. Cliff then shuts the window (and with this small gesture, his desire) as Marion confides that she has been worried about him recently. He replies 'I'm alright now.

You know me better than I know myself', to which Marion adds 'I should – after a lifetime with you'. They link arms and walk past their three children, seated behind a row of spindles dividing the hall from the lounge. Frankie, the youngest, muses contentedly 'They make a handsome couple, don't they?' This emergency narrative closure, coupled with the symbolic closure of the window and the pen-like bars are the only public evocations of Cliff's closeted desires.

The breadwinner's public face is a masquerade, a performance put on to deflect attention from suppressed ambitions and emotions, his conformist appearance obliquely resonant of lost sexuality and what he has renounced. In *The Man in the Gray Flannel Suit*, Tom, while in Italy, had sex for pleasure; he and Maria met not in a twin bedded room, but amid the romantic ruins of a bombed house. What characterises Peck's performance and appearance in the film is his eponymous grey suit, the iconic garment synonymous with his role as provider and through which is conveyed the debilitating effort of preserving the breadwinner masquerade. Psychologist J. C. Flügel's notion of 'The Great Masculine Renunciation' has informed studies of men and dress since it was published in 1930. Flügel dated to the end of the eighteenth century the 'sudden reduction of male sartorial decorativeness' that, he argued, has characterised men's fashion since (110); with the rise of the middle classes and male professional employment, a greater 'uniformity', 'simplification' (112) and democratisation characterised men's attire, as 'Man abandoned his claim to be considered beautiful' and instead wore clothes that 'aimed at being only useful' (111). Male fashions became more inhibited, more functional and less expressive, Flügel arguing that 'modern man's clothing abounds in features which symbolise his devotion to the principles of duty, of renunciation and of self-control' (113). Lundberg and Farnham likewise equated the move among men 'toward more sober and austere garments' with increased work and duty, epitomised by the rise of what they term 'Democratic man' who saw himself 'dedicated to the serious purposes' of work and who 'garbed himself accordingly' (1947: 15). As Cohan has suggested, the grey wool suit is often viewed as a metonym for masculine dullness.

Other specifically fashion writers, however, argue against the notion of male attire as merely functional. Tim Edwards makes the point that the anonymous suit itself can be sexual:

> The main example of the utility of menswear, namely the suit, is as much a symbol of
> masculine sexuality in terms of broadening shoulders and chest and connecting larynx
> to crotch through collar and tie, as it is a practical (if historically uncomfortable) uniform
> of respectability (1997: 3).

There are suits and there are suits, however, and the unremarkable, definitely non-suave ones Tom and Cliff wear (Ed in *Bigger than Life* is sartorially more adventurous with his double-breasted jackets and bowties) are not in the same league as Cary Grant's. The grey flannel suit was respectable and professional, but lacked the dash of the more sharply tailored models it mimicked (in the novel of *The Man in the Gray Flannel Suit*, Tom describes picking up his 'best suit, a freshly cleaned and pressed gray flannel' [Wilson 1955] for a job interview). Tom's suits are the epitome of what dress historian Anne Hollander would term 'non-fashion' which, unlike fashion that 'abhors fixity', 'creates its visual projections primarily to illustrate the confirmation of established custom, and to embody the desire for stable meaning even if custom changes' (1994: 17). Within the context of cinema one can differentiate further between the suave suit and the father's suit. The latter tends to only signal sexuality in the manner Edwards envisages through disavowal, as its relative shapelessness seems openly to acknowledge the need to repress that sexuality. The unfashionableness of this suit symbolises conformity and stands in direct opposition, within the context of the mid-1950s, to the youthful fashions (white t-shirt, jeans and leathers) worn by 'rebels' such as Marlon Brando and James Dean (see Chenoune 1993: 236). As the grey flannel suit became synonymous with the father, so this casual garb became the uniform of the rebellious son.

The symbolic value of the breadwinner's appearance is exemplified by the scene in *The Man in the Gray Flannel Suit* in which Tom and Betsy argue over Tom's lack of ambition. Betsy vents her frustration at Tom's unspectacular $7,000 salary and declares their comfortable suburban home to be a 'graveyard' that 'smells of defeat'. It is manifestly Tom whom she thinks 'smells of defeat', as she continues: 'ever since the war … you've lost your guts and all of a sudden I'm ashamed of you'. Tom counters Betsy's rejection by assuring her that his job is 'an absolutely safe spot' and that 'the war is over, forgotten'. 'Safety' within this context is equated with emasculation. The argument takes place in an oppressively conformist suburban kitchen, Tom the embodiment of Betsy's fears, in his grey tank top, trapped between his aspirant wife and the family fridge. That Tom's emasculation is a corollary of fatherhood is illustrated by his need, after this bitter argument, to seek solace specifically in his role as father, leaving Betsy to go and visit all three children in turn in their beds, bonding, in particular, with his son.

Emotional restraint (the scene in which Tom goes to see the children is virtually without dialogue) and the father's restrained appearance become hysterical symptoms of his unease with his lot. The conjunction of duty, asexuality, dress and social role defines the parameters of a quite particular sense of personal betrayal. The 'man in grey' is a compromised figure and a figure of compromise who must disavow his personal, emotional, sexual needs if he is to become a good father. This tension is most dramatically represented in *Bigger than Life*. Ed is prescribed cortisone for a mysterious arterial complaint; as he starts to abuse the drug he becomes the superman Horkheimer envisaged as the alter ego of the authoritarian male, going from meek family man to the monster who, in the film's penultimate scene, declares that 'God was wrong' to save Isaac from his father Abraham as he himself prepares to kill Lou and Richie.

However, all these films are only superficially resolved by the imposition of a false sense of closure that fails to mask the preceding unhappiness and despair. The films' fathers view their discontent as linked to fathering – and obviously, as they all decide to stay with their families and continue as before (Ed is thwarted in his attempt to kill Lou and Richie by his friend Wally's timely intervention), this is something about their lives that remains unchanged. The clearest attack on fatherhood comes in *There's Always Tomorrow* when, after an unsuccessful evening during which Cliff's children, convinced that their father was having an affair, had behaved rudely towards Norma, Cliff turns to Marion and explains:

> I'm tired of the children taking over, I'm tired of being pushed in the corner, I'm tired of being taken for granted ... I'm becoming like one of my own toys, Clifford Groves the walkie-talkie robot, wind me up in the morning and I walk and talk and I go to work all day. Wind me up again and I come home at night, eat dinner and go to bed. Wind me up the next morning and I drive to the office and work all day to pay the bills ... I'm sick and tired of the sameness, day in day out.

Sirk uses extreme shade to convey Cliff's crisis of insignificance, emphasising the schism between his melting sense of identity (the repetition of 'I'm') and his growing realisation of the anonymity imposed by his social function as breadwinner father.

The most implausible ending is that of *The Man in the Gray Flannel Suit* as Tom and Betsy are reconciled (following the argument in which Tom tells her about his Italian son) when Betsy consents to Tom's plan to set up a monthly standing order to Maria to provide for her and the boy. Typically, at moments of crisis Tom swears how much he loves Betsy and the film closes with him telling his wife 'Would you mind if I tell you I worship you?' But these are desperate declarations. At the end of *Bigger than Life*, Ed goes, in ten fraught minutes of screen time, from being on the point of killing his wife and son to being happily off cortisone and reunited with them in hospital, content to be ordinary again and to have renounced his 'big ideas'. Just as the breadwinner's staid appearance fails to mask the father's repressed sexuality, so the films use shifts in *mise en scène* to connote the ultimate fragility of the closing images of familial contentment. The relative stylistic normality of these endings fails to suppress the marital tensions and paternal discontent previously conveyed through stylistic excess. The canted camera and extreme angles of Ed's Abraham and Isaac outburst far more powerfully evoke the father's hatred of domesticity and mundanity than the image of James Mason smiling benignly swathed in the sterile white of a hospital room manages to affirm his consenting reintegration into that lifestyle.

Another crucial aspect of these breadwinner fathers is that they are the narratives' heroes – not, as was mentioned in the previous chapter, Hollywood's preferred model. Their ever-presentness becomes a facet of their vulnerability; more powerful and more mysterious is the father who is not always there and can thus be reconfigured by and through the child's wishful imagination. However much Tom, Ed and Cliff function as their respective narratives' dominant points of identification, the commuter dad, the teacher dad, the toy manufacturer dad will never work as aspirational models. In Tom, Ed and Cliff, American men would have seen who they were, not who they wanted to be, despite assurances that the American male 'looks to his breadwinner role to confirm his manliness' (Brooks and Gilbert 1995: 266). In 'The New Burdens of Masculinity', published in 1957, Helen Hacker outlined the crisis precipitated by men's unrealistic perceptions of what they could and should achieve, her interviewees revealing that:

> The ideal man is considered by men as being, among other things, a good provider, the ultimate source of knowledge and authority, and strong in character so that he may give a feeling of security, not only financially but emotionally, to his wife and children, and it was evident from their further responses that the respondents found themselves deficient in meeting these demands (227).

Although couched in different terms, Hacker's description of what the contemporary man feels he should be is commensurate with Freud's notion of the symbolic father, the ego-ideal. For behind the ego-ideal 'lies hidden an individual's first and most important identification, his identification with the father in his own prehistory' (Freud 1923: 370). Towards the end of her article, Hacker quotes a female sociologist's definition of a 'real man' as 'one who takes responsibility for a woman and their children' (1957: 233). Hacker admits that such a definition is unlikely to be 'in the forefront of men's consciousness' (233), for *men's* consciousness is in search of something less quotidian. Hollywood in the 1950s certainly offered many more images of fantasy fathers than buffoons and men who take responsibility for their children, and it is to the first category of these – the Oedipal father – that the discussion now turns.

The Oedipal Father: *Rebel Without a Cause, East of Eden*

The story of Oedipus (and more particularly Freud's interpretation of it) underpins much Hollywood cinema and the father–son narrative has proved one of its most enduring motifs. Classically, what, in psychoanalysis, is deemed to occur in much younger children, surfaces in the movies as a key concern of the period of transition from adolescence to adulthood, as children (usually sons) set about detaching themselves from their fathers and families. This detachment is commonly tied to a struggle – an Oedipal struggle with a father figure the sons equivocally wish both to reject and to emulate. It is in this ambivalence towards the father that the dual need for the 'real' father and the symbolic father is contained, the 'real' father being the present, domestic father (such as the breadwinners already discussed or Frank Stark in *Rebel Without a Cause*) and his symbolic counterpart being the unrealistic 'bigger than life' fathers of so many other 1950s' movies: the tycoons, the ranchers, the bullies, the patriarchs.

Growing up is an important element of the youth films of the 1950s and commonly is signalled by two things: the achievement of sexual maturity and the realisation of a rewarding relationship with the father. To Freud, the father's part in this maturation is pivotal, as it is he who delivers the child from the exclusive bond with the mother and into society, and the return of the patriarch in 1950s' cinema signals a desire to reinforce the father's centrality.

The emphasis upon the Oedipal scenario distinguishes films such as *Rebel Without a Cause* from the superficially similar suburban breadwinner films. The narrative dynamics created by the playing out of the Oedipal struggle construct the son as the hero and the father (who in the breadwinner films was the protagonist and primary source of identification) as the figure of authority seen through the son's eyes. The vast majority of Hollywood films about fathers are from the point of view of the younger generation. However, there are exceptions. In the 1950s, these are films which feature younger fathers, such as the breadwinner films, *Shane* (1952) (in which there is both a younger generation father and the more glamorous titular father substitute, played by Alan Ladd), *Take Me to Town* (1952) and *River of No Return*. The last two share the popular Hollywood plot device of having a widower father marry a glamorous woman (in these instances singers) of whom their children approve.[8] Other young fathers (though not particularly important ones) are to be found in *The Big Heat* (1953), *Somebody Up There Likes Me* (1956), *Never Say Goodbye* (1957), *Come Next Spring* (1958) and *Rally Round the Flag, Boys* (1958).

Within the Oedipal films, however, the father is conventionally older. *East of Eden* and *Rebel Without a Cause* (both starring James Dean as the archetypal Oedipal son) succinctly enact the father–son conflicts described by Freud. The foundations of Freud's 'Oedipus complex' hardly need to be rehearsed, except to say that the primary impulse is this: that the infant's exclusive relationship with and attraction to its mother is intruded upon by the father once the child perceives the father as a rival for her love; such an intrusion complicates the infant's attraction to the mother and instructs the child in the ways of the world beyond the dyadic bliss of maternal affiliation, bringing with it both resentment and hatred of the father as well as a desire for him (in girls) and a desire to be him (in boys).[9] This separation is echoed in many films. The father–son narratives focus on masculinity, power and the need to bond with and become the father; the father–daughter relationships (to be discussed later) centre on sexual anxieties and the repression of the incest taboo (an exception being *The Long, Hot Summer*).

Central to an understanding of the implications of the Oedipus complex for the future father–son relationship are two things: how hard it is to effect the dissolution of the complex (to give up the mother as primary object and, for the son, to stop seeing the father as a sexual rival) and what is substituted after the dissolution has taken place. In 'The Dissolution of the Oedipus Complex', Freud makes clear the idea that the 'dissolution' of the complex necessitates the substitution of identification (between father and son) for the sexual bond. As 'The object-cathexes are given up and replaced by identifications', so the father's authority 'is introjected into the ego' where it forms 'the nucleus of the super-ego' and takes on the characteristics of the father – or, more importantly, the characteristics the son presumes the father to possess (1924: 319). The father's position at the time of the dissolution of the Oedipus complex is thereby deeply ambivalent because, the very moment at which he becomes a more important object of identification for his son and thus a means to 'consolidate the masculinity in the boy's character', is also the moment at which the father ceases to be seen by the child as a sexual entity (Freud 1923: 371). This subliminal ambivalence within the father is matched by another felt by the son, namely that he aspires to be like his father but comes to realise that his identification with him will remain forever incomplete. As Freud argues in 'The Ego and the Id', the boy's identification with his father encompasses equivocal impulses as the son is told 'You *ought to be* like this (like your father)' and also 'You *may not be* like this (like your father) – that is, you may not do all that he does; some things are his prerogative' (374). Freud considered the son's desperate 'longing for the father' (376) to be the basis for the ego, but the son must long for a father he can never completely have or be. Such convolutions carry with them fear and self-loathing, as one sees cinematically in James Dean's films. For not only does the son's idealised image of the father retain something of the formidable primal father, but also the son must disavow his fear that the father is not as great as he would like him to be.

The son's disillusionment and his need to reinvent his father to suit his own inter-nalised fantasy inform the relationship between Jim and Frank Stark in *Rebel Without a Cause*. Nicholas Ray's film (made immediately before *Bigger than Life*) has frequently been cited as a parable of its time (see Griswold 1993: 185) and is loosely based on a real psychological case study. Dean's tortured teenager is one of the key images of 1950s' youthful rebellion. As with Philip Cass in *Teresa*, Jim's defining psychological problem is the perceived inadequacy of his father. Although later psychologists modi-fied such claims, in the 1950s and 60s the father's weakness was considered a direct cause of 'problems' with sons such as delinquency, homosexuality and an inability to control aggression (Lamb 1986). In particular, delinquent boys were thought to perceive defects in their fathers, not their mothers (Rapoport *et al.* 1977). Jim Stark is a casebook stereotype and *Rebel Without a Cause* a parable of inadequate fathering.

In the opening scene, three adolescents have been rounded up in the early hours of Easter morning for bad behaviour: Jim is drunk, Judy has been found wandering the streets and Plato, the film's one 'authentic rebel' (Biskind 1974: 35) has killed some pup-pies. As the scene unfolds, it surfaces that here are three children in search of their fathers. All three feel the absence of a father who loves them or who they can emulate, and their misdemeanours are directly symptomatic of this lack. Jim offers the most extended explanation, ranting to Ray, the social worker who befriends him:

I love him. I don't want to hurt him … If he had the guts to knock mom cold once, then maybe she'd be happy and stop picking on him, because they [Jim's mother and grandmother] make mush of him, just mush. I'll tell you one thing, I don't ever want to be like him.

Jim's dissection of his family's psychodynamics is notable for two things: the vitriol he feels towards his mother and anything linked to her (upon leaving the house in a rage it is his grandmother's portrait he kicks in) and the concomitant need he has for a strong father. *Rebel Without a Cause* is only ostensibly about Jim's problematic rebelliousness (the Starks are new to town because they move every time Jim gets in trouble at school); its underpinning subject is the son's desire to have and to become a traditional, authoritative father.

As always in Nicholas Ray's melodramas, the anxieties of the male subject are conveyed through the excesses of his visual style. Frequently, the most stylised sequences are in response to the juxtaposition of Jim's anxiety and his father Frank's weakness, precisely the problem allayed by a successful negotiation of the Oedipus complex, as the son's fears that his father may not be all he would like him to be are repressed. *Rebel Without a Cause* is structured around a series of youthful crises – being apprehended by the police, the fight outside the planetarium, the 'chicken run' in which a schoolmate dies and, finally, the death of Plato. Each crisis precipitates a confrontation between Jim and Frank, and each of these dialogues marks a stage in their mutual journey towards resolving their Oedipal differences.

Following the fight outside the planetarium, Jim returns home. He is drinking some milk when he hears a noise and goes upstairs to find his dad on his knees, donning a floral apron and putting spilt food back on a tray. Jim's mother is ill in bed and Frank has been taking her dinner. The apron and the grovelling on the ground are externalised evocations of Jim's Oedipal anxieties about his weak father. The *mise en scène* accentuates Frank's insignificance; he is sometimes out of focus, often only partly in shot and he is framed by and filmed through the spindles flanking the stairs and landing, an image that renders him both infantile and trapped. Jim, who had presumed that someone in such a prone position wearing an apron must be Mom, is perplexed and rendered inarticulate by the image of fatherhood before him, stuttering 'Dad … stand … don't … I mean don't … what are you?' Here, in all its bald clarity, is the emasculated father as the source of his son's castration anxiety. Particularly problematic in this context is Frank Stark's apparent attachment to the floral apron. A scene later, he is still wearing the apron as he comes into Jim's bedroom for a manly father–son chat. Jim looks distraught and runs from the house. As Russell Lynes, a 1950s' champion of the patriarchal male, notes, 'the man in the apron has no one to blame but himself' (1953: 54).

Jim and Frank are only reconciled after Jim has taken on the attributes of the strong symbolic father he would like to become (and which Frank has failed to be). In an abandoned house, having escaped their dysfunctional, unhappy families, Jim, Judy and

Frank Stark, the rejected father: 'the man in the apron has no one to blame but himself'

Plato establish an alternative surrogate unit. Jim and Judy replace Plato's absent, irresponsible parents, singing him a lullaby and covering him up as he falls asleep. Then, Judy outlines what she wants in a man:

JUDY: What kind of a person do you think a girl wants?

JIM: A man?

JUDY: Yes, but a man who can be gentle and sweet like you are; and someone who doesn't run away when you want them, like being Plato's friend when nobody else wants him. That's being strong.

Jim, upon learning that he can be 'gentle' and 'sweet' without compromising his 'strength', comes to embody the idealised father the film has hitherto lacked, and takes on paternal responsibility for saving Plato. He proves himself to be intensely traditional and not a rebel at all. Just as the traditional father functions as the bridge between the domestic domain and society so Jim, in the final sequence of *Rebel Without a Cause*, negotiates between Plato (armed with a gun) and the assembled police trying to catch him. Jim has usurped the father's role and it is only at this point that reconciliation between him and Frank becomes possible. Plato is shot (the police mistakenly thinking he is still armed) and Jim sobs over his dead body. Now, belatedly, Frank offers Jim the support he craved when he tells Jim: 'You can depend on me, trust me. Whatever comes we'll face it together ... stand up and I'll stand up with you. I'll try and be as strong as you want me'.

In Elia Kazan's adaptation of Steinbeck's *East of Eden*, the father–son relationship is comparably tortured, if constructed around a different set of Oedipal problems. As with *Rebel Without a Cause*, *East of Eden* concludes with the reconciliation between Cal (Dean) and his father Adam Trask (Raymond Massey). Again, the Dean son is involved in a series of Oedipal crises, the basis for which is his desire to talk to and get close to a father who this time is autocratic. Again, stylistic excess marks out the father–son sequences, the text once more proving the hysterical expression of the son's inner turmoil. Kazan uses tilt shots in two crucial father–son confrontations, claiming that they mimicked Adam's 'rigidity – "That's the way it is whether you like it or not" ' (Byron and Rubin 1972: 8). This rigidity serves as a metonym for Adam's severity and functions as a mechanism for distancing us from Adam and his Puritanism. Likewise, the contrasting acting styles of Dean and Massey (the former emotional, extreme, jittery and instinctive; the latter more 'old school', tight and undemonstrative) further express the Oedipal tensions.[10]

As with *Rebel Without a Cause*, these tensions are resolved as father and son are reconciled once the son is content he has assumed the dominant role. Throughout *East of Eden*, Cal's unhappiness has been the indirect result of Adam's inability to talk to him, to establish a dialogue. 'Talking' in this psychological context is the act not just of verbal exchange but also of communicating emotions, feelings and things that otherwise would remain unsaid. Several key father–son arguments centre on words – Adam forcing Cal to read from the Bible, Cal asking Adam to tell him the truth about his estranged mother. The latter exchange concludes with Adam crying after Cal 'We may never talk again', which is true, as, with heavy irony, the next time father and son talk meaningfully is after Adam has suffered a stroke and is lying in bed immobile and incapable of speech. Such a scene in which the son sits by the sick, dying or dead father's bed is the setting for many Hollywood Oedipal reconciliations;[11] here it functions as the moment when Oedipal power is transferred from father to son. Cal is ostensibly happy because Adam has finally asked him to do something for him. Although the task is a mundane one (Adam wants Cal to find him a new nurse), what is important is the subtext of these words. After years of autonomy and autocracy, Adam finally needs Cal.

The assumption of the father's position in both Dean films harks back to the problem at the heart of the Freudian analysis of father–son identification patterns, namely that the son necessarily identifies with a symbolic image of masculinity, an image he internalises, idealises and reinterprets. It becomes this image that the son carries around with him and aspires to and which, in turn, produces a mis-recognition of the father and of masculinity. It is this mis-recognised image that is then reflected back at the father, the father fearing, as Frank Stark does, that he fails to match up. Although Freudian psychoanalysis and 1950s' American society bolstered and promoted patriarchy and the strong father, both also inadvertently furnished others with the tools to dislodge and undermine them by proving such idealised images to be untenable. The masculine preoccupation with symbolic images exacerbates the notion of masculinity – and fatherhood – as performative, lacking as it does a sense of stability, the insecure man needing instead to perform hyper-masculinity in a vain attempt to recapture gender supremacy.

The father–son relationships in the films of the 1950s are fraught, excessive and offer hysterical re-enactments of far more ambitious images of masculinity and fatherhood. For all the images of Dad in his armchair surrounded by an adoring wife and family, the

1950s of the movies, was essentially the era when the father strove to repress his ordinariness, hence the hyperbolic *mise en scène* of *East of Eden*, *Rebel Without a Cause*, *Bigger than Life* or *There's Always Tomorrow*. Similarly, the physical fragilities of Ed Avery or Adam Trask become emblematic symptoms (very like the hysterical ailments of melodrama heroines) for repressed inner turmoil. The cause of this discontent could be identified as both the father's and the son's reluctance to see patriarchy reduced to 'petty domesticity' as Ed terms it. Historian Robert Griswold cites several surveys conducted in the 1950s into what men and fathers actually did around the home and concludes that, 'despite bold claims that "today's husband isn't ashamed to be caught wearing the apron" ... systematic analysis suggests otherwise' (1993: 194). In the 1950s, fewer than 4 per cent of fathers made the beds, only 5 per cent cleaned and dusted, and fewer than 2 per cent did any ironing (194). They fared better when it came to teaching their children right from wrong, which three quarters professed to do, but on the whole 'men's belief in the sanctity of the division of labor' remained sacrosanct (194).

The Name of the Father: *The Long, Hot Summer*, *Giant*, *Written on the Wind*

Fear of the father's ordinariness, feminisation or vulnerability stampedes through 1950s' Hollywood. The most tangible proclamation of the father's supremacy is through the conventional use of his name, traditionally passed onto his family and so a public acknowledgment that his family revolves around him. Display is frequently associated in cinema with the affirmation of masculinity and throughout the 1950s, the film father's name is displayed quite literally. In *A Place in the Sun*, *While the City Sleeps* or *Written on the Wind*, the patriarch's name is put in lights on big corporation buildings and looming spires, flashing imperiously in the faces of the less successful younger generation. In *Giant* and *The Long, Hot Summer*, the 'Benedict' ranch or the town of 'Varner' make their ownership explicit. The phallus has become a place. The name carries psychological weight too; in *The Halliday Brand* and *Home from the Hill* the family name is its brand mark, scarring not just the father's actual territory but also the parameters of his psychological power over his children.

The writings (many of which date from the 1950s) of French psychoanalyst Jacques Lacan illuminate this recurrent trait. In a seminar (delivered in 1956) Lacan states that 'the function of *being a father* is absolutely unthinkable in human experience without the category of the signifier' (1956: 292). He goes on to explain that the 'facts' of fathering (copulation, conception and birth) 'will never lead one to constitute the notion of what it is *to be a father*' (293). Just as Lacan (in 'The Signification of the Phallus') makes a significant distinction between the penis and the phallus, so here he is arguing for the term 'father' as a signifier, as having a symbolic function as well as a physical one. Lacan thereby offers a psychological explanation for the need articulated in many films of the time, to inscribe the landscape or city with the father's name. It is through such statements (distanced from the banality of procreation) that the father is then in a position to reclaim the phallus – when he, as all the patriarchs in the films cited above do, becomes more than the penis, the breadwinner, Dad. Just as, in Lacan's terms, the phallus must remain veiled if it is to retain its power ('it can play its role only when veiled' [Lacan 1958: 288]), so the public proclamation of the father's name masks the actual father's possible lack. It is significant that the majority of fathers in such films are hugely successful but old and physically vulnerable.

Lacan, throughout his writings, describes this notion of the symbolic father as the 'Name-of-the-Father', the signifier onto which are heaped all the idealisations of the father not adequately represented by the 'real' father. The 'Name-of-the-Father' denotes the father's symbolic function as the enforcer of cultural law (see Elliott 1994: 95), and the use of the actual father's name as a manifestation of that power suggests how one can mistake this father for his symbolic counterpart. This is a mis-recognition, an attempt to disavow the limitations of the real father; although, as Lacan also argues, the truly omnipotent paternal figure is the one who 'really has the function of legislator' (1955–6: 218), that is, whose actual role seems to embody some of the signifying force of the 'Name-of-the-Father'. Just as in Freud's writings there is a discrepancy between the muddled, weak fathers of the case histories and the omnipotent, frightening father of the Oedipus essays (see Verhaeghe 2000), so in Lacan there is an endearing mismatch between the fearful 'Name-of-the-Father' and Lacan's preoccupations with his own paternity. His biographer, Elizabeth Roudinesco, identifies as a plausible starting point for his theories of the symbolic father Lacan's own experiences as the father of an illegitimate daughter who, because she was born out of wedlock, could not, under French law in 1941, be recognised as his child or bear his name. In his writings, Lacan swiftly became uninterested in the 'real' biological father and turned his attentions to the symbol that represents phallic power – perhaps to compensate for the law not recognising his own 'real' paternity?

The Long, Hot Summer succinctly narrativises these issues. The action centres on Southern land-owner, Will Varner's (Orson Welles) obsession with his children's ability or not to give him heirs. His son Jody is married but is also an infertile alcoholic, while his daughter Clara is a spinster. Varner's power is explicitly linked to his actual presence as the family and town patriarch, and so the continuation of his bloodline is essential if his 'name' (that is, both what he is called and what he stands for) is to live on. Will pins his hopes on Clara (Joanne Woodward), first trying to pair her off with a wealthy, respectable (though one suspects gay) neighbour, and then with Ben Quick, a stranger whom Varner picks up when driving home one day (Cohan reads sexual connotations into this [1997: 260–1]) and who has a criminal past. Quick, played by Paul Newman in a sweaty white vest, is unmistakeably 'virile', and so the fetishised embodiment of what Varner, who has just come out of hospital, conspicuously lacks. The continuation of the Name-of-the-Father is assured when Ben, Varner's object of identification, finally wins over Clara.

The Name-of-the-Father conventionally signals inflexibility, intransigence and an overreliance on tradition or an attachment to the past. Frequently, as in *The Big Country*, *The Halliday Brand* or *Written on the Wind*, the presiding patriarchs (all in different ways attached to the supposed value of the names they have built) die before the continuation of the family line is assured. In *Written on the Wind* and *Cat on a Hot Tin Roof*, this lack of progeny is related both to infertility and to repressed homosexuality. Then there is an overlapping series of films in which the all-powerful father (often a self-made tycoon) is ill or dying as in *While the City Sleeps*, *The Man in the Gray Flannel Suit* (Tom's boss, who has a troubled relationship with his daughter, has to monitor his heart), *The Long, Hot Summer* and *Cat on a Hot Tin Roof*. The illnesses here are symptomatic of the fathers' inability to secure stable succession. It is only in films (examples would be *Long, Hot Summer*, *While the City Sleeps* and *Giant)* in which the patriarch proves capable of changing with the times that the continuation of his name is assured.

In *Giant*, Jordan 'Bick' Benedict's initial over-identification with his name and his patriarchal position threatens the Name's continuation until he is forced to change. Bick (Rock Hudson) is a charming, unreconstructed cattle rancher who marries Leslie (Elizabeth Taylor), the daughter of an East Coast doctor and takes her back to Texas. The

Newly weds Bick and Leslie arrive at the Benedict ranch

symbiotic relationship between his masculine identity and his land is signalled at the out-set, as Leslie and her family are impressed by the size (500,000 acres) of the Benedict ranch. When the newly weds arrive in Texas, their train alights at 'Benedict' station in the middle of this sprawling wilderness. Bick's sense of ownership extends to Leslie, whom he expects to 'settle down and behave' like 'Mrs Jordan Benedict'. Leslie bears three Benedict children to ensure the continuation of the family line, but she consist-ently challenges Bick's supremacy. At one point, their marriage almost collapses as Leslie leaves Texas with the children after a bitter argument over Bick's regressive masculinity. On his twins' fourth birthday he gives Jordy, his eldest son and heir, a horse. Jordy is afraid of the horse and cries when Bick forces him to ride it with him, remonstrating 'He's a Benedict and he's going to stay in the saddle'. Bick's brutishness as he canters around clutching his screaming son proffers a humiliating portrait of insolent, oppress-ive masculinity, an image not easily nullified by an uncle's pacifying comments to Leslie that Bick, like his father and grandfather before him, does not know 'a damn thing' about raising kids. Leslie's arguments with Bick have consistently centred on his sexism. After a formal dinner, for instance, she shouts at Bick and his friends 'You gentlemen date back one million years', after he has ordered the wives to vacate the rooms and to leave the men to 'politics' and 'man's stuff'.[12] Although Bick manages to woo Leslie back, the marriage only becomes truly stable and successful when he proves willing to modernise.

Bick's modernisation is linked inextricably to his half million acres. His beloved ranch 'Reata' has become a metaphor for the stability of the father, and his disproportionate agitation when his sister Luz leaves ranch-hand Jett Rink (James Dean) a scrappy morsel of it testifies to its symbolic importance. On his portion, Jett strikes oil, igniting the ensu-ing battle over not just the land, but masculinity and paternity. As uncontrollable ejaculations of crude oil drench Jett, the very land that makes up the Benedict power is violated. 'Reata' is literally undermined and with this comes the dismemberment of Bick's tranquil traditionalism. It is not just the jets of oil that scar his land but Rink's wells, der-ricks and 'Jetexas' oil tankers trundling to and fro; Bick must adapt or see his name perish. This he finally does as he renounces cattle farming and agrees (with Leslie) that they too should drill for oil. It is richly significant that Bick reaches this moment as he also realises that Jordy is not interested in taking over the ranch and wants to become a doctor instead. As he moans ruefully, 'I've been keepin' it together all my life, and for who?'

Giant, however, is far from a radical film and equilibrium is re-established by the end not by patriarchy's demise but (as in *Rebel Without a Cause* and many other contem-poraneous films) by its reinvigoration. Having grown to accept the need to change, Bick is finally in a position to reassert his symbolic control, and this he does through the com-ically primitive means of two fistfights. Bick's first fight is with Jett and the second with Sarge, a diner owner who refuses to serve a Mexican family (Jordy's wife, who is with the family party, is Mexican). After the latter, a prolonged fight the aging Bick is on the losing end of, Leslie is breathless with admiration:

> You know all that stuff you used to do to dazzle me? Nothing made you as big a man to me as when you were on the floor of Sarge's hamburger joint. . . . You wound up on the floor, on your back, and I said to myself, "After a hundred years, the Benedict family is really a success".

The significance of the fight is that it finally gives substance to the otherwise hollow idea of preserving the family name by suggesting that it is from *within* the patriarchal structure of the Name, history and masculinity that change is to be wrought. *Giant's* closing image is of two Benedict grandchildren, one white, one mixed race, looking out of their playpen as Bick sits contentedly on the sofa where he has always sat, under the nineteenth-century oil painting of his cattle ranch which has always been there, next to the wife who is now overcome with pride for him. The name of Benedict is preserved through having changed just enough.

In Sirk's *Written on the Wind*, Jasper Hadley's professional success as an oil tycoon fails to secure the continuation of his name. The film opens with the death of Jasper's son Kyle (Robert Stack), and the perceived enormity of the patriarch's power is established swiftly. A drunk Kyle slaloms his yellow sports car from a bar to his home. He streaks by multiple signifiers that collectively connote his father's omnipotence: the neon 'H' adorning the Hadley Oil Co building, the road sign that marks entry to 'Hadley' the town, oil derricks puncturing the landscape, the neo-classical family mansion. When he arrives home, Kyle throws a bottle against the wall. He enters, a shot rings out and he re-emerges falling down dead outside the grand entrance of his father's house. Symptomatic of the son's weakness, Kyle's death nevertheless hangs over *Written on the Wind* as the crowning metaphor for the father's loss of potency. Although Kyle's self-destruction (his drinking, his self-hatred, his death) stems directly from his perceived inability to live up to the Name-of-the-Father, it is through Kyle's desperate waywardness that many of the contradictions and impossibilities of the symbolic father come to be understood.

Kyle is obsessed by the conviction that he is an inadequate substitute for his father and his fears surrounding the issue of succession destroy him. *Written on the Wind* promotes the notion that Jasper, through the external symbols of the Hadley empire, is the phallic embodiment of the power he has amassed (what could be more phallic than a tall building with a neon 'H' emblazoned on its tip?). Conversely Kyle, through his excessive behaviour, turns his back on the patriarchal chain, a distancing from his father reinforced by his later belief that he is impotent and thereby unable to produce a future son and heir. Unlike similarly overwhelmed cinematic sons of the mid-1950s who reject fathers they perceive to be weak in favour of omnipotent fantasy figures, Kyle constructs an inverted fantasy to quell his multiple neuroses in which the all-powerful father is rejected in favour of a more ordinary model. Although Freud's Oedipal father is seemingly impregnable, in other works Freud proved equally alert to the importance of accepting the more ordinary father. In 'Family Romances' he argues, as in the Oedipus complex, that a child needs to achieve liberation 'from the authority of his parents' as 'Indeed, the whole progress of society rests upon the opposition between successive generations' (1909a: 221). Those who have 'failed in this task' are 'neurotics' whose neurosis derives from their idealisation of the parent of the same sex. To compensate for his or her disillusionment, the child concocts 'family romances': daydreams revolving around the replacement of his or her parents with fantasy alternatives which will perpetuate a need to idealise parents. As maternity is 'something unalterable' (223), so the father becomes the focus of these daydreams. The child's 'family romance' is fuelled by disavowal: the child longs for the return to the 'vanished days when his father seemed to him the noblest and strongest of men and his mother the dearest and loveliest of women' (225), but s/he recognises that the father can never be the equal of this symbolic ideal so s/he invents a 'family romance'.

The 'family romance' constructed in *Written on the Wind* centres upon Kyle's fantasy of changing places with his best friend Mitch (Rock Hudson) and so having the much humbler Hoak Wayne as his father. Kyle's fantasy would release him from the bonds of being Jasper's heir and also offers compensation for this father's dependency at work on Mitch, who, unlike Kyle, works tirelessly for Hadley Oil. Jasper and Hoak are old friends, one got rich while the other remained humble. This binary opposition between the rich and the poor father figures is a recurring motif in father movies (see, for example, *Fort Apache* and *Wall Street*). The significance of the oppositional fathers to *Written on the Wind* is that it reinforces the film's exploration of succession and sterility. Success and wealth in *Written on the Wind* (as in many other films of the time) are symbiotically linked to sterility. The two times we see him, Hoak, like his son Mitch, signals the opposite: he is outdoors, an unshackled hunter at one with nature. His fecund environment stands in direct contrast to the luminously strained and introverted Hadley mansion.

It is in this environment that Jasper Hadley dies, immediately after both his children have been returned to him in disgrace. Kyle, who has just met with his doctor and discovered his 'weakness' (that is, a low sperm count), is drunk and is brought in by Mitch, flung over his shoulder. The under-age Marylee (an issue blurred in the film by the casting of Dorothy Malone) has been escorted home by the Hadley police for having propositioned a petrol pump attendant. Jasper is in his study with Mitch, his surrogate son, recounting how his wife died in childbirth and how he has 'failed' as a father. This sense of failure is emphasised by Jasper's physical frailty (he stumbles as he gets up from his chair) and by the insignificance of his appearance. Dressed in brown cardigan, trousers and tie, Jasper blends seamlessly with the brownness of his library walls and shelves. It is as if the father is disappearing into the material trappings his wealth and social standing have brought, a debilitation further exacerbated by Sirk's use of framing in this scene, often positioning Jasper so low in the frame that he seems in danger of sliding out of shot. Jasper then goes upstairs. At the top he falters, collapses and tumbles all the way down again, already dead as Mitch rolls him over on the hall floor.

Is not the point here the realisation that the father can never be the Name-of-the-Father and that the sterility which pervades *Written on the Wind* stems from the other characters' collective inability to recognise this? In the very final scene this argument is reiterated as Kyle's sister Marylee, in whose hands the Hadley estate is left, sits at her father's desk holding a model oil tower under a portrait of Jasper holding the same tower. Of this closing image Sirk commented:

> Malone (Marylee) has lost everything. And I have put a sign there indicating this –
> Malone, alone, sitting there hugging that goddammed oil well, having nothing. The oil
> well is, I think, a rather frightening symbol of American society (Halliday 1997: 133).

One can extend this further and propose that, in clutching the symbol of her father's power and potency, Marylee is upholding the belief in the Name-of-the-Father while simultaneously indicating the sterility of this attachment, as what she possesses is the phallic symbol and not the phallus.

The Death of the Father: *Gunman's Walk*, *Broken Lance*, *The Halliday Brand*, *The Big Country*

Amid the 1950s' obsession with the omnipotence of the father resided an equally consuming interest in the father's death. On occasion, the father's death is a means of testing the son and heir and proving, as happens in *While the City Sleeps*, that he does not match up. The scene in the basement between Big Daddy and Brick towards the end of *Cat on a Hot Tin Roof* is all about the dying father coming to terms with his son's failings while recalling that his own father had died happy because, as Brick hypothesises, he had his son with him. To intentionally over-simplify, the father's death either signals closure or a new beginning. In *Written on the Wind*, Jasper Hadley's death brings closure, while in other Sirk melodramas such as *Magnificent Obsession* (1954) and *All that Heaven Allows*, the patriarch's death is liberating, a time of renewal.[13] This balancing of death and renewal forms the basis for the battles with the father in many of the decade's Westerns, the genre in which the representation of the father is at its most extreme.

The archetypal schema adopted by the patriarchal Westerns of the 1950s is a powerful father (more often than not an irrational, despotic caricature) surrounded by a posse (commonly) of feuding sons. The prevalence of this model is demonstrated by its appearance in A-features and B-features alike. Such a dynamic carries clear biblical and mythic overtones. In films such as *Gunman's Walk* (1958), *Broken Lance*, *The Halliday Brand* and *The Big Country*, the ruling fathers (like T. C. in *The Furies*) offer undiluted images of hyper-masculinity. The sons who, whether grudgingly or willingly follow in their wake, are lesser men, crude and corrupt versions of their fathers, paternal power seemingly diluted between them. In several of these Westerns (for instance *Broken Lance*, *The Halliday Brand* and *Gunman's Walk*) there is a relatively sensitive, better-natured son who has taken on the more generous traits of the father who is contrasted with at least one (in *Gunman's Walk* there are only two brothers) oafish and violent brother who has become a crude version of the more brutal and irrational side of the father's character. It is in how the sons turn out that the bruising power of primal masculinity is understood.

This dissipation of the father's power (and Name) is resolved in these Westerns in two contrasting ways: either the father must die in order to bring his bad bloodline to an end, or he feels compelled to kill the worst son, usually before dying himself (Lee Hackett in *Gunman's Walk* kills his son Ed in a duel, but he survives, perhaps as the result of learning belatedly to accept his other son Davey). Through this archetypal father–son relationship, these Westerns parody their own image of masculinity, the destructive symbiosis between autocracy (the father) and resentful acquiescence (the sons) acting as a parable for how masculinity should not be handed down through the generations. The Western has conventionally been viewed as a genre dominated by binary oppositions, definitively expressed in Jim Kitses' twin lists, 'The Wilderness' and 'Civilization' (Kitses 1969: 11). By the 1950s, masculinity in the Western had become polarised, as the machismo of the West was becoming outmoded and passé; in *The Big Country* (as in *Giant*) this is characterised as the opposition between the old West and the modern East. There is a significant opposition in these Westerns between the law of the father (based upon brute force, conservatism, the need to settle old scores) and the law of the son (expressed as reason, negotiation, the desire to move on). The death of the father (and of the unreconstructed sons) is necessary if patriarchal masculinity is to survive and evolve.

The relationship between the fathers and the law in these films is fundamental, as all these father figures believe the law is answerable to them rather than vice versa. All also, more or less explicitly, come into direct confrontation with the law. In *Broken Lance* (a remake of *House of Strangers*)[14] the father Matt Devereaux (Spencer Tracy) is brought to trial because he, his sons and his ranch-hands have burnt down a copper plant that is contaminating his cattle's water. Like Gino Monetti before him, Matt (and this becomes a symptom of his unreconstructedness) fails to realise the seriousness of the charges against him or of his powerlessness in the face of the legal system. He still believes himself to be untouchable, as he had been years before, when he hanged three men without the authority of the sheriff. In burning down the copper plant, Matt again applied the anarchic, arbitrary rules of the 'Wild West' and in court he comically threatens to run the lawyer out of town. Matt, needless to say, is held in contempt of court and, just as in *House of Strangers*, it is his favoured son, Joe, who takes the rap for him,

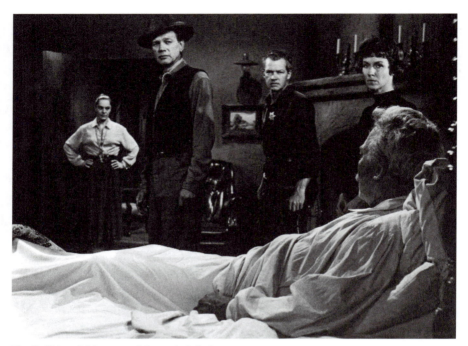

The Halliday children recoil from their father

swearing under oath that it was he and not his father who fired the first shot at the copper plant.

Likewise, in *Gunman's Walk*, Lee Hackett believes he can flout the laws of society – as one bystander in Jackson City comments Hackett was around before the war and so is not answerable to the rules established since it ended. Here again, though, the law of the father comes up against the law of the state. Lee's favoured son, Ed, has caused the death of a half-Sioux ranch-hand but denies culpability. The Sioux's family hire a lawyer and Ed is brought to trial. Ed is acquitted, but turns against Lee, believing (erroneously) that he must have fixed the trial for him. After shooting a man and failing to convince the sheriff he had done so in self-defence, Ed is imprisoned, but then shoots the sheriff's deputy. Lee gets to Ed before the sheriff's posse (thereby standing one last time for an alternative law) and Ed, who, it is clear, only admires his father for his prowess with the gun, challenges him to a duel. Lee is faster on the draw and wins; he cradles the dying Ed in his arms – a potently emotional action of remorse performed again in *The Big Country* – and, in this gesture, acknowledges that it was his own contempt for the law that led to his son's death.

A reversal of the above pietà concludes *The Halliday Brand*, in which the confrontation between father and the law is acted out most elaborately. The despotic father in this Joseph H. Lewis B-movie[15] is also the town sheriff whose 'hard hand' built the town.

A common characteristic among these fathers is their racism and after sheriff Halliday has sanctioned the killing of mixed-race prisoner Gevaro (for being in love with his daughter Martha), his eldest son Daniel (Joseph Cotten) becomes an outlaw, turning his back on his father and going in search of a place where no one knows the name 'Halliday'. Daniel starts a vendetta against his own father, leaving 'the Halliday brand' of a tomahawk outside the jailhouse, hanging a noose in his father's office and setting fire to his farm. In challenging his father's supremacy so directly, Daniel is in danger of becoming the man he despises. He is saved, however, by the film's finale, a scene reminiscent of Jacobean tragedy in its heightened absurdity and venomous intensity. His father, who lies dying in his bed, draws a gun on Daniel, accusing him of having no respect for the Halliday name. Daniel's retort is to remind him that he has 'cheated . . . and killed with it'. Both his siblings, Clay and Martha, rally round Daniel. The siblings' shared revulsion for their father is emphasised by a classic Joseph H. Lewis shot of the bed-ridden Halliday, his children looming menacingly over him. Lewis uses a low angle and deep focus to make the father, in the extreme foreground and slipping in and out of shot, appear expendable and vulnerable. This image forms a prelude to the final act of parricide. The children reject their debilitated father and walk away, only for Halliday to struggle out of bed one last time and come out of his bedroom brandishing a gun. Framed from the same (gun level) low angle, the final stand-off between Daniel and his father ends with the supremacy of the child as Halliday admits that he cannot shoot Daniel because 'it'd be too much like shooting myself'. He dies in Daniel's arms, the son only reconciled with his violent father when he is finally overthrown.

The generational battle is starkly (though not crudely) drawn in this low budget Western. A year later, in the more ambitious and expensive *The Big Country* there are various battles which radiate out from one central feud between two opposing fathers: rich and superficially refined land-owner Henry Terrill (Charles Bickford) and the rougher Rufus Hennessey (Burl Ives), whose family is referred to by Terrill's daughter as 'local trash'. Because it is never fully explained, this old feud exemplifies the danger brought by a lack of moral anchorage, of a closed society run by fathers who consider themselves above the law. Terrill has the outward trappings of civility, while Hennessey, though outwardly uncouth, possesses a greater sense of moral purpose. He kills his eldest son, Buck, for example, for trying to shoot Terrill's intended son-in-law Jim McKay (Gregory Peck) in the back during a duel – a duel that had begun with Rufus bellowing at Buck 'For the first time, try to be the man I'd like you to be'. Having warned Buck, after he had discovered him in the process of trying to rape Julie Maragon (Jean Simmons), that he would have to kill him, Rufus is left cradling Buck saying, 'I told you I'd do it'. *The Big Country* concludes with the deaths of both patriarchs, signalling the futility of their motiveless feud as well as the arbitrary masculine codes the two fathers live by. In an ironic, deflating finale, the patriarchs meet face to face in a distant, powdery canyon. Both fire and both fall to the other's bullets, but they are filmed in such excessive long shot that they seem of little more significance than beetles grubbing about in the chalky dust. For what, all these futile, savage deaths? These Westerns highlight the delusory power of the Name-of-the-Father. The resurgent primal father brings with him barbarism and primitivism that, as in myths and fables, need to be repressed. It is within the confines of the Western genre that gentility and metaphor have been dispensed with, as men can slug it out or fathers and sons can kill each other. The crude, old-fashioned patriarchal position has become untenable; the father (as well as the scarred son) must die if subsequent generations are to be liberated from their subservience to the brutalising ideology he symbolises.

Fathers and Daughters: *Peyton Place, The Furies, The Big Country, Bonjour Tristesse*

The other form of paternal brutality found in 1950s' Hollywood is incestuous desire (or, more commonly, implied incestuous desire) between father and daughter. Although in the 1940s the father–daughter relationship was still common, in the 1950s it was superseded by the father–son dyad, illustrative of the decade's growing tendency towards viewing fathering as a vehicle for examining issues of masculinity. The sexual father in films such as *The Furies, Rebel Without a Cause, Peyton Place* or *Bonjour Tristesse* raises the notion of incestuous desire and is quite different from the largely positive father–daughter relations Wolfenstein and Leites detected in the cinema of the 1940s (1950: 113). Stephanie Coontz maintains that incest was probably far more prevalent in the 1950s than we will ever know (2000: 35). As if affirming this, various films of the time seem neurotically compelled to suppress any eroticisation of the father–daughter bond. *Angel Face* couches the daughter's fixation with the father in terms of hero-worship, although Dianne's violent, obsessive hatred of her stepmother also suggests sexual intent. *Peyton Place*, in which stepfather Lucas Cross rapes and impregnates his stepdaughter Selina, offers an explicit portrayal of the illegal father–daughter bond. It is in grandly Foucauldian terms (in that the film's narrative suggests that to bring incest out into the open is to contain its threat) that *Peyton Place* ultimately embraces Selina and condemns the sexual father. Again, the 'bad' father is brought to justice, although only in a roundabout way as it is Selina who is put on trial for Lucas's subsequent murder. At first Selina is unwilling to talk of either the rape or her subsequent abortion, although the town doctor finally persuades her to let him tell the court the details, rounding on Peyton Place for its gossipy, destructive ways, ways that had shielded Lucas by making Selina too scared to speak out. In their belated support of Selina, the inhabitants of Peyton Place once more suppress the 'problem' of incest.

It is crucial that Lucas is not Selina's biological father and that the biological fathers in *Peyton Place* are absent or pronounced to be, with trembling hysteria, asexual. The stepfather is often the family member who poses the biggest (and overtly sexual) threat, as in another 1950s' film, *The Night of the Hunter*. Within the intrinsically patriarchal framework of Hollywood in the 1950s, the biological fathers do not consciously mani-fest such desires, although many share the characteristic of exerting a significant influence over their daughters' sexuality or sexual maturation: Stanley giving Kay away in *Father of the Bride*, Charles' dependency upon Dianne for artistic inspiration in *Angel Face*, Varner bullying Clara into a relationship with Ben Quick in *The Long, Hot Summer*. On occasion the sexual bond between biological father and daughter is barely repressed, as when Pat Terrill, at her own engagement party, tells her father he is 'still the hand-somest man in the room' or when P. J. returns home and puts a string of pearls around his excited daughter Vance's neck at the start of *The Furies*. In such cases, needless to say, the incestuous overtones are intensified by the absence of a biological mother as well as the daughters' demonstrable innocence. These fathers are allowed to become excessive and brutal because their masculinity has gone unchecked. An exception to this pattern is the father–daughter relationship in *The Long, Hot Summer*, which remains uneroticised – but then here there is no stepmother, the potential rival for the father's love. In several films, however, the daughters win the battle: in *The Furies*, Vance throws a pair of scissors at her stepmother and maims her, in *Angel Face*, Dianne plots to mur-der her stepmother and in *Bonjour Tristesse*, the stepmother commits suicide, indirectly as a result of her stepdaughter's antagonism.

The confusion of the father's role in relation to his daughter is exemplified by Judy's fraught relationship with her father in *Rebel Without a Cause*. Judy becomes provoca-tively sexual as a means of countering her father's rejection of her demonstrative shows of affection. In the opening scene, she has exaggeratedly red lipstick and an equally vibrant red coat at the same time as she is crying to Ray that her father called her a tramp. In a later scene, Judy wants to hug and kiss her father as she used to. Her father, mindful of the fact that his daughter is no longer prepubescent, rebuffs her kiss with a brusque 'Aren't you too old for that kind of thing?', to which Judy retorts, 'Girls don't love their fathers? Since when?' As Judy tries again to kiss him, her father slaps her and she runs off, only for the father to call after her 'Hey, glamour puss . . .', thus blurring the boundaries between sex and affection once more. Both father and daughter could have benefited from a short lesson in psychoanalysis. In 'Transformations of Puberty', Freud outlines the need to respect the culturally defined 'barrier against incest' and also of allowing girls in particular to outgrow their period of childish affection for their par-ents as it is 'precisely these girls who in their later marriage lack the capacity to give their husbands what is due to them' (Freud 1905b: 150). Having said this, in an alarming passage in the 1958 edition of *Baby and Child Care*, Dr Spock, in the section 'A girl needs a Father Too', states that a girl 'gains confidence in herself as a girl and a woman from feeling his [her father's] approval. I'm thinking of little things he can do, like com-plimenting her on her dress, or hair-do, or the cake she's made' (1958: 321). The father–daughter dyad, it seems, was too readily understood exclusively in relation to the erotic.

Dancing with her father at her engagement ball, Pat Terrill is worried at the prospect of having to live apart from him

Several father–daughter relationships in 1950s' Hollywood are inappropriately sexual and demonstrate a problem with separation between father and daughter (see Chodorow 1978), perhaps because (through the death of the mother) the requisite distance between them has been eroded. In both *The Furies* and *The Big Country*, the intimacy between father and daughter is pronounced and revolves around dress, appearance and mutual flattery. At the beginning of *The Furies*, Vance (Barbara Stanwyck), grown-up daughter of T. C. Jeffords, skips excitedly down the stairs to greet her returning father. He comments 'her gown befits you', and we learn that Vance's dress belonged to her dead mother. T. C. then produces the necklace he has brought back and Vance puts it around her neck, admiring herself in the mirror as a lover might. Father and daughter then discuss Vance's marital possibilities with both playfulness and a flirtatious intensity (they are physically close and gaze at each other intently) that render the scene uncomfortable to watch.

In *The Big Country*, Pat Terrill's admiration for her father ultimately gets in the way of her intended marriage to Jim McKay. Major Henry Terrill is an ambiguous figure, suave and not that much older than his intended son-in-law. Pat's inability to detach herself from him is thereby tinged with plausible sexual attraction, although her cheery disposition indicates such an attraction to be profoundly repressed. Their attachment, though not consciously expressed, is indicated through dialogue, so to Pat's confession that she finds her father still the handsomest man in the room, the Major replies 'And do you know what makes it so nice is that I think my little girl really means it'. Neither the distance created by Terill's use of the third person nor his reference to 'my little girl' is easily brushed aside. Costume accentuates the narcissism inherent within the Major's acceptance of Pat's dependency. As in *The Furies*, there is an uneasy sense that the Major and Pat are made for each other, his distinctive claret suit, brocade waistcoat and silk tie – intended, one presumes, to cut a dash and mark Terrill out as a different type of man from the understated McKay – being matched by Pat's figure-hugging black dress with a plunging scallop-neckline and diaphanous top. They are both showing off.

Narcissism conventionally is a dubious quality in the heterosexual male; as the bread-winner's donning of the tank-top implies, Hollywood's 'good' fathers have their minds on loftier things than whether or not the fleck in their suit picks out the colour of their tie. In *Bonjour Tristesse*, the most uncomfortably tragic of the decade's father–daughter films, such trivial considerations form the basis for the portrayal of the charmingly self-absorbed father Raymond (David Niven) who, for most of the film, is holidaying on the French Riviera with his daughter Cecile (Jean Seberg), who is in her late teens. Once again, there is no mother and Raymond, a playboy, is in a relationship at the start of the film with a younger woman, Elsa. *Bonjour Tristesse* is recounted in flashback by Cecile and, at first, father and daughter are very happy. Cecile, who at the start is unattached, meets Philippe; the daughter's lover, however, is not the problem as, in a reworking of the Oedipal scenario, what intrudes upon the father–daughter dyad is Raymond's sub-sequent relationship with Ann (Deborah Kerr). Ann is both an older woman and an old friend of Cecile's mother: the stereotypical stepmother. Raymond and Ann are due to marry and the latter takes on an overtly maternal role with Cecile. Cecile starts to hate Ann and concocts a scheme for getting rid of her which involves reuniting Raymond and Elsa by making Raymond believe Elsa and Philippe are attracted to each other. Cecile engineers it so that Ann overhears Raymond with Elsa, revealing that his love for Ann is a passing phase. Although Cecile regrets her actions, it is too late: Ann, distraught, leaves and her car crashes along the rocky Riviera coast. Raymond and Cecile believe Ann's death to be suicide, but never talk about it. It is instructive to outline the narra-tive of *Bonjour Tristesse* because it appears so schematic, so like a psychoanalytic case study.[16]

The boldest feature of the film's *mise en scène* is the inversion of the mono-chrome/colour convention. Preminger uses black and white for the present and lush colour stock for the flashbacks. The present is tense and de-sensualised, while the past is glamorous and sensual. This dichotomy, however, is contradicted by the significant implication that the journey Raymond and Cecile have undergone is from innocence to experience, not vice versa – the past being more vibrant than the stagnant present but also characterised by an innocent suppression of sexual consciousness. The pivotal moment is Ann's death, an event that conjoins Raymond and Cecile through mutual guilt. Cecile terms her lifestyle with Raymond before this tragedy an 'unusual set-up'. Most unusual is Raymond's regressive narcissism. However urbane and glamorous both Raymond and his lifestyle are, it is his disavowal of his paternal role that imprisons Cecile. The later Raymond in the monochrome present and wearing conventional evening attire is in stark contrast to the Raymond of the Riviera, where he performs stomach-flattening exercises, pats the maid's behind and swans about in tight swim-ming trunks and a showily initialled shirt knotted just above his svelte waist.

Into this idyllic father–daughter relationship (which resembles an established marriage) intrudes Ann. Raymond's short-lived liaison with a woman his own age compels him briefly to remember his age and his paternal duties. Ann (who, despite being a couturier,[17] is definitely matronly) adds sobriety to Raymond's frivolous suaveness; in short, she behaves like the breadwinner man. Cecile's reaction to Ann is comically orthodox Freud: she makes a chart comparing herself to Ann and she sticks pins in a Voodoo doll; she proclaims a second marriage would be a 'disaster' for Raymond and she likens Ann to a mother-in-law, as if she, Cecile, is Raymond's wife. The very stereotypical quality of this hatred serves to highlight the untenability of the sexual father–daughter relationship and the irretrievability (not to mention taboo) of their pre-Ann contentment. *Bonjour Tristesse*, however, is a mesmeric film that works on its audience in much the same way as Raymond works on the characters around him: we are persuaded to love Raymond and the pre-Ann fantasy existence, couched as it is in the sumptuous luminosity and colour of the flashbacks, as striking and overpowering as Raymond's grace and bright shirts. The combination of joy and sensuality present in the *mise en scène* substitutes for the disavowed sexuality that binds father and daughter; it also suggests a world not constrained by modern morality or, indeed, the guilt and introspection induced by modern psychoanalysis. The limpid blue of the sun-stroked sea, the jollity are as lost to Cecile and Raymond as Paradise is to Adam and Eve after the temptation. Cecile's worry that 'it's gone too far', that her plan to restore the symbiosis she had with Raymond is too extreme, becomes a pregnant phrase that explains the ramifications of this lost world; Ann's painful rejection and her subsequent suicide simply provide an acceptable motive for the mutual guilt of father and daughter.

Home from the Hill

Later psychoanalysts such as Jessica Benjamin have asked of Freud and Freudians 'why the phallus and the father have this exclusive power, this monopoly on desire, subjectivity and individuation', positing that 'the oedipal world is not the whole world' (1988: 93–4). Hollywood seldom appears to have probed its own phallocentricity in this way, and yet, towards the end of the 1950s, *Home from the Hill* – and, to a lesser extent, *Pillow Talk* – function as swan songs (one melodramatic, one comedic) to the patriarchal male. In *Home from the Hill*, Rafe (George Peppard) has the opposite problem to Cecile: he is the illegitimate son of a father, Wade Hunnicutt (Robert Mitchum), whom he resembles and remains close to but who, to his death, denies Rafe is his son. Unlike Cecile, Rafe survives his father's inadequacies to become a parent himself (to a child that, again, is not biologically his own), thereby taking on the sense of responsibility Wade conspicuously lacked. At the cusp of the 1960s, a decade that rebuffed the traditional patriarch, *Home from the Hill* posits the possibility of leaving the arrogant,

Wade in his hyper-masculine den

oppressive male behind. The plot centres on the relationships between Southern land-owner, Wade, and his two sons, Theron (George Hamilton), the legitimate son of his unhappy marriage to Hannah, and Rafe, the child from an earlier liaison. The second half deals with Theron's courtship of Libby Halstead, who, unbeknown to Theron, gets pregnant before they separate and eventually marries Rafe, who is fully aware Theron is the father of her child. The two stories collide as Libby's father shoots Wade, believing *him* (the town's great philanderer) to be his grandson's father.

Like Raymond, Wade refuses to grow up, a refusal suggested by his continual need to prove his virility. As a father figure he is deeply ambivalent. As with many older 1950s' fathers, he is the town's pivotal patriarch (an ex-soldier, a hunter and a land-owner); he also displays a macho, brutish masculinity (symbolised by his hunting) which contrasts with the civilised nature of the town and home in which he lives. His rebelliousness is represented by his unchecked promiscuity, and at the outset these two facets of Wade's character are linked as he is hunted and shot by a husband who assumes Wade has had sex with his wife. Wade does not want to be trapped by his identity as father. A common thread running through Minnelli's work of the 1950s is a concern with the overthrow of machismo, in *Home from the Hill* suggested by a belief in the masculine alternatives to the unreconstructed father.

Civility is here linked to femininity while masculinity breeds uncivilised machismo, a primitive struggle that is acted out by Wade and Hannah's arguments over their son Theron. When he takes it upon himself to show Theron how to be a man (when Theron is seventeen), Wade is in his den, a sanguineous room bedecked with the skins of the dead animals he has shot and the guns he has shot them with. Wade, horrified at the sissy-ness of his son's bedroom, has brought Theron here to show him 'how a man lives'. Although Rafe, despite his illegitimacy (or perhaps because of it, being the offspring of lust not duty) is Wade's more 'natural' heir, Theron is eager to prove himself a man in his father's eyes. His desired identification with Wade comes when he shoots, unaided, a wild boar. Wade, who is in pursuit, catches up with Theron – who looks more like he has just had sex for the first time – for a bonding manly chat about real fear.

The community's attitude to Wade's sexual history is that it is a sin that will not be forgiven, so when Theron goes courting Libby, her father spurns him for being his father's son. As Hannah says, 'your name is all he saw'. While the tone of *Home from the Hill* might indicate sympathy for Wade (Hannah's gentility is smothering) his past eventually brings about his – and Theron's – downfall. Theron and Libby start to see each other in secret and in one scene – one assumes when their baby is conceived – Theron, in his unbuttoned shirt and rolled-up trousers, has changed visibly from prim, clean-cut boy to sexualised, desirable man. Theron's post-coital image signals his sexual liberation (resembling as he does Rafe, who consistently and quite ostentatiously wears his shirt undone to his stomach) but also his fateful identification with his father. By unwittingly getting Libby pregnant, he mimics his father's indiscretions, and, again unknowingly, kills ('hunts down' in the symbolic, sexual tangled wood) his son's grandfather, an action that makes Theron an exile in much the same way Wade has been from the domesticity of his own home.

The sins of the father are revisited on the son. In a quintessential 1950s' confrontation between the macho father figure and the sensitive, more feminine son, Theron, having learnt Rafe is his brother, stands up to Wade and tells him 'If you'd been any kind of a man you'd love him'. The two men face each other in profile, Wade's old, traditional masculinity exemplified by Mitchum's barrel chest, hair gel and cigarette, Theron's gentler alternative by Hamilton's sunken stomach, rounded bony shoulders and soft hair. Minnelli's enduring interest in the sissy boy (the John Kerr characters in both *Tea and Sympathy* and *The Cobweb*, for example) lends this confrontation a radical intention: the desire to disprove the centrality and finality of the father. As a crucial exchange within a melodrama, this masculine confrontation is then subsumed into *Home from the Hill*'s ultimate endorsement of the feminine. Theron's rebellion proves the stupidity of that linchpin of patriarchal ideology: 'like father, like son'. However, the son's symbolic transferral from masculine to feminine domain is narrativised through Rafe, Wade's surviving son. The end of *Home from the Hill* offers a fraught conclusion to its discussions of patriarchy and gender. Wade dies never having proclaimed Rafe as his son and it is Hannah who, despite despising her late husband's promiscuity, engineers a public acknowledgment of Rafe's paternity when, on Wade's tombstone she has engraved: 'Husband of Hannah. Beloved father of Raphael and Theron'. Rafe's response to this inscription is ambiguous. Ed Gallafent surmises from George Peppard's expression indicates that 'There is apparently no doubt that Rafe welcomes this final reintegration into patriarchy' (1990: 81), a view countered by Laura Mulvey who sees in this graveside exchange the melodramatic rejection of 'rampant virility' and the 'unmitigated power of the father' (1977–8: 76). What one gets at the end of *Home from the Hill* (as with many of the 1950s' male melodramas) is the resurgence of a benevolent patriarchy. Having criticised the patriarch throughout, as Michael Walker notes (2004: 34), the film closes with the re-centralisation of 'the family line' through the final reunion of Hannah and Rafe, who leave together at the end 'to raise the patriarch's grandson' (34).

There are two quite different ways in which Hollywood at this time finally chose to turn its back on the crusty patriarch: through resuscitating the new father as happens with Rafe and through celebrating bachelordom, the ultimate rejection of paternal responsibility. These two images inform the representation of masculinity in *Pillow Talk*, a comedy that neatly surmises the concerns of the late 1950s around fathering and independence. The bachelor image had been made much of in the 1950s as an antidote to the drudgery and enslavement of family life. Popularised by Hugh Hefner's *Playboy*, which first appeared in December 1953, the bachelor became synonymous with male freedom. Hefner's first celebratory editorial warned:

We want to make it clear from the very start, we aren't a 'family magazine'. If you're somebody's sister, wife or mother-in-law and picked us up by mistake, please pass us along to the man in your life and get back to your *Ladies' Home Companion* (quoted in Ehrenreich 1983: 43).

Playboy was brazenly anti-conformist. It called all the 'grey flannel-suited' men and fathers to take a stand against breadwinning and domestic responsibility and Hefner's 'new fun morality' (45) centred on the vilification and exclusion of women and the trumpeting of bachelordom as an alternative to marriage – 'the biggest mistake of a man's life' (Burt Zollo in *Playboy* June 1954, Ehrenreich 1983: 48). In *Pillow Talk* this conflict is revisited as Brad Allen (Rock Hudson), at first the quintessential unreformed bachelor, rails against marriage and fatherhood to his best friend Jonathan:

Before a man gets married he's like a tree in the forest, he stands there independent, an entity unto himself. And then he's chopped down, his branches are cut off, he's stripped of his bark and he's thrown into the river with the rest of the logs. Then this tree's taken to the mill, and when it comes out, it's no longer a tree – it's a vanity table, the breakfast nook, the baby crib and the newspaper that lines the family garbage can.

Fatherhood means a loss of identity, a loss of masculinity and a loss of life. Brad, however, reforms his opinions after meeting his perfect woman, and at the end of *Pillow Talk* is jubilantly announcing his impending fatherhood. Fatherhood, though, has been in this film the subject of a running gag. In order to avoid bumping into Jan (his future wife) in Jonathan's office, Brad has sought refuge in the office next door, a gynaecologist's waiting room. Here, his complaints about stomach pains are taken to be the signs of an extraordinary pregnancy. Two more encounters with the gynaecologist and his nurse occur, providing the film's final image. Brad, on his way to tell Jonathan his news, tells the nurse 'I'm going to have a baby'. This time, the nurse and doctor do not let him escape, each taking one arm and dragging Brad off. His expression turns from pleasure to panic; the taming of the bachelor becomes fatherhood as farce.

The 1950s' nebulous traditionalism was, by the end, under scrutiny and femininity was becoming more acceptable and more important. Clara, the proto-feminist daughter in *The Long, Hot Summer*, articulates best the reasons for this shift when she says to Ben Quick 'I've spent my whole life around men who push and shove and shout and think they can make anything happen just by being aggressive, and I'm not anxious to have another one around the place'. Even such a residually patriarchal institution as Hollywood started to be of this opinion as the films produced during the era of women's liberation, far more mindful of the female perspective, attest.

Notes

1. Germaine Greer had argued much the same in 1970, when writing in *The Female Eunuch* that the nuclear family 'is possibly the shortest-lived familial system ever developed' (1970: 248). See Chapter 3 for a fuller discussion of Greer's comments on the nuclear family.

2. See Dorothy Thompson 'Is Morality "Normal"?', *Ladies' Home Journal*, March 1958, 11, 20, 169.

3. See also Cohan 1997, pp. 52–3.

4. This was a recurrent concern in *Ladies' Home Journal* and *McCall's* (see 'How America Lives: "My Work Doesn't Hurt Anyone" ', *LHJ*, October 1958 in which a working mother justifies the fact that she has continued to work).

5. See for example, John Bowlby (1969) *Attachment and Loss, Volume I: Attachment*: 179–80 etc.

6. See Dorothy Thompson 'Is Morality "Normal"?', *Ladies' Home Journal*, March 1958, 11, 20, 169.

7. In the film, Tom tells Betsy his affair with Maria took place in June 1945, but this is probably a factual error and in the book the affair takes place at the end of 1944, just prior to Tom and others being posted to the Pacific. In the original novel, Tom knows before leaving Italy that Maria is pregnant.

8. Children helping their father to select a new mother or wife is a recurrent Hollywood motif. See *The Courtship of Eddie's Father* and *Sleepless in Seattle*.

9. An extremely lucid and succinct account of the Oedipus complex is offered in Freud (1923) 'The Ego and the Id': 371.

10. For two discussions of the narrative use of Dean's acting style see Mellen 1977 and Wexman 1993.

11. Other examples include: *The Halliday Brand*, *Wall Street*, *Magnolia*.

12. See Biskind 1983 for an extended discussion of the binary oppositions in *Giant*.

13. In a television interview with Mark Shivas (reproduced in part on the American DVD of *All that Heaven Allows*) Sirk mentions his fascination with the metaphysical idea borrowed from Euripides that one person dies so that another can live.

14. See Chapter 1 for a discussion of *House of Strangers*, including the plot, which *Broken Lance* adheres to closely.

15. Despite the casting of the already well-known Joseph Cotten as Daniel, *The Halliday Brand* is a B-movie, as demonstrated by its budget and production values. By the 1950s, the Hollywood majors were phasing out B-features – productions that in the late 1930s, for example, had made up 52.6 per cent of the major studios' output (see Maltby 2003: 133; 163).

16. The Freud case history *Bonjour Tristesse* most obviously resembles is 'Dora' (Freud 1905a), in which a female patient's hysteria is attributed by Freud to her lasting attachment to her father. The section of Dora's story that is closest to *Bonjour Tristesse*

tells of Dora's objections to her father's affair with Frau K and Dora's subsequent belief (backed up by Freud) that she had been offered to Herr K in return for his wife being offered to her father. Dora's hatred for Frau K is recent, and Freud deduces from this that the hatred she feels towards her father's mistress – in conjunction with the love Freud believes Dora has for Herr K – have revived earlier feelings of 'being completely in love with' her father, an attachment Dora has repressed.

17. Jobs in the fashion industry were often used in Hollywood in the 1950s to connote the relatively liberated, independent career woman: *Rear Window*, *Designing Woman* and *There's Always Tomorrow* offer other examples. Presumably such jobs were seen to be both feminine enough and economically credible.

3

Revolution and Feminist Unrest: Fatherhood under Attack in the 1960s and 1970s

This chapter will look at these two decades together, with a view to understanding the father in relation to feminism. Women had lent ballast to the patriarchal mythology that prevailed during the 1950s; they married early, raised children and looked after the home. As women started to question this existence, so the dynamics of family life altered and the figure of the father entered a period of reassessment. The first extended explanation of women's growing unease with their lot came in Betty Friedan's *The Feminine Mystique*, published in 1963 and a catalyst to the women's liberation movement. In it, Friedan, an American journalist and mother, identified what she termed 'the problem that has no name': the dissatisfaction of the middle-class mother and housewife with the mundanity of her supposedly privileged and comfortable suburban lifestyle, wanting to take pride in saying 'Occupation: housewife' but being secretly ashamed at not feeling fulfilled by housework and childcare (1963: 16–17). Asking at the beginning of *The Feminine Mystique* 'Is this all?' (13), Friedan put in train a movement that, by the end of the 1970s, was to effect irreversible changes in how American families were run and how parental roles were conceived. Whereas, at the end of the 1950s and beginning of the 1960s, American women were still being taught that 'truly feminine women do not want careers, higher education, political rights – the independence and the opportunities that old-fashioned feminists fought for' (13), by the close of the 1970s, the majority of married women in America were in employment, around 50 per cent of marriages ended in divorce and 10 per cent of single-parent families were headed by men. One of the battlegrounds of the women's liberation movement, inevitably and naturally, was fatherhood – what was expected of the father, his inadequacies and how much more he could do for his children.

Friedan argued that '*The Feminine Mystique* has succeeded in burying millions of American women alive' (293) and she mounted an eloquent attack against the very foundations of American patriarchy, a system sustained by a highly prescriptive notion of femininity – and an equally prescriptive (though more self-serving) image of paternity. She blamed women's unhappiness on categoric divisions of labour, singling out such concepts as 'togetherness', which the magazine *McCall's* invented in the mid-1950s to express how fathers and mothers worked as a unit by doing different but equal tasks, never questioning the distribution of such tasks and their effects (Friedan 1963: 42–3). Friedan also challenged the idea that femininity precluded such masculine traits as wanting an education or a job, being independent and being interested in ideas, a notion championed in a favoured target – Lundberg and Farnham's *Modern Woman: The Lost Sex* (1947) in which education and careers are explicitly blamed for masculinising women, with damaging consequences for family life and even for a married couple's ability to gain sexual gratification (Friedan 1963: 37).

In talking about American women, Friedan's target was American men, for in talking about the discontent of the suburban housewife, the image of her oppressor became all the more clear. The stay-at-home woman was an essential component (as also expressed a decade earlier by Simone de Beauvoir) of the perpetuation of the big patriarch and breadwinner ideal, what could be termed the 1950s' masculine mystique. The dutiful homebound mother and the working but detached father had an intense symbiosis, and so in telling women to break free of the shackles of domesticity, Friedan was effectively telling them to reject the patriarchal structure in which they held a secure place. For the fulfilment of women's political, social, personal desires and needs proved incompatible with the traditional family model, a model that was inevitably threatened as women questioned what they were doing with their lives and decided to look beyond their husbands, their children and their home. The position of the 'head of the household' thereby became vulnerable from the moment Friedan, in the last paragraph of *The Feminine Mystique*, asked 'Who knows what women can be when they are finally free to become themselves?' (331). In no small way Friedan neatly turned the tables on men. As women sought out their identities independent of men so men became seen through and defined by their relationship to women.

Women's liberation caused the re-examination of patriarchy as a term and institution and of the father's role within it. Juliet Mitchell in *Woman's Estate* attributed to Kate Millett a shift away from an understanding of 'patriarchy' to mean specifically 'the rule of the father' to signify more generally 'the rule of men' (1971: 64). Patriarchy or 'the sexual politics whereby men establish their power and maintain control' (65) thus came to imply that the father, as head of the family, exemplified the system of ownership and oppression that characterised it and that, in turn, all men were potential fathers: innately capable of calling for and effecting the subjugation of women.

Directly and indirectly reflective of the rejection of the old-fashioned patriarch is the fact that relatively few father films were produced in the 1960s and 70s compared with the previous decade. Perhaps this was hardly surprising at a time when the Hollywood studio system (the great cinematic emblem of patriarchal control) was in turmoil as the big studios, after a string of financial disasters, were under threat from new producers, directors and independent production companies (see Monaco 2001). In what was not a period of masculine confidence, the father films that were produced did not follow a particularly clear trajectory, although common features exist. In the 1960s, for instance, several films were released in which images of archetypal masculinity were dismantled or undermined. The traditional father Sam Bowden is threatened almost irretrievably in

Cape Fear and between 1962 and 1965 Hollywood produced three films (not in any sense backed up by social reality) about single fathers, thereby positing an alternative to the beleaguered Bowden. *The Courtship of Eddie's Father*, *To Kill a Mockingbird* and *The Sound of Music* are not radical films and they are all, to varying degrees, concerned with reinventing the patriarch to ensure his longevity. But they also acknowledge that the father must change if he is to survive. The early 1960s also saw the release of films such as two Warren Beatty vehicles, *Splendor in the Grass* (1961) and *All Fall Down* (John Frankenheimer, 1962) in which the masculine model the fathers represent are, for opposing reasons, rejected. The issue of needing to impose change on gender relations is also evident in the films that feature a generational battle between father and children. As with many films of the 1950s, these sometimes centre on rebellious teenagers, but less predictably the late 1960s especially seemed to produce a number of significant films in which the child (in these instances the son) rebels far later. In films such as Arthur Penn's *The Chase* (1966), Gilbert Cates' *I Never Sang for my Father* (1968) and Elia Kazan's *The Arrangement* (1969), adult sons leave it until well into adulthood to stand up to their fathers. These films are depressing and characterised by irresolution (the tortured relationship with the father is unfinished business). In marked contrast are the energetic youthful rebellions against the family in more youth-centred films such as *The Graduate* (1967). In two other films that concentrate on generational conflict, *Bloodbrothers* (1979) and *Breaking Away* (1978), the former concludes with the rare abandonment of a brutal father and the latter with the equally rare establishment of a particularly close father–son relationship.

The impact of the women's liberation movement on Hollywood film is almost immediately apparent, but not perhaps in the ways one might expect. One important image of masculinity and paternity in the 70s, for example, was the belligerent and conservative father who steadfastly refuses to give up his old patriarchal ways. In films such as *Sometimes a Great Notion* (1971) and *The Great Santini* (1979) these values are initially critiqued, only for both films to end by supporting the outmoded values the fathers represent. As indicated by other early 70s' films such as *The Godfather* and *Junior Bonner* (both 1972), Hollywood was not averse to recuperating the entrenched masculinity under attack from feminists and liberals at the time. The unexpected salvation of a doubtful patriarch also emerges at the end of Steven Spielberg's *Jaws* (1975) and, in another Spielberg film, *Close Encounters of the Third Kind* (1977), the regression of the father is portrayed as encroaching infantilism. *Kramer vs. Kramer*, assumed by many sociologists and psychologists to be such a significant film, actually proved a far more influential social document than it did a movie, its Academy Awards notwithstanding. *Kramer* was one of surprisingly few father films of the 70s (Hollywood caught up in later decades) to fully acknowledge the women's liberation movement and the changes feminism had wrought to familial and gender relations.

The Troubled Patriarch: *Splendor in the Grass*, *All Fall Down*, *Cape Fear*

Feminist reform in the 1960s was slow. Despite being reputedly 'smitten' by Eleanor Roosevelt in 1960, President Kennedy had very few women in his cabinet and his reforms and changes hardly included women at all, although he did agree to Roosevelt founding the Commission on the Status of Women in 1961, a year before her death (Rowbotham 1999: 371). In 1963, the Commission produced a report opposing sexual discrimination in government employment and demanding 'equal pay for comparable work' (371). Between 1963 and 1967, it continued to press for equality and under President Johnson the Equal Opportunities Commission was set up and in 1966 Friedan founded the National Organization for Women.

A residual attachment to the paternal role models of the 1950s as well as the contemporary reassessments of gender and familial relations are dramatised in films such as *Splendor in the Grass* or *Love with the Proper Stranger* (1963) as the younger generation's fraught battles with the father, the father in these instances being the symbolic father who embodied the hypocrisy and oppressiveness of the older generation and its 1950s' values. Both films also end with the younger generation siring children of their own – and promising to do things differently. What is being signalled here is the unsustainability of the autocratic paternal model, although in John Frankenheimer's contemporaneous *All Fall Down*, the rejection of the father is quite different as here the once 'brilliant' man has become a depleted, passive alcoholic whose nightly retreats to his den serve as another metaphoric embodiment of the retreat from the symbolic primal father of the 1950s. The first time we see Ralph, the father in *All Fall Down*, he is dishevelled and downing a scotch while doing a jigsaw. An old leftie whose two sons call him by his first name, he is an unconventional father who presides over a fragmented family unit. One son, Berry-Berry (Beatty), in jail at the start of the film, is compulsively violent towards women; the other, Clint, is a compulsive eavesdropper who notes down the conversations of other family members. *All Fall Down* is in part a 'Momism' film after its time, in that the sons' problems are implicitly the result of an overbearing and oppressively adoring mother. Visually, though, it is the image of wasted masculinity (Berry-Berry as well as Ralph) that predominates – their dirty vests, Ralph's retreat to his den to drink, Berry-Berry's sexual violence. Masculinity appears to have nowhere to go.

Elia Kazan's *Splendor in the Grass* is the quintessential early 1960s' film about tortured teenage love, the heady relationship between Bud Stamper (Warren Beatty) and Deanie Loomis (Natalie Wood) being opposed and thwarted by the intervention of Bud's father Ace. Its hyperbolic tone can be interpreted as a hysterical response to the oppressive law of the father personified in Ace, the by now conventionalised, rich tyrant. Ace's opposition to Bud and Deanie, however, is unexpected, in that he does not insist his son settles down but that he sows his wild oats for a while before doing so. The generational difference in *Splendor* is thus reminiscent of the central father–son battles in *Home from the Hill*. What the later film adds to Minnelli's generational conflict are the trauma and pain of the transition to adulthood when the father is oppressive and intent on holding the children back. The reactions to the father's intervention in *Splendor* are extreme as Deanie has a nervous breakdown and Bud a seizure. That the autocratic paternal model is likewise unsustainable, though, is also demonstrated, as Ace's own demise is itself richly symbolic. Upon hearing that the 1929 Wall Street crash has bankrupted him, Ace takes Bud out of Yale for a weekend of revelry before committing suicide by jumping out of the hotel window, with his son in the next room in bed with a dancer he, as his last act of paternal love, had procured for him. The crash, because it bankrupts the father, functions here as a stark metaphor for the redundancy and necessary death of the bullying patriarch, a notion underscored by Bud's actions following his father's death as he returns to the humble farm where Ace started out to start his own family choosing to lead the simpler, less grandiloquent life his own father had rejected.

The loss of patriarchal dominance and the concomitant representation of patriarchy as lack is, out of the films of the early 1960s, most eloquently visualised in J. Lee Thompson's version of *Cape Fear*. Here, Sam Bowden (another Gregory Peck father) is a lawyer, confident in his dual role of protector and defender of his family and clients until the arrival in town of Max Cady, a rapist recently released from jail. Played by Robert Mitchum, Cady instantly recalls the violence, sexual attraction and menace of Mitchum's character, Harry Powell, in *The Night of the Hunter*. Cady blames Bowden for his conviction, as Bowden provided crucial evidence against him, and he begins to stalk and torment him, Betty his wife and Nancy his teenage daughter. Cady becomes the symbolic reminder of Bowden's loss; he is sexual, criminal and violent while Bowden is asexual, civilised and law abiding. The struggle between these polarities is fraught, and *Cape Fear*'s conclusion – in which Sam finally defeats Cady and returns home with his terrified family – is unconvincing.

The reason for this lies in the film's persistent suggestion that Cady is Bowden's repressed, the unacceptable side of masculinity that the respectable father must deny. *Cape Fear* opens with Cady, in an ostentatious white suit and Panama hat, strutting nonchalantly towards the courthouse to the menacing strains of Bernard Herrmann's score. Bowden is in court and has not seen Cady; he is self-assured, suave and oozes the unctuous superiority of a man who feels in control. He jokes easily with his presiding judge and then walks to his car. Cady follows Bowden and catches him unawares, stretching in through the open car window to whip his keys from the safety of their lock. Bowden swiftly becomes vulnerable as Cady demonstrates his capacity for slipping through the cordon of power and legitimacy the lawyer assumes protects and shrouds him in the same way that he, as father, protects and shrouds his family. Cady's threat cannot be countered through the deployment of legal and legitimate tactics, which is why it is both actual and figurative. He eludes capture for his crimes because he is never caught in the act; the patriarch's fear of Cady is patched together from insinuation, innuendo and supposition, and although *Cape Fear* is on the surface a conventional suspense tale, this generic framework couches the symbolic death of the good, stable, trustworthy, traditional father.

Within any binary opposition, power rests with one element at the expense of the other. Cady's power against the legitimised father figure is exemplified by his difference from Bowden. Bowden conforms to the specific paternal archetype Peck establishes in *Gentleman's Agreement*, *The Man in the Gray Flannel Suit* and *To Kill a Mockingbird* and his appearance exemplifies his role: at work he wears a classic single-breasted dark suit over a stiff-collared white shirt and tie, while at home he dons a series of clichés from within the narrow confines of the middle-class gentleman's 'smart casuals' wardrobe: cardigans, slacks and comfortable, white deck shoes, too pristine to have ever been seriously used. Conversely, Cady dresses extravagantly in pale colours, striped t-shirts and his signature Panama; his clothes are unstructured, suggestive of freedom or carelessness, complementing Mitchum's swaggering sexuality, an overall image rounded off by the succulent cigar which snuggles between his lips. The respective wardrobes also imply very different relationships between clothes and bodies. Whereas the grey-suited anonymity represses Bowden's sexuality and hides his body (even when dressed for bed Bowden is fully covered up), Cady's carefree, open-necked style draws attention to both his body and his masculinity. That the father's power is in part founded upon the renunciation of his sexuality and his potential allure has always seemed to stem from an uneasy compromise: the father has 'proved' his sexuality and desirability by siring a child, but in order to conform to the symbolic need for the father to no longer pose a sexual threat to the family (but rather to protect that family from the sexual threat of others) he must give that active masculinity up. The father's strength is stable only as long as this 'lack' is accepted rather than challenged.[1]

Cady is strip-searched and the emasculation of the father (Bowden) is complete

In *Cape Fear*, Cady's overt sexualisation stands in defiance of the de-eroticised father and his hegemonic position. In an early scene, in which Bowden still thinks it will be possible to stop Cady from within the parameters of the law, Cady is strip-searched. Rather than disempowering Cady as intended, getting him to take off his clothes down to his boxer shorts (and Panama hat) has the effect of emphasising what the sombre-suited father figure has conspicuously forfeited. Cady is happy to be strip-searched, ultimately because it enables him to flaunt his possession of the phallus and thus to question the father's impregnability. In several films, Mitchum's swelled, muscular chest comes to connote virility and untamed masculinity, and on those rare occasions when he is the father or father figure (*The Night of the Hunter*, *River of No Return*, *Home from the Hill*), his virility undermines his claims to paternity. Thompson's framing in the strip-search sequence takes to an extreme the notion that the tough body is the phallic body. Mitchum stands, often in the foreground, with his waist sucked in and his pectoral muscles puffed up; his image is cropped at the waist to prioritise a chest whose fullness and smooth contours throw into sharp relief the comparative emptiness under Bowden's respectable wool jacket. Having renounced aggressive masculinity, Bowden belatedly discovers that he has also renounced the means to combat it, a failure that explains Bowden's deep-rooted fear that Cady intends to destroy his family and violate his teenage daughter.

Bowden swiftly recognises that, if Cady is to be effectively challenged, he must renounce his own trust in morality, law and goodness and become more like Cady. Cady's threat therefore precipitates the internalised disintegration of the good father and the terminal destabilisation of his family. Bowden is initially appalled by his private detective Sievers' proposal that he should think about paying some men to rough Cady up, but instead does something just as dubious, which is to offer Cady money for leaving town. When this fails, Bowden follows Sievers' plan, but unsuccessfully. Bowden's rectitude crumbles as he starts to think like Cady; it is Bowden himself who assumes Cady's intention is to attack his family – as Cady replies, 'Now that's your train of thought, counsellor, not mine'. Cady's intention has insinuated itself into Bowden's imagination: he has become the good father's repressed symbiotic Other.[2] This symbiosis is confirmed in the scene after the strip-search in which Bowden returns home and talks through with Betty the possible consequences of their daughter Nancy being raped by Cady and being asked to testify against him. By bringing up the subject, by going through the as yet hypothetical judicial process in such depth, by raising the issue of the 'clinical details' Nancy would, in such a situation, be called upon to give in court, it is Sam Bowden and not Max Cady who seems perverse and violent. Bowden, who had told his wife and daughter, 'Thinking isn't knowing' when they assumed that it was Cady who had poisoned their dog, should know better than to let a hypothesis run away with him.

The good father is thus put in the position of having to defend his family from an aspect of himself – the physical, sexual father who lies buried beneath a socially imposed patina of respectability. The *mise en scène* of *Cape Fear*, with its emphasis upon long, noir-ish shadows, is suggestive of this doubleness. Fear of the sexual father and the use of shadows come together in the film's final, long sequence on the lake '*Cape Fear*', Bowden having lured Cady to his houseboat in a last, desperate attempt to ensnare him. These final chiaroscuro scenes amid tangled trees and with indistinct figures slipping through water that glistens in the moonlight contain Cady's most direct attacks on the Bowden family as he molests Betty in order to get Bowden away from Nancy, before going after Nancy as well. The trauma of the father's dual desire for the mother and the daughter is the incestuous pattern the myth of the de-sexualised father is striving to bury. But here, in the primal form of Cady, it rises again, and it seems no accident, in the final fight between Cady and Bowden or a little earlier when Cady strangles the deputy sheriff supposedly standing guard over the women, that levels and the distinction between under the line of the water (what is buried, repressed) and what is above it (what is permissible, in the open) become so important.

In these last scenes, and prior to Bowden's final defeat of Cady, Thompson's predilection for ellipses as means of generating suspense is most amply manifested. Some of the ellipses are narrative based, but mainly they are to do with visual representation: tight framing and editing from one close-up to another to disorientate and break up a scene; using such extreme darkness that it is hard to make figures out until they are too close for comfort. *Cape Fear* culminates in the inevitable watery duel between Cady and Bowden that, against the odds, Bowden wins. The duel takes place within the film's by now conventionalised noir *mise en scène*. Although, after having been left for dead under water, Bowden resurfaces to club Cady on the head, incapacitate him and finally to hold him at gunpoint, his decision not to shoot Cady, letting him face life imprisonment instead, leaves open the threat of his return (Cady had wanted to inflict on Bowden's family 'death by a thousand cuts' and this is Sam's reciprocal gesture). In the concluding shot, the Bowden family leave '*Cape Fear*' in a motorboat, a family superficially safe and secure but now profoundly undermined, their fracturedness conveyed, as it has been previously, by the three of them sitting together but looking in different directions. At the heart of this unease is Sam Bowden, who cannot, after having, at least on the level of fantasy, descended to Cady's level, re-establish himself as the upright patriarch or indeed as the unimpeachable lawyer. His stern, defiant stare out from the boat at the end of *Cape Fear* may indicate his desire to resume his role as the family's great protector, but the look is also one of haunted resignation.

Single Fathers: *The Courtship of Eddie's Father, To Kill a Mockingbird, The Sound of Music*

It is notable that Hollywood, at a transitional time between the intensely conservative 1950s and the late 1960s, released three major films that focused on the single, widowed father. The good single father is a potent and popular cinematic myth and one that counters the threat of the 'bad' single mother, one of Hollywood's favoured objects of hatred and distrust. *To Kill a Mockingbird*, *The Courtship of Eddie's Father* and *The Sound of Music* offer three early prototypes of a figure Hollywood frequently idealises (an earlier film *Houseboat* [1958] also features a single father and after the ground-breaking *Kramer vs. Kramer* [1979] there followed many more). Such adulation of the lone father flies in the face of historical fact as statistically only one in ten single parents now are fathers and the figure was lower before the 1970s. It has also never been considered preferable for children to be brought up by one parent rather than two,[3] and in both *Eddie's Father* and *The Sound of Music*, the father actively seeks a replacement mother. The single father in movies can in part be argued to be a symptom of gender definitions moving away from the traditional binary of the working father and stay-at-home mother. However, he has also become a potent and repeatedly used imaginative motif within Hollywood, a figure of fantasy that serves a political function in proving the adaptability and resilience of patriarchy, but which is also purely romantic.

Why is the father left alone to tend his children such an attractive image? Within film history this is an obsession peculiar to Hollywood (the divorced father in the British 1950s' film *The Spanish Gardener*, for example, is a cruelly inept parent). In the 1980s and 90s, the father alone with his child became a recurrent love object in romantic comedy – *Three Men and a Baby*, *Three Men and a Little Lady*, *One Fine Day* (1996) and *Sleepless in Seattle*. The first way in which Hollywood valorises the single father is to create out of the least likely man a romantic love object, the narrative motive (as it was in *Gentleman's Agreement*) in both *Eddie's Father* and *The Sound of Music*. Frequently, as in *The Courtship of Eddie's Father* or *The Sound of Music* and *Chitty Chitty Bang Bang* (1968), it is the children who desire and instigate the search for a new mother; as Caractacus Potts, the father in the last of these, observes to his soon-to-be new partner Truly Scrumptious, he is everything to his children 'except what they need most'. The second way Hollywood valorises the lone father is to make him into a romantic ideal, the perfect composite parent (the maternal surrogate as well) who has renounced any need for sexual attachment or a new wife because his family is all he needs. This is the model followed in *To Kill a Mockingbird*.

Atticus Finch in *To Kill a Mockingbird* is the perfect fairytale father, who, despite the availability of Maudy across the street (a character who is younger and so more eligible in the film than she is in Harper Lee's novel), never contemplates remarriage. The single father of fairytales feeds a tremendous need not to devalue or forget the symbolic father – and implies a residual fear at his imminent loss. There are countless children's tales, old and new, in which the benevolent parent is the father (frequently contrasted with the wicked stepmother as in 'Hansel and Gretel' and 'Cinderella') or in which the father is the only parent (as in 'Beauty and the Beast'). There are fewer stories in which the parents' roles are reversed. Christopher Hill has observed that, while the father of myth is often tyrannical, the father of fairytales is often benevolent (cited in Burgess 1997: 6).

Psychology has traditionally been overly concerned with the mythic father, but the child's view – echoed by the fairytale fathers – tends towards seeing the father as kind and protective. Lacan believed, for example, in the 'ravaging effects' on the child of the father who is also the 'legislator' (1957–8: 218–9), the pillar of the community – the social father – making the most awesome individual father. Atticus is a benevolent version of Lacan's fearsome father, both an idealised father and an idealised lawyer. Unlike Sam Bowden (also a lawyer and also played by Gregory Peck), Atticus, a public defender in 1930s' Alabama, is responsible and fearless, not hesitating when asked by the sheriff to defend Tom Robinson, an African-American wrongly accused of raping a white girl, Mayella Ewell. The romanticisation of Atticus extends to his liberalism and *Mockingbird*'s concerns resonate with those of the Civil Rights movement. In this context, Atticus becomes a multiple figure of identification for the film's audience. As noted earlier, Peck brings to the role his own specific history of playing sober, upright and gentle fathers. Just as Bowden in *Cape Fear* was threatened by Max Cady, in *Mockingbird,* Atticus is similarly threatened by and favourably compared to 'bad' fathers such as Bob Ewell, Mr Cunningham and the punitive father of 'Boo' Radley. Ewell is the film's extended portrait of bad fathering, a single father, like Atticus, who beats his daughter Mayella, forces her to perjure herself in order to convict Robinson (it was Ewell who beat Mayella) and who later tries to kill Atticus's children, Jem and Scout.

Despite his favourable positioning within the narrative, Atticus has been interpreted negatively, as an establishment figure who stands in the way of ideological change. In bringing together the personal role of the father and the law, Amy Lawrence has used a Lacanian interpretation of the paternal signifier to condemn Atticus as the prime motivator in suppressing feminine independence and for being implicit in the film's benign racism. Lawrence proposes '. . . a feminist reading that resists the film's smooth liberal surface by examining how women are distorted and fragmented . . . by the racist and patriarchal system delineated in the film' (1991: 176). These arguments are insightful, but this reading downplays the romanticisation of Atticus and the extent to which the daughter Scout (who narrates the film) adores him and makes the audience adore him too. Lawrence's interpretation is extremely useful for the trial scene, but Robinson's trial (in terms of pace, *mise en scène* and tone) stands apart from the remainder of Mulligan's film, and so is not entirely representative of it.

Within the trial Atticus does, as Lawrence posits, become the Lacanian father, the awesome legislator who represents and is bent upon upholding the patriarchal system within which he operates. Lawrence's contestation is that the figure of the father is key to silencing the feminine, and she notes how, during the trial, Scout and her narrator's voice are 'shunted aside' as the male characters – especially the father–son identification between Atticus and Jem – predominate (1991: 174). This reading, however, sidelines the film's clear intention to glorify Atticus, and so sidesteps the issue of why he is such an attractive father figure. Atticus stands for so much we the audience might wish to identify with. He leads the fight against racism and bigotry, he upholds the liberal ideals of the American judicial system and he has taught Scout and Jem right from wrong. Defeat in this case notwithstanding, the packed African-American gallery in the segregated courtroom rises to its feet to honour Atticus as he leaves. With reverence a black minister has told Scout: 'Miss Jean Louise (her real name), stand up – your father's passing'. Atticus is Piero della Francesca's 'Madonna della Misericordia', with the needy and bereft sheltering under her ample cape. He is the great protector who stands up for the weak and the good.

The one time when Atticus does embody the intimidating legislator–father is during his cross-examination of Mayella Ewell. Mayella is terrified; she has learnt by rote her story that it was Tom and not her father who beat her, although her mannerisms – perching precariously on the edge of her chair, pointing an accusing finger at Tom but unable to disguise her affection for him – betray her. Atticus probes this ambivalence and in so doing pries into the suppressed source of Mayella's pain, notably the abuse she suffers at the hands of her father. In a final, extraordinary outburst, prompted by Atticus asking 'Do you want to tell us what *really* happened?' (Atticus's patronising tone towards his defenceless witness makes this the moment when we feel truly equivocal towards him) Mayella, never uttering Robinson's name, blurts out,

> I got something to say, and then I ain't gonna say no more. He took advantage of me, and if you fine, fancy gentlemen ain't gonna do nothing about it, you're just a bunch of lousy, yellow stinking cowards.

The *mise en scène* here is deeply emotive and emphasises the rawness of Mayella's testimony. As she begins, a slow zoom-in starts, coming to rest on her face in an extreme, slightly soft close-up, a framing that is broken only once by a reverse shot of Atticus standing over her. Just as she is trapped by the camera, Mayella is imprisoned within the complex unspoken laws of the father. The 'he' in her statement is overtly Tom Robinson, although it could also be her father or even the figurative male (Atticus, the male court) who refuses to hear what she is saying.

A tortuous series of unspoken but readable signs leads one to understand Mayella's anger and motivation to be fear and loathing of her father and equally to understand Atticus's decision not to protect the unprotected daughter, whose testimony eventually condemns his client. The conjunction of the law and the father is fleetingly permitted to resemble the failure Lacan ascribes it and Mayella, realising the good father will not offer her protection, bolts from the witness chair, only to be caught and ushered to her place by her own 'bad' father, who does not quite have the gall to put a comforting arm around her, leaving it instead equivocally hovering along the back of her seat.

Mockingbird (both within the trial scene and beyond it) wants its audience to believe in the peculiar brand of patriarchy and paternity Atticus represents – benevolent, just, but innately traditional. In an early bedtime scene after he has listened to Scout read falteringly from *Huckleberry Finn*, he sets about explaining gender difference to his tomboy daughter. Scout has asked Atticus what he is going to leave her when he dies, knowing that Jem is going to inherit his watch. Atticus tells her that she will not inherit from him but will receive her mother's jewellery. When Atticus has left and the link between femininity and inheritance established, Scout is prompted to ask Jem whether or not their mother was pretty. In the small details of this exchange – Scout cupping Atticus's watch between her clumsy, innocent hands, Atticus on the porch listening in to his children's conversation about their mother – lie the seeds of *Mockingbird*'s attitude to fathering: the father is there to coax his children towards a safe, conventional world.

He is also there to protect Jem and Scout from the brutalising adult world Mayella's father embodies (there is, for instance, the scene in which Atticus takes Jem with him to see Robinson's family; Jem is left in the car and Ewell, who is staggering drunk, lurches menacingly towards the vehicle and then spits at Atticus when he comes over to protect his son). Unlike Ewell who has (like the rapist stepfather in *Peyton Place*) propelled Mayella into adulthood too early, Atticus acts as a go-between for Jem and Scout, facilitating, rationalising the adult world for them. A repeated motif in *Mockingbird* is Atticus sitting down with Scout (as in the bedtime scene) to explain to her the adult world. In one such scene, after Scout has been caught fighting in the playground for defending her father's name against taunts that he defends 'niggers', Atticus sits her down on the front steps and teaches her white liberal ideology: how she should substitute 'Negro' for 'nigger' and how he 'couldn't hold my head up in this town. I couldn't even tell you and Jem not to do something again' if he did not defend Robinson. It is through its blurring of the roles of father and lawyer (both instruments of protection) that *Mockingbird* argues for the goodness of patriarchy.

Atticus explains to Scout why he is defending Tom Robinson

That Atticus is the complete, composite parent is illustrated by an earlier bathetic sequence in which he shoots a rabid dog. Here, Atticus enacts the potent masculine myth that the hitherto feminine and sensitive man can also, if required, reveal his repressed macho side. Mostly Atticus uses words to teach Scout and Jem; as Scout the narrator says just prior to the dog sequence:

> There just didn't seem to be anyone or thing Atticus couldn't explain. Though it wasn't a talent that would arouse the admiration of any of our friends, Jem and I had to admit he was very good at that. But that was all he was good at, we thought.

A prevailing image of masculinity in American popular culture is that expressed in Kenny Rogers' song 'The Coward of the County', in which the 'cowardly' son (instructed by his father not to prove his masculinity through fighting, as he has done) finally rises up against the brutes who have raped his wife and, in the barroom, floors the whole lot of them. Non-aggression has its limitations and men are at some point going to have to wield a gun. In a wry parody of the 'coward' being compelled by exceptional circumstance to use violence, Peck has trouble getting his lawyer's glasses to rest on his head as he steadies his aim, finally resolving the problem by throwing them to the ground. Unencumbered by his benign lawyer–fatherliness, Atticus then kills the prancing dog with a single shot, the sheriff remarking to his flabbergasted children, 'Didn't you know your daddy was the best shot in the county?'

Atticus's goodness is thus the result of a successful compromise – for what marks and sustains his fathering and concomitant liberalism is an inherent desire to reconfigure traditional patriarchy. Psychoanalyst Helene Deutsch noted in the early 1960s that her student grandson's generation 'bemoaned the way fathers seemed to be increasingly taking a back-seat in childrearing, and the way they have become devalued along with the society they represent' (Sayers 1992: 79). The suggestion here – as in *Mockingbird* – is that traditional fathering and active involvement with childcare can and should co-exist. The potency of Atticus Finch is that he is both a symbolic, fantasy father-ideal and a 'real' father, one who performs – albeit with the assistance of the family's black maid Calpurnia – the quotidian tasks of parenthood as well.

Compared to Atticus, Tom Corbett (Glenn Ford) in *The Courtship of Eddie's Father*, though by no means evil, offers an image of imperfect parenting. Like Tom Winston (Cary Grant) in *Houseboat*, Corbett is the slightly inept widowed father who urgently needs the help of a substitute mother. Both Toms are considered highly desirable. Corbett has the pick of three very different women: Elizabeth, a homely neighbour who was best friends with Eddie's dead mother; Dollye, a sexy redhead; and Rita, a financially independent career woman, while Winston has a choice of two: his dead wife's sister; and a voluptuous Italian played by Sophia Loren. It may come as little surprise that Tom Corbett (and Eddie) in the end choose Elizabeth, the one who most closely resembles the lost mother and who can thereby most consummately restore completeness to the Corbett family. Less predictably, but rather refreshingly, *Houseboat* concludes with the rejection of the homely woman in favour of Loren.

Tom Corbett's singleness, unlike Atticus's, is the source of his and Eddie's troubles, hence the search for a replacement mother. That Tom is unaccustomed to performing the nurturing role is demonstrated in an early scene, as Tom and Eddie prepare lunch on what is Eddie's first day back at school since his mother died and Tom's first day back at work. As he is taking a cup and saucer down from a kitchen cupboard, Eddie explains to Tom how he had wanted to cry at school; as Victor Perkins points out, 'Eddie's precarious physical position on the stool, his careful handling of two fragile objects, counterpoint his attempt at emotional poise' (1972b: 76). Deborah Thomas, in a more recent discussion of this scene, finds Tom to be 'clearly moved' by his son's stoicism, his response only interrupted by the doorbell and the arrival of the housekeeper (2000: 112). Tom, as Thomas suggests, bottles up his feelings, but whereas Thomas views this with sympathy (believing that Tom wants to establish intimacy with Eddie but lacks the necessary emotional articulacy and confidence), it is possible to interpret Tom's fathering more negatively.

Upon finding his goldfish dead Eddie becomes hysterical

Compared to Atticus Finch, Tom Corbett is an old-fashioned single father; he is undemonstrative and considers childrearing to be woman's work, much like Phil Green does in *Gentleman's Agreement*. The role of the substitute mother in both films is also comparable; in *Gentleman's Agreement*, when Phil's son Tommy is taunted at school for (supposedly) being Jewish, Phil's fiancée, Kathy is the one to physically comfort him, just as it becomes Elizabeth who comforts Eddie. Although Tom learns to be a caring father (when he finally prioritises Eddie over Rita when Eddie has run away from summer camp), it is difficult to gloss over his deficiencies, as the film to an extent does. Early on, he has, for example, failed to notice that Eddie has come into his bed during the night and later he uses his housekeeper Mrs Livingston to babysit on New Year's Eve while he goes out with Rita. It is only because both Mrs Livingston and Elizabeth refuse to look after Eddie that Tom does not do the same on Eddie's birthday. There are various crisis moments throughout *Eddie's Father* that signal Tom's paternal shortcomings, the first coming the evening of Eddie's first day back at school. Upon finding a dead goldfish in his tank, Eddie screams. Tom's response here is to slap Eddie, much as a nineteenth-century doctor might a hysteric; conversely, Elizabeth's approach is to talk to Eddie and ask him, 'You were thinking of your mother, weren't you?' When Eddie's hysteria has abated, father and son share a brief, rather stiff exchange during which Eddie reveals he realises how much Tom misses his mother and the two make a secret pact always to tell each other everything. As in this scene, it is always another character (most frequently Eddie) who functions as the catalyst for a shift in Tom towards greater emotional openness, just as it is others who instruct him in the art of parenting.

In a sequence that demonstrates just how different Tom is from Atticus, Eddie falls ill with a fever. Rather than sit over his bed all night as Atticus does with Jem at the end of *Mockingbird*, Tom fetches Elizabeth (a nurse) to stay with Eddie through the night while he gets a good night's sleep. Through such moments it is hard to sustain Thomas's view that it is Elizabeth (and not Tom himself) who is the major obstacle to father–son bonding. Both Atticus and Tom are traditional, but whereas the former is also liberal and enlightened, Tom is unreconstructed and deeply reactionary, an attitude demonstrated by his ultimate rejection of Rita, an independent career woman. While they are still dating, Rita tells Tom she wants a man who will 'love me on equal terms', to which Tom retorts she should be satisfied with the vote for now, as her call for equality will never 'become a national movement'. This exchange could well be ironic, as of course equality in 1962 was just on the verge of becoming a 'national movement', but in terms of what it says about Tom, his response indicates his desire to re-establish the traditional patriarchal family unit and erase the 'problem' of the independent woman. Frequently Hollywood's sons endorse their fathers' reactionariness and here, Eddie gets what he wants by ensuring that Tom gets together with Elizabeth. *The Courtship of Eddie's Father* closes on a close-up of a contented son looking on as Tom and Elizabeth chat on the telephone like old friends. Tom, serenely unaware of the dramatic social changes brewing, effortlessly returns to his old life; he is restored to the role of breadwinner and he has found in Elizabeth a traditional feminine substitute for his wife.

Captain von Trapp in *The Sound of Music* is another of these conventional and gently incompetent fathers of Hollywood comedies. Like Tom, von Trapp needs either the support of nannies or a new wife to help with the care of his seven children and, again like Tom, he gets both in the form of one sweet-natured and unthreatening woman, the novice nun Maria. Deborah Thomas is as harsh on von Trapp as she is kind to Tom Corbett, arguing that his nationalism is akin to the Nazism he ostensibly despises and suggesting that, in marrying him, Maria is 'significantly diminished' (2000: 135–6). In the early 1960s, British psychoanalyst D. W. Winnicott observed that it was necessary for a child to be 'let down gently' by their father and to realise that the real father is flawed and can never conform to the imaginary ideal he, in the eyes of his children, had come to represent. It is only after this realisation, Winnicott argues, that a fruitful relationship can be established (1964: 117). Both *Eddie's Father* and *The Sound of Music* let their respective audiences 'down gently' in terms of Tom and von Trapp and their over-attachment to chauvinism.

The chauvinistic but lovable autocratic father who is eventually softened by the persistent attentions of a kindly woman is a recurrent figure in Rodgers and Hammerstein musicals (see also *The King and I*, made into a film in 1956). A positive interpretation of *The Sound of Music* could focus on how music and Maria change von Trapp for the better, and how, under their twin influences, the Captain is transformed from wooden patriarch to warm husband and father, his prior deficiencies becoming attributable (as they are in *Eddie's Father*) to grief. Von Trapp's initial traditionalism is telegraphed through *mise en scène*. Wise uses straight lines (in both blocking and set design) to signal his rigidity and a low-angle camera to signal his autocratic condescension as he literally looms over everyone else. When Maria, fresh from the abbey, arrives at his house, von Trapp catches her in the ballroom, a room unused since the death of his wife. He stands imperiously straight-backed in the doorway (a stance emphasised by the low-angle camera) and half obscured by the chiaroscuro lighting. He then ushers her out, before introducing her to his children, whom he calls with the aid of his naval whistle, arranging them in an orderly line ready for inspection.

This linearity is broken down as von Trapp falls in love with Maria; more fluid, rounded movements and soft, romantic lighting supplant the hitherto militaristic lines, low angles and sharp lighting. The point of mollification comes as the Captain has just sacked Maria for presumption (he has been away and comes back to find that she has allowed the children to cavort around Salzburg in clothes made from old curtains). He hears the children singing 'The Sound of Music' to his then fiancée, Baroness Schreider (*The Sound of Music* also has an unsuitable woman who needs to be dispatched). The Captain is irresistibly drawn to the sound of his children singing and, although he marches as usual into the house, his gait is swiftly transformed into a reverential tiptoe the closer he gets.

Now he hovers in the doorway (humbled, contained by it rather than imposing himself upon it) smiling joyously. There is then the first of several soft-focus close-ups of von Trapp, accentuating his softening and re-eroticisation, a transformation that here culminates in his spontaneous, happy embrace with his children (again creating a rounded, relaxed shape as opposed to a neat line) and which eventually prompts him to reintroduce dancing into his home.

Although Hollywood's adoption of the single father was in some respects ahead of its time, like other reformed Hollywood fathers, what Atticus, Tom and von Trapp represent is the continuity of patriarchy as opposed to its displacement. Sarah Harwood (after Virginia Wright Wexman) has noted how in Hollywood romances the convention has been 'to achieve closure through incipient families' and to end with the establishment of the heterosexual couple, a form of closure that Harwood terms the 'Final Romance' (1997: 61–2). It is through such a 'Final Romance' that patriarchal stability is reaffirmed at the end of *The Sound of Music* or *The Courtship of Eddie's Father*. Imbedded within such a structure is the desire, by the 1960s, to recuperate not merely patriarchy and heterosexual conformity, but to establish a minutely modified version of traditionalism that makes the dominant masculine archetype just about acceptable to those more radical forces calling for social and political change.

The Family under Threat: *Mary Poppins*, *The Chase*

This necessary compromise is exemplified by the change that occurs in a patriarch such as George Banks in Disney's 1964 adaptation of *Mary Poppins*, a film that illustrates how hard it was to displace the patriarchal model. Here, the magical eponymous nanny – a more literal *deus* (or *dea*) *ex machina* than Maria in *The Sound of Music*, who arrives to help avert catastrophe – descends from the fairytale clouds hanging over London in order to steer a classic Edwardian family towards modernisation by aiding the metamorphosis of its aloof paterfamilias into a loving, fun father. Mary Poppins is not the love interest as Maria (or Truly in *Chitty Chitty Bang Bang*) is; there is a Mrs Banks, a fervent, if ditsy, Suffragette, whom Mary helps to steer away from the feminist cause.

We first encounter George Banks as he returns from work, as always, on the strike of 6 o'clock. He immediately proclaims his attention to duty, routine and a blinkered, steadfast patriarchal hierarchy through the words of his first song ('I feel a surge of deep satisfaction, much as a king astride a noble steed . . .'). His outmoded ideology is mocked and must be replaced. As a father, he is of the 'children must be seen but not heard' variety and his wife, in response to her husband's stiffness, spends more time with the Suffragettes than at home. Poppins, as befits her fairytale status, is also a force for liberalisation who, alongside the Banks children, Jane and Michael, articulates their need for better, less neglectful parenting. As a force for change, Poppins considers her work done when the family is content – and changed. In the final scene, Banks returns home in an implausibly jolly mood for a man who has just been sacked. With his bowler hat punched through, his stiff collar unbuttoned, his tie askew, he now offers a parody of the staid banker he was. Having realised the errors of his autocratic ways he hoists his family off to the park to fly their kite, a kite that for the duration of the film has been broken and condemned to the cellar. With the father safely restored, Mrs Banks' nascent feminism can now be quashed, a defeat symbolised by her 'Votes for Women' sash becoming the kite's tail. Mrs Banks, like her husband, has exchanged one cause for another (the family), which is, as Poppins declares before soaring up once more to the clouds, 'as it should be'. Any shift in family dynamics Poppins masterminds is desired more or less consciously by Mrs Banks and the children; her support of the Suffragette movement is fragile and she seems more excited by the daring exploits of her sisters than anything else. The parable of *Mary Poppins* is confirmed by the 'Let's Go Fly a Kite' finale. As his reintegration into the patriarchal system is complete, Banks finds himself re-employed at the bank and promoted to the position of partner. The depressing conclusion of Disney's *Mary Poppins* is that what women's liberation (of whatever era) wants more than anything is not a monumental change in how gender roles are conceived, but merely a traditional father who is also sometimes available for play. This is the ideology behind Hollywood's 'Final Romance'.

While the revolutionary movements started in the 1960s did herald the restructuring of the traditional family, they did not effect its demise, and as Mary Poppins suggests, a little change in the father was greeted with much joy. From the publication of *The Feminine Mystique* in 1963, the typical domestic unit came under predictable attack and, by 1971, the influential British psychologist R. D. Laing talked of the ' "family" as merely a fantasy structure' (1971: 5). The nuclear family had become a concept instead of a working reality and the late 1960s and 70s saw a burgeoning of the debates around the values, role and validity of the traditional familial unit. In the *New York Times*, for example, there appeared an interesting series of articles about the increase in homosexuality and the repercussions of this for 'family values': could the 'ineffective father' cause a son's homosexuality (*New York Times* 1968: 69)? Was the increased acceptance of homosexuality a symptom of a general dissatisfaction with heterosexuality and the family (*New York Times* 1975b: 31)?[4] Ann Roiphe thought not, arguing that, despite the rise in homosexuality, anti-family sentiment and women's liberation, the traditional familial structure should not be devalued as this was what most people still desired (*New York Times* 1971b). Another article then maintained that gender divisions among hippy families were not so very different from those in traditional 1950s-style families (*New York Times* 1972: 325). Elsewhere, women's liberation and the greater education and employment of women were blamed for blinding people to the reality that 'without the family our society loses its substance' (*New York Times* 1975a: 17).

This residual conservatism is ambivalently treated in the films of the time. The probing of traditional family values is greatly in evidence in the films of the late 1960s. In *The Graduate*, eminently respectable families are built around deceit and unhappiness;

in *Guess Who's Coming to Dinner* (1967), the inherent racism of an ostensibly liberal white middle-class family comes to the surface; in *The Arrangement*, a veneer of affluent respectability is rejected in favour of potential happiness within an alternative, non-traditional family; and in *Love Story* (1970) father and son enact the stereotypical 1960s' battle between the generations. In *The Arrangement* (one of several Elia Kazan movies to feature a turbulent relationship between father and son)[5] this struggle becomes internalised within Eddie (Kirk Douglas), an advertising executive who deliberately crashes his Alfa Spider and nearly kills himself. Eddie realises that he cannot simply return to the 'bullshit' of his old life, and in his imagination he constructs the 'bad' alter ego of who he used to be, a loathsome figure with slicked hair, moustache and sharp suits. This alter ego was a cheating husband and a neglectful son and father; the new Eddie turns his back on this life and image. He ends up a psychiatric patient but also forms an alternative family unit with his mistress and her baby. Eddie's infantilisation and his abnegation of responsibility resemble the similar regressions of Benjamin in *The Graduate* or later Roy in *Close Encounters of the Third Kind*. Characters such as Eddie no longer want to be or become the conventional father; they commit symbolic parricide, much as the younger generation was perceived to be doing through the youth movements of the late 1960s.

Arthur Penn's *The Chase* bleakly suggests what might have befallen Kyle and Jasper Hadley from *Written on the Wind* had they stumbled into the 1960s. Val Rogers is the 1950s-style tycoon whose name is burnt into the local landscape and consciousness. He owns land and commandeers people: his son Jake, Sheriff Calder who owes his job to him, much of the town and its immigrant labour force. Rogers at one point throws a lavish birthday party for the 'in' crowd of those he favours and who, reciprocally, curry favour with him. Jake unveils the consummate metaphor for the repressive extended patriarchal family his father is seeking to establish: a model of a local college Val is funding that will mean the town's children will no longer have to leave home to complete their education. Just as Val has trapped the adult Jake, so the father will become the whole town's Big Brother, an early shot of a billboard proclaiming 'Val Rogers Properties' now seeming heavily ironic. It is, however, the extent of Val's ignorance rather than his omniscience that signals his defeat, for not only does Sheriff Calder finally bite the hand that fed him and rebel against being Rogers' stooge, but also Val belatedly learns that his son's marriage is a sham and that Jake is in love with the wife of Bubba Reeves, the town's infamous bad son and escaped convict. As it is in *The Graduate* or *The Arrangement*, the foundations upon which 1950s' paternal omnipotence was based are ultimately exposed.

Rogers' redundancy is unmasked by the chaotic, ambling rise of Calder as an alternative, more contemporary and far less didactic patriarch. The last part of *The Chase* is dark, violent and shambolic; although it is ostensibly Bubba who is the object of the titular 'chase', the subject of the 'chase' is the moribund order Rogers represents. As

Calder defies his symbolic father, he also assumes the mantle of modern (or modernising) protector. Repeatedly, the lumbering but nevertheless graceful bulk of Marlon Brando as Calder physically stands between the forces of tradition (Rogers, the town, the mob) and those driven into hiding by its narrow and shallow rules (Bubba, his black friend Lester, Jake and Anna Reeves). At one point – on the jail steps, significantly – Calder is reduced to a bloodied heap, his face disfigured by the pummelling he has received. But, martyr-like, he still gets up and staggers on, the hysterical embodiment of defiance against the father. Calder's painful uprising suddenly makes sense of his decision not to adopt children because he did not want to bring them up 'over a jail' where he lives: the whole rotten town is a jail and one that, in the form of the fire that engulfs the car pound at the end, needs to be razed to the ground before it can change. The conclusion of *The Chase* expresses the need for revolution and the decimation of the old order as, amid the cars engulfed by flames, Jake is fatally injured and, just in front of those jailhouse steps again, Bubba is shot. So, as both of the town's unhappy sons ultimately die, its two fathers, Rogers and Calder, live on – the former to view the devastation and waste he has wrought, the latter to finally escape the jail.

In *The American Male*, contemporaneous with *The Chase*, Myron Brenton articulates male doubts and grievances as he attacks both the 'invisible straightjacket that still keeps him [the American male] bound to antiquated patriarchal notions of what he must do or be' and the fact that 'suddenly the world is seen only through the feminist prism' (Brenton 1967: 13–4). The specific paradox, according to Brenton, to have beset the American father, is that his responsibility 'has enlarged in inverse ratio to his authority. In other words, his duties have expanded while his rights have diminished' (134). Following Brenton, it becomes apparent that the traditional father perceived his authority to lie in his aloofness from the home, that once he was called upon to acquire other, more domestic, responsibilities, he felt his authority to be under threat. His greater presence in the home corrodes the father's old symbolic value. Brenton, well before the 1970s' 'men's movement', realised that fatherhood suffered from being defined for and by women rather than for and by men, leading him to balk at the 'ludicrous conclusion … that fatherhood is somehow feminine!' (139), that, the more a man derives 'emotional gratification' from fathering, the more he is likely to be found 'lacking in masculinity' (139). If one compares some of the film images of fatherhood from the 1960s, there is a discernible difference between those, such as the lone fathers in *To Kill a Mockingbird*, *The Courtship of Eddie's Father* or *The Sound of Music*, which offer feminine fantasies of fathering and those, such as *The Chase*, which are masculinity-centred and markedly more chaotic and morose. An imperative for men and fathers in the 1970s became to make feminism and its requirements work for and not against them. Many feminists have suggested cynically that the impetus behind the 1970s' men's movement and its new ideal of caring fatherhood was not the desire to work out how better to bring up children but to discover an arena in which men could talk about themselves and their own feelings, the consummate cinematic expression of which is a film such as *Kramer vs. Kramer*. The majority of fathers and film fathers, however, still failed to discover the joys of practical parenthood, the debates becoming increasingly divisive and heated as the women's liberation movement hit its stride in 1970.

1970 and All That

Australian feminist, Dale Spender called 1970 'a very good year for women' (1985: 19). It saw the publication of several key feminist texts including Germaine Greer's *The Female Eunuch* and Kate Millett's *Sexual Politics*, new members flocked to the National Organization for Women (NOW) and (although it subsequently fell three states short of ratification) in 1972 the US Congress passed the Equal Rights Amendment (stipulating that 'Equality of rights under the law shall not be denied or abridged by the United States or by any State on account on sex').[6] It was not that women had shown no dissatisfaction in the 1960s – the divorce rate increased steadily after 1960, following years of decline – but they were now choosing to become more vocal on their own account. The language of the revolutionary forces of the 1960s had been male; as Rowbotham wrote in 1973: 'As soon as we learn words we find ourselves outside them ... Language is part of the political and ideological power of the rulers' (1973: 32–3). In the 1960s, 'Men led the marches and made the speeches and expected their female comrades to lick the envelopes and listen' (Coote and Campbell 1982: 13). Now women wanted liberation for themselves.

Fathers and the traditional family came under particular attack: to Millett, the family was 'a patriarchal unit within a patriarchal whole' (1970: 33), while Greer parodied the patriarchal family thus: 'Mother duck, father duck and all the little baby ducks. The family, ruled over and provided for by father, suckled and nurtured by mother seems to us inherent in the natural order' (Greer 1970: 246). This 'natural order' Greer argued was the foundation for our social, religious and political hierarchies, following on from Engels' belief that the 'modern individual family' (247) was founded on the enslavement of the wife and traditional class hierarchy. Greer initiated a fundamental renegotiation of the father's role, as she argued that 'paternity is not an intrinsic relationship' (247) and that the nuclear family 'is possibly the shortest-lived familial system ever developed' (248). Her utopian alternative of a Tuscan-based commune, an 'unbreakable home' that 'did not rest on the frail shoulders of two bewildered individuals trying to apply a contradictory blueprint' (265) is a beautiful piece of 1970s' feminist idealism. Greer proclaimed in *The Female Eunuch,* 'women have very little idea of how much men hate them' (1970: 279); perhaps it is also true that fathers had very little idea how much women and children hated *them*. As Valerie Solanas wrote in the *SCUM*[7] *Manifesto*: 'The effect of fathers, in sum, has been to corrode the world with maleness. The male has a negative Midas touch – everything he touches turns to shit' (1967: 11).

If fatherhood as a function and not just an institution was to regain power and credibility it had to reconfigure itself – or at least be seen to reconfigure itself. It is popularly believed that, phoenix-like from the ashes, 'new man' rose out of the men's movement of the early 1970s to replace the vilified patriarch of student and feminist mythology. 'New man' did arrive, but the actual changes in image brought about were minimal. For all the positive aspects of the new nurturing father image, under 50 per cent of men questioned for one 1976 survey had a 'positive orientation' towards fatherhood, compared to 63 per cent in the late 1950s (Griswold 1993: 229). Millett remarked that 'Perhaps patriarchy's greatest psychological weapon is simply its universality and its longevity' (1970: 58) – for all the words of the women's and men's movements stating that men had to fundamentally alter their ways, men and fathers proved extremely resistant to doing anything of the sort.

The Unacceptable Father: *Sometimes a Great Notion, Jaws, Close Encounters of the Third Kind, The Great Santini*

When thinking of 1970s' father films, *Kramer vs. Kramer* usually comes to mind. However, although *Kramer* became the seminal example of new fathering and ostensibly reflected the social changes that had been wrought by feminism, the same decade also produced a series of quite different films in which the fathers are 'grumpy old men' who remain belligerently unreconstructed to the end. The men and fathers of *Sometimes a Great Notion*, *The Great Santini* or *I Never Sang for my Father* fight for and celebrate a pre-feminist masculinity, and the films, rather than condemn them, offer them a strange form of redemption. The fathers in these films are recuperated by being configured as 'mad' as opposed to 'bad'; madness and eccentricity become the convenient means by which characters such as Bull in *The Great Santini*, Henry in *Sometimes a Great Notion* and Roy in *Close Encounters of the Third Kind* come to be exonerated. This is essentially to let the fathers off the hook and there are fewer than expected examples of the father in 1970s' Hollywood suffering out and out rejection, although this occurs in *The Missouri Breaks* (1976), *Alice Doesn't Live Here Anymore* (1974) and Robert Mulligan's *Bloodbrothers*, which will be discussed later.

Paul Newman's adaptation of Ken Kesey's *Sometimes a Great Notion*[8] tells the story of the Stamper family of Oregon lumberjacks who defy a local union strike by continuing to cut and sell timber. The film's exposition of masculinity is constructed around a binary opposition between the masculinist Stamper clan huddled around its paterfamilias Henry (Henry Fonda), and the forces of political modernisation, represented by his estranged son Leelan (Michael Sarrazin). With Henry reside his eldest son Hank (Newman), Hank's wife Viv (Lee Remick) and Hank's cousin Joe Ben. Their house is literally ostracised from society, on the other side of the river from the town: a castle (the last bastion of masculinity) protected by its moat. Leelan, a college-educated hippy comes to stay and intrudes upon Henry and Hank's gruesome parody of old machismo. This old machismo is also symbolised by the broken arm Henry suffers for most of the film. Standing out proudly but absurdly at right angles to his body, the failing limb becomes a belligerent, performative enactment of fading masculinity.

Betty Friedan in *The Second Stage* equated the emergence of the 'long-haired young men' (like Leelan) who supported women's liberation and who marched against the war in Vietnam and Cambodia with the death of primal masculinity in the US and with the realisation that men could be 'sensitive, tender, compassionate' without forfeiting their rights to be called 'men' (1981: 118). Sadly, *Sometimes a Great Notion* as a whole retains a residual admiration for Henry and Hank's brand of intransigent chauvinism, most succinctly illustrated in two protracted tree-felling sequences – tender and virtually mute anthems to the art of lumbering and, by implication, traditional masculinity. Although *Deliverance* (1972) is a far superior film, there is a similarity between the two contemporaneous films' aesthetic enjoyment of 'real' men in the great outdoors, recalling Brad Allen's speech in *Pillow Talk* in which the strong tree is evoked as a metaphor for the independent man before marriage and fatherhood emasculate and fell him.

Sometimes a Great Notion is equivocal, at ease with unreconstructed masculinity while simultaneously aware that such an attitude is problematic. It signals the inevitable expiration of patriarchy through a series of deaths and departures: acts of leaving this life behind. Henry, like the 'real man' he is, has taken his already symbolic arm out of its plaster himself, only to return to work and die, when his other arm is severed by a split tree. The parodic appositeness of Henry's demise – to be killed by the film's enduring metaphor for the outmoded manliness he epitomises – is tragicomic divine retribution. Lumbering also causes the death of Joe Ben who, in the same accident, is trapped under a tree trunk in the river and drowns, and indirectly the suicide of a neighbour, financially ruined by the Stampers' strike-breaking. Rejection of this entrenched masculinity ultimately proves the catalyst for Viv's decision to finally leave Hank. Why, therefore, after this richly bathetic portrayal of Henry and Hank's absurd rearguard action against modernisation, does *Sometimes a Great Notion* conclude on a note of compromise? Having functioned as the by now conventionalised *deus ex machina,* compelling the Stampers to face the errors of their ideological ways, Leelan in the end helps out Hank (with whom he had been barely on speaking terms) when he wants to steer logs down the river to sell them. This is one of several implausible reversals imposed on the ends of films to make a misogynist brute seem not too bad after all. That just two men and their chug boat could guide so many logs safely downstream is assumed, by all the townsfolk looking on, to be an impossible feat, as impossible, perhaps, as the two diametrically opposed archetypes of masculinity finding common ground. But Hank and Leelan succeed. With one last defiant swipe at modernisation, Hank straps his father's severed arm to his chug's mast, his dead fingers flipping the world the bird: triumphalism joined with rigor mortis.

The portrait of masculinity in Spielberg's *Jaws* and *Close Encounters of the Third Kind* is similarly linked to madness and eccentricity. In *Jaws*, it is most obviously Quint who is mad, not Brody, the father (although Brody's neuroses could be construed as such) while in *Close Encounters*, it is Roy the father who is sent off the edge by his obsession with the alien spaceship. Roy is immature from the start, not a father so much as a naughty son, but it is his obsession with the UFOs that prompts his descent into madness as immaturity and insanity bond to form the basis for his emotional and psychological detachment from his family. Roy regresses and begins to fill the family den with a replica of the rock where a vision tells him the mother ship will land. After his biological family have left him, Roy establishes an alternative triad with a fellow alien-believer and her son, the infant who was abducted by the aliens at the beginning and is relinquished by them at the end. That Roy is awaiting the mother ship and boards it at the end (thus abandoning the surrogate family as well) can straightforwardly be interpreted as yet another example of the father's latent infantilism – desiring the return to the mother ship, the womb and the company of children. This communion with the feminine is inevitably at the expense of fathering; as Vivian Sobchack argues, 'the traditional bourgeois family [in *Close Encounters*] is seen in terms of failed paternity' (1996: 157). 'Failure' here is abdication in favour of childish adventure.

Issues of masculine and paternal failure are more pronounced in Spielberg's earlier *Jaws*. Perhaps because of its narrative simplicity (the duel between men and the man-eating shark) *Jaws* has, on several occasions, been interpreted metaphorically: 'It is the ritual retelling of an essential patriarchal myth – male vanquishment of the female symbolized as a sea monster' (Caputi, 1978: 305), it 'reflects a disguised hatred of women and the preoccupation of our society with sadistic sexuality' (Rubey 1976: 20) or it stands for the 'distinctive anxieties associated with the end of the Vietnam era' (Torry 1993: 32). As Fredric Jameson warns, however, 'none of these readings [that focus on what the shark represents] can be said to be wrong or aberrant, but their very multiplicity suggests that the vocation of the symbol – the killer shark – lies less in any single message or meaning than in its very capacity to absorb and organize all of these quite distinct anxieties together' (1990: 26). Similarly, Andrew Britton (1976) warns against the uncomplicated genderisation and sexualisation of the shark. Both Jameson and Britton go on to discuss the relationship between the three male protagonists who join forces to kill the Great White – Brody (Roy Scheider, Amity Island's chief of police), Hooper (Richard Dreyfuss, a middle-class oceanographer) and Quint (Robert Shaw, a local shark-hunter). As Britton observes, the shark's prime target is the family ('the basic unit of American democracy' [27]) which it is the collective fathers' job to protect. Brody is the central father of the trio – not only is he a father, but his position as the town's chief of police marks him out as the social, administrative father. However, in another unexpected reversal, he rises up at the end and kills the shark single-handedly. Before this, Brody has been identified as weak and, in a film so preoccupied with masculine potency, to have relinquished possession of the phallus.

In Benchley's novel, Hooper has an affair with Brody's wife Ellen; with the removal of this detail Spielberg, as Britton notes, removes 'all trace of conflict within Brody's family' (27). Despite strengthening his position within the family, the film's Brody is still vulnerable and attacked from all sides: he is afraid of water, he is an outsider recently arrived from New York to become the Mayor and Amity's establishment do not heed his urgent requests to close the beaches after the shark has struck for the first time. As their symbolic father, he fails to offer children and families protection. In many ways Brody resembles Sam Bowden in *Cape Fear*: both are honourable if flawed fathers pitted against monsters who, because they in some way represent their own repressed fears, almost bring about the fathers' demise. The shark as reflective of Brody's unconscious helps to explain one awful lapse of parenting – when Brody looks after the public beach and lets his two sons swim in the 'pond' nearby, designated the safe area. As Brody sits in his deckchair looking out to sea, a voice hails the arrival of the shark in the pond. A man is killed, though Brody's two sons escape. Brody is forever warning his children and forever proving to be their inadequate protector.

Brody regains his sense of masculine control when he leaves the family and island behind and boards the *Orca* with Quint and Hooper for the final, protracted assault on the shark. At sea (figuratively as well as literally), Brody confronts his inner demons, most obviously his fear of water, a neurosis that he specifically does not want to pass on to his children. In their battles against the Great White, Quint dies and Hooper almost dies, so Brody (like Bowden against Cady) is left on his own to slay the monster. What Brody achieves by this final triumphant act is the reclamation of the phallus and the restitution of the father's importance: he has slain his inner demons and he can finally offer both the families of Amity and his own some protection. True belief in the father is established, as Britton implies, through Brody having acted on his own: he had told Hooper that in Amity, unlike in New York, 'one man can make a difference' and now he has proved that 'individual action by the one just man is still a viable force for social change' (Britton 1976: 31). Just as Quint's death is important to Brody's resurgence, so it is telling

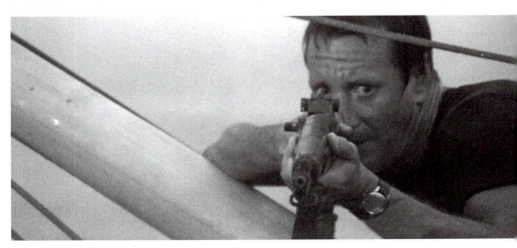

Brody slays the shark and conquers his inner demons

that the socially privileged Hooper survives. Quint, as well as the shark, represents the dark side of civilised masculinity while the success of the educated Hooper is in keeping with Hollywood's belief in and over-valuation of the privileged and traditional male (class as an issue that impinges on fatherhood will be returned to later in this chapter). As Brody and Hooper float back to shore on what remains of Quint's boat, equilibrium or 'order' has been restored.

At the end of *The Great Santini*, it is specifically antiquated order that is restored. Set in 1962 and so before JFK, Vietnam and all that we would now consider to constitute 'the 1960s', *The Great Santini* centres on a father, Bull Meachum (Robert Duvall) who is an ex-Marine pilot who served in the Korean War and finds it impossible to adapt to civilian and family life. Nicknamed '*The Great Santini*', Bull is, for the bulk of the film, feared by his family and hated by his eldest son, Ben. He is, in 1979 when the film was made, the embodiment of US imperialism (see Britton 1986: 25). But, as in *Sometimes a Great Notion*, Bull's flaws are in the end suppressed as the family unite behind the memory of the dead father. Dale Spender (after Greer) has remarked that 'men would not act as if they had power if women treated them as if they didn't' (1985: 66). Bull, to start with, is just such a disempowered caricature, and *The Great Santini* opens with a sequence that belittles and ridicules masculinity. Following some dare-devil practice flying, Bull (at an armed forces do) leads his equally puerile colleagues through a tired routine of men behaving badly: quaffing drinks, getting rowdy, throwing glasses into the fire; rounded off by Bull pretending to vomit over the genteel orchestra. Although *The Great Santini*

Bull Meachum taunts his son Ben after a game of basketball

is set in 1962, when it was released in 1979 this retrogressive attachment to machismo would have been viewed more negatively. One American psychologist of the time developed an androgyny scale, arguing that men or women who were either 'strongly masculine' or 'strongly feminine' have 'limited or crippled personalities' (Clinebell 1977: 177) and in *Woman's Estate*, Juliet Mitchell defined male chauvinism as being 'too much of a man' (1971: 63). Bull is over-attached to masculinity.

Sport is often used in Hollywood films as a metaphor for, a means of externalising the psychological conflicts between sons and their fathers, particularly fathers who are overly preoccupied with the need to prove masculinity. In Robert Mulligan's *Fear Strikes Out* (1957), a domineering father pushes his son Jimmy (Boston Red Sox outfielder, Jimmy Piersall, played by Anthony Hopkins) so hard that Jimmy suffers a nervous breakdown. Jimmy only manages to salvage his life and baseball career after distancing himself from his father. A similar crisis befalls Bud Stamper on the basketball court in *Splendor in the Grass*. Bud collapses and although he is diagnosed as debilitated by anaemia, the root psychological cause of his breakdown is that he, at his father Ace's request, has stopped seeing Deanie, the love of his life. Then again in *Field of Dreams* (1989), the baseball pitch Kevin Costner builds on his cornfield brings back his hero, 'Shoeless Joe' Jackson but it also enables him to reach a point of reconciliation with his dead father. In *The Great Santini*, the failures of patriarchy are played out in Bull's protracted Oedipal battles with Ben on various basketball courts. Bull's battles with Ben offer some compensation for feelings of inadequacy and redundancy; as his friend Virge puts it, Bull is the 'war hero without a war'. A Meachum tradition has been the backyard basketball contest between father and son. Commonly, as is the case when Steve Martin has one last dunking session with his daughter on the eve of her wedding in the remake of *Father of the Bride*, the backyard sessions are playful bonding opportunities. In *The Great Santini*, they are highly competitive. When Ben finally wins one of these games, Bull finds it impossible to accept defeat, taunting Ben and calling him 'the sweetest little girl' when he cries. The idea that he should be aiding his son's passage to manhood is not countenanced by Bull, who instead sees his aim as being to preserve both his dominance and Ben's submissiveness. The father–son crisis reaches its peak during Ben's varsity basketball match. Bull becomes enraged at Ben's rough treatment at the hands of a member of the opposite team and, from first the touchline, then the court itself, goads Ben into punching his opponent to the ground. This gets Ben disqualified. As he bestrides Ben like a comic colossus, Bull has literally as well as figuratively overstepped the mark; he transgresses the boundary between off- and on-court space in much the same way as he encroaches on Ben's personal space as a son. In a reversal of the Oedipal scenario, Bull needs this identification with his eldest son and, when Ben finally turns his back on his father, he goes off the rails and, in a parody of his already parodic self, becomes as unacceptable as possible.

It is disappointing that such a pitiful monster is reconciled to the son and family he has so abused, but perhaps this is just acceptable as Bull dies soon after. Bull has fled the family home after beating up his wife Lillian in front of their terrified children. It is Lillian who then asks Ben to go in search of his father, and Ben finds him under a tree babbling nonsense. As Bull has finally lost all sense of the difference between himself and his alter ego 'the great Santini', so Ben cannot find it in himself to abandon the father after all. Instead, he helps him up and reassures him (in one of the most grossly sentimental exit lines): 'I love you Dad, and there ain't nothin' you're gonna do about it'. Fulfilled (or is it lobotomised?) by this rapprochement with his ghastly father, Ben has secured the smooth passage of patriarchal power from Bull to him. Betty Friedan, in *The Second Stage*, briefly comments on *The Great Santini*, calling this scene the film's 'real ending' (1981: 128). Friedan's adjustment, however, represses the film's bleak Oedipal conclusion. After Bull's death, the Meachums prepare to drive to a new home (*The Great Santini* had started with Bull driving them to the house they are leaving). Ben decides they should drive in the dead of night, just as Bull would have done, to avoid the traffic. The son, notwithstanding the endless battles with Bull when he was alive, has assimilated the absurd and maniacal idiosyncrasies of his deranged, deluded father.

The Working-Class Father: *Bloodbrothers, Breaking Away*

The need to so often exonerate the bad father in Hollywood movies is an emotional one. In its reworking of the scene in which the son goes to visit the sick or dying father in bed and is reconciled with him, *Bloodbrothers* is atypical in that the father, Tommy DeCoco, is left once and for all alone. *Bloodbrothers* is the story of a working-class Italian-American family: Tommy, his wife Maria and sons, Stony (a young Richard Gere) and Albert. The bedside scene takes place in hospital, which is where Tommy ends up after fighting with the police summoned to arrest him for beating up Maria so badly that she had to go to hospital. The family is dysfunctional, most clearly articulated through Albert's anorexia, a dysfunctionality directly attributable to Tommy's violence. As Maureen Green argued in the 1970s, 'A good father is a blessing; an inadequate father may be worse than no father at all' (1976: 149). After Tommy's battering of Maria, his family desert him, recoiling from his monstrousness much as Halliday's children do in *The Halliday Brand*. Stony, like Ben in *The Great Santini*, is on the verge of taking his father back as, in the hospital scene Tommy is penitent, promising 'I'll make it up to her – all of you'. Stony's girlfriend is the one to persuade him that Tommy will never change and Stony ultimately turns his back on Tommy and so also the brutish, regressive masculinity he represents.

Tommy is a particular brand of Hollywood caricature. He is an adulterous Italian-American whose ignorance, inarticulacy and brutality are uncomfortably symptomatic of his working-class-ness. When comparing Tommy DeCoco to Atticus Finch, it becomes clearer that Tommy's deficiency is a corollary of his class. In *Mockingbird*, Atticus stands out from the other fathers not just because he is good, but also because he is middle class. As with the characterisation of Tommy, the bad fathers in *Mockingbird* are all working-class farmers and corollaries of this seem to be their racism and violence. Atticus is enlightened, but he is also privileged, a result of class divisions that the narrative does not critique. Hollywood has played its part in perpetuating the myth that working-class fathers are, more often than not, bad. Tommy, like Henry in *Sometimes a Great Notion* or Eddie's 'self-made' businessman father in *The Arrangement*, lacks the finesse of a father like Atticus. Griswold offers a historical overview of this position when he comments:

> The message to fathers . . . could hardly be clearer. Men's commitment to and involvement with their children had a decisive impact on personality development and on social order. But not all fathers, sociologists concluded, were so committed. It was middle-class men who most often treated their children in ways that promoted self-reliance, democracy, emotional stability, heterosexuality, and tolerance. If affluent blue-collar workers could drive their new cars to their new homes in Levittown, the parental dimensions of their lives lacked the expressive, affective, and egalitarian richness that allegedly characterized middle-class men's lives (1993: 211).

In 1974, David Lynn in a book on fatherhood and the child, made precisely Griswold's point when he remarked that 'Working men are much less likely than professional–executive fathers to see childrearing as part of their parental duties. They are more likely to regard children as the wife's domain' (7). Despite such faith in the middle-class father, there is no substantive proof that middle-class men make more successful fathers (Griswold 1993: 253).

Within the class struggle, Stony is the proto-middle-class son who challenges his father in part because he wants to turn his back on all he signifies. Since the gangster films of the early 1930s, the Italian-American has proved a particular racial and cultural configuration that, within Hollywood, has functioned as shorthand for the most unsalvageable and unpalatable brand of masculinity. The closest the Italian-American father gets to manifesting middle-class fathering sensibilities is when Vito Corleone in *The Godfather* (once again from his bed) tells his son Michael 'I never wanted this for you', meaning a life of organised crime. As it would be for Michael Corleone if he did not get sucked back into the Mafia, liberation and happiness can only come to Stony if he leaves Tommy and his Italian-Americanness behind. Stony is an honorary member of the middle class, he takes a job working with children in a hospital rather than following Tommy into the construction business and, whereas Tommy is primitive and gestural (a manual labourer and violent adulterer), Stony is verbal. Stony's articulacy conforms to the archetype of the educated man who, in the 1970s, felt trapped by his masculinity. As the 'Berkeley Men's Center Manifesto' declared:

We, as men, want to take back our full humanity. We no longer want to strain and compete to live up to an impossible oppressive masculine image – strong, silent, cool, handsome, unemotional, successful ... We no longer want to feel the need to perform sexually, socially, or in any way to live up to an imposed male role, from a traditional American society or a 'counterculture'. We want to love ourselves ... ('Berkeley Men's Center Manifesto' 1974: 173).

Stony usurps his father's position, leaving home and taking care of Albert. Whereas Tommy and Maria had merely resorted to shouting at him to eat, it is Stony and then the hospital doctors who explain and make sense of his condition. In abandoning Tommy and his values and taking Albert with him at the end of the film, Stony clarifies many things: his usurpation of the paternal role, his middle-class aspirations, his rejection of his upbringing and his feminine tenderness.

As it sides with Stony, *Bloodbrothers* ignores the socio-political issues that might have created Tommy. During one argument Tommy tells Stony what a job is. Stony has just revealed his desire to work with children, which Tommy manifestly does not consider to be man's work. A job to Tommy has little to do with personal growth or emotional ful-filment; instead it is being able to provide food for one's children and put a roof over their heads. He would pour scorn on a 1977 description of the 'liberated' father as 'one who finds as much satisfaction in relationships with his children and takes as much responsibility for their physical and emotional care as he does in and for his job, career or other activities' (Clinebell 1977: 173). Like the majority of 'concerned' liberal films of the 1970s, *Bloodbrothers* ultimately puts its faith in the middle class as a liberating force, but leaves Tommy trapped by his class and education. It is Stony and not Tommy who, at the end, is permitted to escape the limitations of his surroundings (see Considine 1985: 105) and to flee the unhappy domain of the father, 'presumably heading for the middle class' (Ehrenreich 1983: 138).

The sympathetic working-class father in *Breaking Away* is a rare exception to the Hollywood class model. Peter Yates' film takes place over the summer between school and college. Dave hangs out in Minneapolis with his three buddies Mike, Cyril and Moocher. Dave and Cyril have slightly loftier social expectations than their two mates and are the products of a more aspirational working-class upbringing. Dave, for most of the film, is obsessed with everything Italian; he speaks Italian, he addresses his father as 'Papà', his days are consumed with cycling, he listens to opera and insists that his mother cook him Italian food. By the end of the film, he becomes disillusioned with Italians after a run-in with the Italian Cinzano cycling team and takes up French. Dave's preoccupation with Italianness is important to *Breaking Away* as it foregrounds what is traditionally most important about Italians: family. Dave even persuades his parents to try for another baby and by the end, his mother is pregnant.

Dave's relationship with his father is particularly expressive on the subject of class (he is simply 'Dad' in the end credits). Dad, though ambivalent about this, wants his son to have more than he had; he is happy when Dave accepts his college place, although earlier he had remarked to his wife (as if resenting his son's difference): 'He [Dave] is never tired, he's never miserable. I was tired and miserable'. Dave's sensibilities are already different from Dad's, and yet, unlike *Bloodbrothers*, in which such differences are traumatic, here they are handled comically. Dave loves opera but is useless at flogging his father's second-hand cars (so much so that, when some rich students bring a car back, Dave tells Dad he should give them a refund; an act that precipitates his father's physical collapse). Dad likewise treats Dave's Italian affectations with incomprehension, stammering to his wife Evelyn after venturing into Dave's room: 'He's shaving . . .', 'So what?', 'He's shaving his *legs*'.

Breaking Away, however, stresses the fragility of Dave's aspirational identity, as when he lies to Cathy, a student at Indiana University and pretends to be 'Enrico' in an attempt to make himself more interesting. And it is to Dad that Dave turns after the Cinzano race. Dad is recuperating after his collapse; Dave returns home and asks 'How are you feeling, *Dad*' before crying on his father's shoulder. The gesture of filial need, in conjunction with the use of the English rather than the Italian term of address, signal that Dave has returned to the father and what he stands for, a symbolic reunion cemented by the film's denouement, the Minneapolis cycling race in which, for the first time, 'townies' take on student teams from Indiana University. Dave's team 'The Cutters' (their very name affirms his solidarity with Dad as it refers to his father's stonecutting past and to the local quarry industry) eventually wins the race. Dad is jubilant, Mom is pregnant and the working class are victorious. After reconciling with Dad and his roots, Dave is free to go to college, and *Breaking Away* ends on a freeze frame of Dad's shocked expression as Dave cycles by shouting 'Bonjour, papa'.

Kramer vs. Kramer

A film that more than any other affirms the supremacy of the middle-class paternal model as a liberating ideal is Robert Benton's *Kramer vs. Kramer*, also made in 1979 and arguably the most influential and important cinematic depiction of the father. *Kramer* crystallises the persistent central paradox of the post-women's liberation male: the dual desire to re-ignite belief in masculinity and patriarchy alongside the urge to discard traditional masculinity as inadequate. That patriarchy was a moribund ideology in its death throes is evident in films throughout the 1970s; but whereas the majority remains transfixed by the Oedipal mess the woebegone patriarch has bequeathed to the generation he has sired, *Kramer* forgets the old patriarch and posits an alternative model of fatherhood. In films such as *Sometimes a Great Notion* and *The Great Santini*, the only way in which the elder sons can negotiate the future is by explicitly taking their fathers' place. But where are Hank and Ben going? As Andrew Britton notes about Luke Skywalker's battles with Darth Vader in the *Star Wars* trilogy, 'How on earth, if one's father is Darth

Vader, can one wish to inherit the phallus?' (Britton 1986: 26). Although embarking on journeys, neither Hank nor Ben at the end of their respective narratives suggest purpose or independence. Instead, their inheritance is to redeem the monstrous patriarch, a similar capitulation occurring at the end of *Return of the Jedi*. In *Kramer vs. Kramer*, the transition to the future and the restoration of the phallus is more delicately and astutely handled, with the father appropriating the traditional female role of nurturer and becoming a 'new man'. However, *Kramer*'s complexity and power lie in its concomitant desire to reassert male dominance and so recapture men's patriarchal supremacy without recourse to pre-feminist, Darth Vader-like archetypes.

Kramer vs. Kramer has possibly proved more significant as a social document than as a film and it is forever being invoked as the most significant cultural image of liberal post-feminist fathering. Although a few films followed directly in its wake (*Ordinary People, Author! Author!, Table for Five*), *Kramer* proved far less influential as a film. Benton's film captured the evolving contemporary views of fatherhood and contained (as if ticking them off a social worker's checklist) all the important contemporary issues of childrearing: divorce, custody, women's independence, calls for men to become more emotionally involved fathers. *Kramer* deftly managed to reflect current thinking on divorce policy and childrearing (questioning, for example, the assumption that mothers make better parents than fathers and the view that it was imperative to effect a reconciliation between child and absent parent as soon as possible) at the same time as it proposed the father's inherent superiority. The latter went against social reality, as in the late 1970s (as now) nine out of ten single-parent families were headed by mothers. *Kramer*, however, did reflect the fact that, despite the infrequency of this, when fathers did fight for custody of their children they increasingly, in the 1970s, got it (Griswold 1993: 26).

Its indebtedness to feminism notwithstanding, *Kramer* is constitutionally conservative and demonstrates an insidious ideological position whose central tenet is that men, through heeding feminism, can change, become exemplary fathers and in so doing dispense with the psychological and actual need for the mother. Although comparable in its idealisation of the lone father, *Kramer vs. Kramer* is a more aggressively anti-feminist, single-father movie than *To Kill a Mockingbird*, and yet it manages to be less systematically patriarchal than either *The Courtship of Eddie's Father* or *The Sound of Music*. In the first scene, Joanna Kramer leaves the family home in New York to 'find herself' in California. Ted is left to bring up their six-year-old son Billy alone. Joanna then returns to New York a year later, determined to get back her son. Following a protracted courtroom hearing, she is granted custody only to decide, on the day she is supposed to be picking him up, that Billy is better off with Ted.

Kramer's relationship to feminism is complex. Rowbotham has remarked that 'by the late 1970s the conviction that Women's Liberation held clear answers to a better society was gone' (1999: 444) and *Kramer*, in its treatment of Joanna, endorses such a view.

Joanna offers a stereotypical portrait of the unfulfilled woman who stopped work immediately after marriage and felt that her identity had become subsumed into her dual roles of mother and wife. Upon returning to New York, she also illustrates what Betty Friedan herself was arguing in 1979, namely that women were 'finding that it's not so easy to live with – *or without* – men and children' (my italics; *New York Times* 1979: 40). In the aftermath of women's liberation, Friedan in 1981 returned specifically to *Kramer vs. Kramer*, hailing its triumphant reconfiguration of masculinity (to encompass man's 'tender prowess as a parent') as 'a feminist triumph, surely?' (1981: 122). But is this the case? Joanna's need to escape her traditional role was no longer, in the 1970s, an uncommon one.[9] However, the film implicitly but strongly suggests – for all the director's protestations that Joanna is heroic[10] – that Joanna is wrong in what she does, and so formulates a powerful critique of feminism and feminist doctrine. In that *Kramer vs. Kramer* is a film and not a social document, this seals Joanna's fate as the inadequate parent and, as a film, it suggests that the courts are wrong to award her custody. *Kramer* denies Joanna's right and overturns the court's verdict. As with the judgment of Solomon, there is more than a passing sense that Billy is eventually left with the 'right' and 'real' parent.

Like earlier lone-father films, *Kramer* is a melodrama; its melodramatic content centres on Ted and his relationship with Billy while Joanna is, quite deliberately, ostracised from this and instead becomes its ideological target. As with comparable single-father melodramas, Ted is the archetypal figure who fulfils both social and fictive fantasies. He is not bound by traditional definitions of the father and is just as likely to display maternal characteristics as paternal ones (so echoing the words of one early 1980s' single father who referred to himself as 'a mother, because there is no male, no name for men, doing the job that I'm doing' [O'Brien 1982: 184]). Ted Kramer was the supreme fantasy figure for the generation of 'latchkey kids', children whose fathers were leaving in increasing numbers and whose working mothers left them to fend for themselves. Thus *Kramer*'s significance as a film stems from its realism; as David A. Cook wrote in a caption to a still from *Kramer*: 'Before they would reach the age of sixteen, fully half of the children born in the United States between 1970 and 1980 would see their parents divorce' (2000: 293). From 1970 to 1975 the divorce rate in the United States increased by 40 per cent while the number of marriages fell by 30 per cent. *Kramer* reflected the failure of the institution of marriage and was one of several Hollywood movies of the late 1970s to centre on divorce (Cook cites films such as *Manhattan*, *The Goodbye Girl* and *Starting Over* as other top-grossing movies to feature divorce [2000: 294]). *Kramer* was the year's top box-office film, and although Benton has expressed surprise at how popular it proved with teenagers,[11] it seems likely that the teenagers who willingly sat through a melodrama about a messy custody battle had lived through much the same themselves, and that what they saw on the screen was what they most obviously lacked: a devoted and ever-present father who put his child before his work, who fought for that child in the courts and who was devastated when the judge granted his ex-wife custody. As one study on the effect of divorce asserts, children 'have a powerful need to create a protective, loving father ... Without any sense of contradiction, they are able to maintain a benign image of the loving father side by side with a history of repeated rejections and failures' (quoted in Griswold 1993: 235).

In keeping with this emotional need, Ted's inadequacies as a father are swiftly dispatched. In the opening scene, he stays late at the office exchanging chauvinist jokes with his boss, then, the morning after Joanna's departure, he proves to be inept in the kitchen, failing to make the French toast he has promised Billy. There is a neat play on Ted's machismo in this scene as, prior to mucking everything up, he shows off to Billy his technique for whisking eggs with one hand ('it's all in the wrist'). Shortly after, Ted presents Billy with a 'TV dinner', which he refuses to eat, but Ted rapidly becomes a model parent. The late 1970s and early 1980s have been referred to as the era of 'paternal rediscovery' (Lamb 1986: 3); in transforming himself, Ted metamorphoses into the type of new father feminists had been calling for. A key facet of *Kramer*'s melodramatic fantasy is, however, that Ted usurps rather than complements the female position by taking over the mother's role. When, just after Joanna has left, his neighbour Margaret comes to the door and reminds Ted that it 'took a lot of courage' on his wife's part to walk out, Ted's stern reply – to which Margaret, a single divorced mother, has no riposte – is 'How much courage does it take to walk out on your kid?' Ted offers the counter argument to feminism, here suggesting (going totally against perceived social reality) that he could not have done such a thing, and that he, the father, is going to do what mothers usually do in such situations: stay with the children.

Within the framework of melodrama, Ted becomes the conventionally abandoned mother struggling to bring up the family alone, forfeiting a job in order to take care of his child and urgently needing to get a lesser job in order to support them both. But whereas Alice, in a similar predicament in *Alice Doesn't Live Here Anymore*, needs a replacement father to help raise her son, Ted is self-sufficient. Countering the feminist call for women to have more than a husband, a child and a home, *Kramer vs. Kramer* – through its portrayal of Ted, not of Joanna – elevates and sanctifies the routine, mundane acts associated with traditional motherhood. Feminists argued vociferously that the traditional feminine role was oppressive, demeaning and dull, a standpoint articulated cinematically in the 1970s by a film such as Chantal Akerman's *Jeanne Dielman* (1975) in which the monotony of the housewife's existence is taken to surreal extremes. In *Kramer*, Margaret (who has by now become Ted's friend and confidante) testifies at the divorce hearing (directly to Joanna) that Ted and Billy are 'beautiful together'. *Kramer* appropriates the feminine by glorifying routine, ritual and repetition, the means by which the 'beauty' of Ted and Billy's relationship is expressed.

One scene (just after the TV-dinner sequence, during which Ted and Billy get on badly) exemplifies this attitude and functions as the transitional moment in the father–son relationship – when routine comes to signal father and son having reached a point of mutual trust. It is morning. The first shot is of a board on Billy's wall, packed with photos of Joanna and assorted cards and letters from her (demonstrating that what had come between father and son – anger and a sense of loss at the mother's departure – have since become integral components of their lives). Recalling the first morning after Joanna's departure, there is then the rumble of a dustcart outside. The image then cuts to the corridor; Billy, in vest and pants, enters the bathroom and we hear him urinate. He emerges from the bathroom without having flushed and goes into Ted's room to wake him up. Billy then walks into the living room/kitchen and we see Ted in the background emerge from his bedroom, go into the bathroom, urinate and this time flush. The camera then pans to follow Ted going to the front door to retrieve the newspaper, and pans again in the opposite direction to the kitchen table. Here the camera rests, showing father and son getting together the breakfast things (Billy puts the doughnuts on the plates while Ted pours out milk and juice), sitting down and immersing themselves in their respective bits of the newspaper as they eat, Ted finally pulling up a chair (without looking up) on which to rest his feet. There is then a fade to black. This mute sequence contains only one edit, long takes and fluid camera moves serving to unify Ted and Billy, underscoring their relationship's newfound cohesion and solidity. The scene's content – the trivia of everyday life, characters' gestures, the minute changes to Billy and Ted's way of interacting with each other – all also denote a fascination with, a fetishisation and veneration of the man performing such tasks in place of the woman. Nestor Almendros's camerawork, though covert and observational, is a key component of this, delicately drawing one's gaze towards an ostensibly insignificant or private gesture. The domestic father–son bonding scenes in *Kramer* are relatively silent and filled with repetitive and incidental gestures, contrasting crucially with Joanna's reciprocal dependence upon words as a means of communication. In the café scene when she tells Ted she wants Billy back she launches into a pre-prepared speech. Likewise, in the courtroom and right at the end as she explains to Ted why she cannot take Billy, Joanna is entirely dependent on words. Ted is shown to be much more physical (and this *Kramer* shows to be a good parenting trait): in the café he smashes a glass against the wall when Joanna reveals that she wants Billy back and there is the film's signature father–son bonding sequence when Ted runs several blocks with the injured Billy in his arms to a hospital. Joanna, like any sensible mother, would probably have hailed a cab.

The love of gesture in *Kramer* is signalled through its use of repetition, and repetition, in turn, is used to indicate both the appropriation of the feminine domain Joanna has renounced and the 'beauty' of Ted's relationship with Billy. In an inversion of feminism's depiction of domestic drudgery as the enslavement of women, routine and repetition (dropping Billy off at school, going to the park) here affirm the closeness of father and son. By the time the court has granted custody to Joanna, Ted and Billy's relationship, the beauty in banality that *Kramer* finds endlessly fascinating, has become

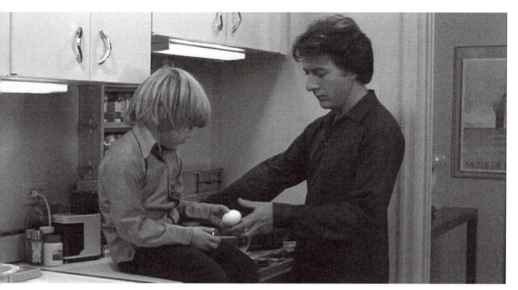

Ted and Billy make breakfast together for what they think is the last time

the counter argument to the pervasive feminist claim that a parent could possibly want anything more than to look after a child. On the eve of the custody hearing, Ted's lawyer asks him to draw up a list of 'pros' and 'cons' for why he wants to retain custody of Billy; the 'cons' column is full of traditional parental gripes such as 'no social life' while the 'pros' column is empty. Ted then visits Billy in bed and cradles him, whispering 'I love you'. The film's message is clear: this is all the parent wants and all the child wants to hear, alongside which lurks the implied question posed to Joanna, the unfulfilled mother: 'How could any parent need more than this?'

In a frequently insidious way, *Kramer vs. Kramer* has mounted, through its sensuous attention to the details of Ted and Billy's everyday life, both an argument against the feminist position and an argument for the elevation of the father–child relationship over any other. The perfection of this bond is exemplified by the film's conclusion: one final, poignant repetition and the mother's renunciation of her legal rights. The final repetition shows Ted and Billy, on what they think is their last morning together as an everyday father and son, making French toast, the meal Ted got so disastrously wrong on their first morning alone. This time, they are in practised, silent synchronicity as Billy throws the bread in the egg mix while Ted cooks. In court, Ted had warned Joanna that, if she chooses to destroy the life he has built with Billy, 'it may be irreparable'. The tense silence of the second egg breakfast scene is only broken by Ted saying with forced joviality, 'Let's get this show on the road'; but Billy starts to whimper and Ted holds him, giving him a traditional buddy's pat on the back. Joanna taking Billy would damage irreparably the sanctity of the father–son relationship and in terms of the underlying ideology of the film, Joanna's decision not to take Billy away from Ted and his home is metaphor-ically symptomatic of feminism's encroaching realisation that what it had called for might be destructive and wrong. The challenge *Kramer* poses serves both progressive and regressive ends; it suggests that men and fathers have changed, while simul-taneously intimating that such change will ensure the continuation of the father's predominance within the home. In the end, despite the relative narrative importance of an alternative familial structure (the single-parent family), *Kramer* is far from being a pro-gressive text. Although it does not call for the restoration of the traditional nuclear family, it does advocate, in its final rejection of the mother, a return to what Millett termed the imaginary 'golden age' of patriarchy when men existed contentedly together before the arrival of women (1970: 35).

Kramer touches upon a range of important aspects of the father in the late 1970s: Ted is the archetypal nurturing, post-liberation Dad; he answers fears that the father has been made redundant by feminism and he proves how significant the presence of a father is to the child's development. Ted proves not that the father is an essential com-ponent of a two-parent family, but that he is the *most* important parent. This is obviously hugely contentious. When, for example, research in the 1970s uncovered the positive impact of 'the father who cares' on his child's school success (*New York Times* 1976: 20), what was relevant was not the father per se, but rather that his presence indicated that there were two parents involved with their child. In both socio-political and cine-matic terms, *Kramer vs. Kramer* concludes a decade of liberalism, uncertainty and upheaval, ushering in a period as deeply conservative and regressive as the 1950s. It does this, however, by astutely deploying the language and sensibility given to men by feminism and two decades of revolution and change. And so Ted Kramer deftly avoids being Tommy DeCoco or Bull Meacham – fathers from the dark ages.

Despite the pattern of the family in America having been forced to change, in two short decades, beyond recognition (Rowbotham 1999: 444–5), the 1970s ended with women's economic situation worsening and with conservative political factions such as the Christian Right and the Pro-Family movement gaining ground. Notwithstanding the social upheaval triggered by feminism, men and the society they had built around them-selves did not want to change nearly as much as women's liberation had wanted. As Kate Millett stated in 1970, patriarchy's greatest psychological weapon is its longevity, to which one could add its consummate ability to reconstruct itself. As the message on the old T-shirt goes: 'I'll be a post-feminist in post-patriarchy'. For all the changes wrought to public perception of the father's role, for all the bragging about new-man-ism, Ted Kramer negated the feminist threat more convincingly than all the macho patriarchs of the 1950s. Like the family, the image at least of the father had changed over the 1960s and 1970s beyond recognition, but how much had men actually changed in terms of what they did? Although, between 1975 and 1981 the time spent by fathers on childcare and household work increased by 20 to 30 per cent, the amount of time fathers were spending on childcare in 1981 was still only a third of that spent by mothers (Bronstein 1988: 5) despite the fact that, by 1980, only 15 per cent of American families were composed of a father who worked and a mother who stayed at home (Rowbotham 1999: 454). Men and fathers had learnt to defeat feminists at their own game.

Notes

1. See previous chapter for a fuller discussion of the paradox of the asexual breadwinner father.
2. The film's symbolic power is demonstrated by the censorship battles that preceded its British release. The BBFC imposed 161 cuts before allowing *Cape Fear* to be released with an 'X' certificate (a restored version was released in the 1990s, to coincide with Martin Scorsese's remake). Nonetheless, one critic still believed the film should have been banned altogether. See James C. Robertson 'Unspeakable Acts: the BBFC and *Cape Fear*', *Journal of Popular British Cinema* no. 3, 2000: 69–76.
3. McLanahan and Sandefur argue that 'Children who grow up in a household with just one biological parent are worse off, on average, than children who grow up in a household with both of their biological parents' (1994: 1).
4. Cf. also Brenton 1967: '. . . if the father remains passive, weaker than the mother, or rejecting as the boy grows up and if the mother remains or becomes dominating and overprotective – the boy either develops into a weak, passive man basically fearful of women or actually becomes a practicing homosexual' (148).
5. For a discussion of *East of Eden* see Chapter 2.
6. See Steven J. Ross (ed.) *Movies and American Society*, Oxford: Blackwell, 2002: 336–7.
7. The Society for Cutting Up Men.
8. UK release title *Never Give an Inch*.
9. Cf. *New York Times* 1973a. In 1963 it is suggested that only approximately one in 100 wives left home. In the 1970s, the wives' departure was usually a 'declaration of discontent and lack of personal fulfilment' much like Joanna's is.
10. Benton in the documentary on the *Kramer vs. Kramer* DVD (UK edition).
11. Ibid.

4

Back to the Future: Nostalgia, Tradition and Masculinity in the 1980s

In 1988, British writer Jonathan Rutherford expressed a central male concern with the effects of feminism on men and masculinity. Rutherford quotes a man who left a workshop on the politics of the family upset and confused:

> A group of women were saying that they didn't trust men to look after their children. It was as though they were saying that all men were child molesters. Surely women want men to look after children more. I don't know what these feminists want (1988: 21).

Subsequently, Rutherford posits that men and women 'seemed to be talking different languages' (22). The 1980s was a time of crisis for masculinity and fatherhood, but it also proved to be a time of male resurgence as one of the notable features of the decade's films is that fatherhood, having been defined in the 1960s and 1970s through feminism and women's issues, came once again to be defined, as it had been in the 1950s, by and for men. The father films of the 1980s – for all their diversity – congregated around a central suspicion not merely of feminism (the whole Reagan decade dismissed feminism) but of the changes to masculinity that feminism had hoped to implement. As another pro-feminist male commentator wrote in 1990, America in the 1980s

> ... brought pause to the pace of change, after fifteen years of feminist outcry and varied male response. Public culture encouraged the approval of images of violent, aggressive, silent men, and the prestige of military values escalated (Stearns 1990: 230).

The 1980s was a time when the tensions surrounding the liberal revolutions of the previous decades surfaced: feminism had threatened the male sense of masculinity, of what was meant by 'being a man', but it had also left unresolved the role of the father, the nurturing male (see Seidler 1985). Fatherhood had, in the 1970s, been an important battleground: women successfully demanded that men did more of the childcare and more around the home, while both the emergent new Right in America and new father groups such as Families Need Fathers in the UK began to argue that feminism corroded masculinity and that the ideal family was the male-headed nuclear one. In the 1980s, traditional fatherhood reasserted itself.

As in the 1950s, the resurgence within popular iconography during the 1980s of a tougher masculinity reflected the contemporary political and social atmosphere. In 1980,

President Jimmy Carter was defeated by Ronald Reagan, the latter's landslide victory ushering in an era of aggressive right-wing policies, bolstered by the demise of women's liberation and the emergence of a strong Christian Right. As Susan Faludi stated in her seminal study of 1980s' gender politics *Backlash: The Undeclared War against Women*:

> The media's pseudo-feminist cheerleading stopped suddenly in the early 1980s – and the press soon struck up a dirge. Feminism is 'dead', the banner headlines announced all over again. 'The women's movement is over,' began a cover story in the *New York Times Magazine* (1991: 101).

Robert Griswold identified Charles Murray's 1984 book *Losing Ground: American Social Policy 1950–1980* as an important influence on Reagan's traditionalism and his systematic attack on the welfare state. Contained within Murray's zealously right-wing arguments is an essential tenet of post-feminist masculinity studies: that the Great Society programmes of the 1960s 'undercut male responsibility and thereby brought on the catastrophic rise in the number of female-headed families, out-of-wedlock births, welfare dependency, unemployment, crime, and poverty' (Griswold 1993: 237). Murray speculated (as did consecutive conservative governments in the UK) that young fathers acted irresponsibly *because* the welfare state made it 'economically illogical' for them to marry their pregnant girlfriends or take menial jobs 'to support their families' (237), going on to suggest that 'Big, liberal, free-spending government inadvertently, perhaps with the best of intentions, destroyed homes and promoted paternal neglect' (237). British Conservative Prime Minister Margaret Thatcher sympathetically declared in the mid-1980s that there was 'no such thing as society, only families and individuals'. The two Reagan administrations championed traditional families and conventional masculinity, set about dismantling the Democrat Welfare programme, built up America's nuclear arsenal and pursued an aggressive, militaristic foreign policy. Carter's liberalism was ridiculed; he had pardoned Vietnam deserters and conscientious objectors, brought in legislation to help single parents, declared – despite his Christian faith – that homosexuality was not a threat to family values and, on the eve of Reagan's victory, had proclaimed the day before Labor Day as Working Mothers Day.[1]

In terms of cinema's representation of the father, a cycle is emerging. Both in the immediate post-war years and the era of women's liberation, good fathering became synonymous with nurturing, kindness and gentleness; in the more male-driven and economically buoyant 1950s that divides them and again in the 1980s that come after, autocratic, traditional images of fathering predominated. This would suggest (unsurprisingly) that Hollywood output is affected by political and social trends; it does not, however, mean that anomalous texts do not also emerge and, as has been argued in the Introduction, Hollywood's own history (the recurring narratives that films rather than society have made popular) at times goes against the broader trends intimated above.

The 1980s, however, has been interpreted as a peculiarly cohesive era for Hollywood, during which films were quite conspicuously reflective of the politics and sociology of the time, hence the many books already published that highlight this link; Susan Jeffords' *Hard Bodies: Hollywood Masculinity in the Reagan Era* (1994), Robin Wood's *Hollywood from Vietnam to Reagan* (1986), Elizabeth Traube's *Dreaming Identities: Class, Gender and Generation in 1980s Hollywood Movies* or Sarah Harwood's *Family Fictions: Representations of the Family in 1980s Hollywood Cinema* are a few that are particularly pertinent to this study.

In terms of the representation of fathers, the 1980s opened with a series of films that mimicked the success of *Kramer vs. Kramer* by championing the liberal, caring father. As with *Kramer*, however, *Ordinary People, Author! Author!* and *Table for Five* (1983) offer equivocal messages about fathering and family values, as the fathers' greater involvement with childcare is, in all three films, tightly linked to the rejection or disappearance of the mothers. The maternal influence had likewise been marginalised throughout the 1950s, in many of its Westerns, its tycoon films and its Oedipal father–son dramas. This preoccupation with the independence of masculinity (and concomitantly fatherhood) came further to the fore in the 1980s in many of its action films, films in which fathering became an anomalous and marginalised form of masculinity and something that men did, in extremis, on their own. Fatherhood problematises and hampers the expression of strong masculinity in such films as the *Indiana Jones* trilogy (1981, 1984, 1989), *The Terminator* and *Terminator 2: Judgment Day* (1984, 1991), *Lethal Weapon* (1987) and *Die Hard* (1988).

Robin Wood has argued that the 'Restoration of the Father' became the 'dominant project, ad infinitum and post nauseam, of contemporary Hollywood cinema' (1986: 172); that, in the 1980s, the father in all his guises – 'symbolic, literal, potential' (172) – infiltrated all genres (much as he had done in the 1950s). The restoration of the father in the 1980s primarily came about through his romanticisation by the son, often in films – such as *Top Gun* (1986) and *Field of Dreams* – in which the father is dead and the son's relationship with him remains unresolved until, through a surrogate figure, he comes to understand and identify with the paternal ideal he has constructed. This twin attachment to and assimilation of an idealised father is likewise present in Steven Spielberg's *Indiana Jones and the Last Crusade* in which father and son even fall for the same girl. This nostalgic attitude to the father draws together a number of things, the first being a yearning for a past national identity; as Jeffords argues 'Invoking the days before that [national] power waned, Ronald Reagan, Colonel Trautman, Doc Brown, Dr Jones and Obi-Wan Kenobe all stand as emblems of a personal and national identity that could be recaptured' (1994: 87). The films of the 1980s also display a yearning for a stronger father, as in the *Back to the Future* trilogy (1985, 1989, 1990) and for equilibrium, and through this for traditional family values. This last tendency links a number of key 1980s' films: *Fatal Attraction, Wall Street* (1987), *The Untouchables* (1987) and *Parenthood*

(1989). Accordingly, the 1980s was also the decade that most emphatically rejected extremes, whether the despotic fathers of *The Shining* (1981) or *The Mosquito Coast* (1986) or the wimpy dad of *Back to the Future*. These conformist tendencies were cemented at the end of the decade with a series of comedies centring on the trans-formation of unreconstructed men into 'new men' through fatherhood: *Three Men and a Baby* (1987), *Baby Boom* (1987), *Look Who's Talking* (1989) and *Parenthood*.

Nice Dads: *Ordinary People, Author! Author!, Table for Five*

Sheila Rowbotham in *A Century of Women* quotes the American 'Mary Donnelly' (the pseudonym of a Catholic Reagan supporter) telling women to 'Beware of the guy who likes to hang curtains. Look for the masculine guy' (1999: 514). Following the success of *Kramer vs. Kramer* and the popularity of the new father image Ted Kramer exemplified, a handful of American films were produced that valorised the nurturing, domestic father and the 'guy who likes to hang curtains'. Soon these were to be superseded by movies that centred on 'the masculine guy'. As Lynn Segal observed, masculinity became a tense issue as the involved, feminist-inspired model of father-hood that emerged in the 1980s precipitated men into 'crisis', threatening their 'whole perception of themselves as adults' (1997: 42). Segal reasons that the feelings active fathering aroused in men, such as tenderness and sensuality, had been 'utterly tabooed' among men (42), and so they found themselves in an equivocal position. Vic Seidler agreed: 'As boys, we [men] learn constantly to prove our masculinity . . . Fear is defined as an unacceptable emotion. But in disowning our fear and learning to put a brave face on the world we learn to despise all forms of weakness' (1985: 155). Like Segal, Seidler concluded that, although feminist magazine *Spare Rib* (which he is quoting) might advocate that men should accept that 'real strength is recog-nising your own weakness', this very recognition 'threatens our very sense of masculinity' (156). To permit intimacy, men have learnt, is to be weak; and so all the traits of the 'good father' are signs of timidity and unmanliness. Such fears lurk around the tender father movies of the early 1980s. These films lacked the utopi-anism Betty Friedan expressed in *The Second Stage* when she describes the 'quiet movement of American men . . . on the edge of a momentous change in their very identity as men' (1981: 112), for whom the disastrous Vietnam War would prove 'the beginning of the end of the hunter–caveman, gun-toting, he-man mystique' (118). Considering that *Rambo* proved one of the most successful films of the 1980s, Friedan's belief that 'machismo was dying' (118) was no more than quaint feminist optimism. The 1970s had the opposite effect on the representation of men and fathers.

Author! Author! and *Table for Five* centre on non-traditional families – ones in which the parents have divorced and remarried, in which offspring from various sexual part-nerships are brought together and in which the fathers end up being the families' primary carers. In *Author! Author!*, playwright Ivan Travalian (Al Pacino) is compelled to become the stable, attentive father of a chaotic brood of kids after his second wife Gloria leaves home for another man. Gloria (like Joanna in *Kramer*) offers a negative representation of the liberated woman who renounces domesticity in favour of personal happiness. Against this, it is easy to idealise Ivan, in a similar way as *Kramer* idealised Joanna's abandoned husband Ted. Even before Gloria leaves, Ivan is a fun, involved parent who plays freely with his children and takes them on work dinners when Gloria is not there. After Gloria's departure, Ivan insists that he should look after their children, even though he is not the biological father of all of them, also refusing (during a farcical rooftop custody siege) to surrender his stepchildren to their biological father. Ivan is the paternal role model Friedan and other feminists might have envisaged for the 1980s: he is non-authoritarian, his children interchangeably address him as 'Dad' and 'Ivan' and, when he confesses to two of his sons that he is 'still hung up on your mother', one boy enquires, 'Mine or his?'.

In *Table for Five*, the effect of the 1970s on the father is reflected differently, as Jamie (Jon Voight) is not a 'new' father but, at least at first, a negligent one. Like Ivan, he becomes the attentive single parent of a gaggle of children to whom he is diversely attached (biological children, stepchildren, one adopted son) and as in *Author!*, *Table for Five* presents the father-led family as an idyllic alternative commune, a haven of diversity. Here, Jamie's transformation from neglectful father (a wayward and irresponsible ex-golf pro who has squandered his winnings in dodgy business schemes) to attentive parent is prompted by the death of his ex-wife in an accident while he and the children are on a cruise. Though not an innately conscientious parent in the way Ivan is (his initial intention on the cruise is to leave the children in their cabins at night while he goes to the bar in pursuit of women), when Jamie has learnt to be a good father and to put his children first, he offers a similar anti-traditional paternal ideal.

For all the importance of *Kramer vs. Kramer*, films such as *Author! Author!*, *Table for Five* and *Mr Mom* in which Michael Keaton plays a father who has lost his job and so becomes the homemaker and childcarer while his wife works as an advertising executive, proved blips in the history of Hollywood's representation of the father. As several critics have noted (Jeffords 1994, Wood 1986, Rattigan and McManus 1992), the 1980s saw Hollywood reinvigorate the father–son narrative. Jeffords links this resurgence to the rise of conservatism and to Reagan's desire – which she likens to Darth Vader's – to 'extend his influence beyond his own generation' (65). This intertwining of the father's traditionalism with longevity is illustrated in the series of trilogies the 1980s spawned: *Indiana Jones*, *Star Wars*, *Rambo* and *Back to the Future*. The serial nature of these films proposes and exalts the immortal father. Hollywood was moving, along with the Right, towards the belief that society needed the re-emergence of traditional paternal authority, although (unlike the autocratic model of fatherhood prevalent in the 1950s) this traditionalism was tempered by greater sensitivity and involvement in childcare. This revised traditionalism ensured the active promotion of 'family values' – a term invariably and euphemistically used to signify the conventional heterosexual values of the nuclear family – and the restitution of the father as the linchpin of that unit.

Robert Redford's *Ordinary People* is the most important nurturing father film in the post-*Kramer* group, although here Calvin (Donald Sutherland) is a more conventional breadwinner father than either Ivan or Jamie. His wife Beth (Mary Tyler Moore) is a housewife and his surviving son Conrad (Timothy Hutton) is now, following the death of his brother Buck, an only child. Arguably *Ordinary People*'s critical and popular success (it won several Academy Awards) was due in part – as was the case with *Kramer* – to its inherent traditionalism. Again, as in *Kramer vs. Kramer, Author! Author!* and *Table for Five*, the father becomes a nurturing, sensitive parent following an unexpected and, for the family, cataclysmic event: the death of an eldest son. Buck's death motivates the narrative and leads indirectly to the disintegration of the family unit, culminating again in the eventual departure of the mother. As in the other films, Calvin is not merely the better parent, he is the only one Conrad has left; his idealisation is contingent upon crisis and, as in both *Kramer* and *Author!*, upon the vilification of the mother. As Robin Wood observes, if the woman in such films 'can't accept her subordination, she must be expelled from the narrative altogether ... leaving the father to develop his beautiful relationship with his offspring untrammelled by female complications' (1986: 173). The deification of the father in films such as *Ordinary People* goes against specific social realities (that is that, by 1983, the number of fathers who refused to comply with court rulings on maintenance payments, for example, had reached 'epidemic proportions')[2] although it reflects the feminist trend towards more involved fathers.[3]

Ordinary People is the first in a notable line of gently traditional father–son films directed by Robert Redford, later examples being *A River Runs Through It* and *Quiz Show*. Calvin Jarrett conveniently straddles the liberalism of the 1970s and the encroaching conservatism of the 1980s. Not innately capable of good parenting, he has to be instructed in the art by, most significantly, Conrad, his surviving son, but also by Conrad's psychotherapist Dr Berger, who functions in the film as an alternative father figure. From the outset, Calvin is compromised and a compromise, an uneasy blend of what a son would ideally want and what he knows he has. His deficiency is presented as passivity. He is of conformist appearance, dressed in sombre suits and ties, he pursues the equally conformist leisure activities of golf and jogging and manifests an intransigent traditionalism in his distrust of psychotherapy – a science rooted in emotional commitment and exchange. Calvin is thus provoked, even challenged, by emotional and psychological circumstances into becoming an actively engaged father.

The contrast between Berger and Calvin as father figures is pronounced. Berger is everything Calvin is not: he listens to music loudly, he smokes, he wears casual clothes, he slouches, he uses expansive hand gestures and he raises his voice. Calvin is measured, reticent and quiet. All Berger's characteristics function as metonyms for what is truly

important about him, namely that he (not Calvin) is capable of helping Conrad overcome his overwhelming, irrational sense of guilt over his brother's death (Conrad feels
guilty for having survived the boating accident that killed Buck and imagines – rightly –
that his mother would have rather Buck had survived).[4] Berger also offers Conrad pre-
sent-ness and stability. He is there for Conrad, and at a particularly charged moment,
just after Conrad has discovered that a friend from psychiatric hospital has killed herself
while Calvin and Beth are in Texas on a New Year golfing holiday, it is Berger to whom
Conrad turns. In Hollywood, a father's lack of paternal success is frequently measured
by the amount of extra-familial support the troubled child needs in order to survive; Conrad's investment in therapy indirectly indicates his emotional need, as does his
membership of the school choir and, to a lesser extent (for this is the activity he has to
forego if he is to continue seeing Berger), his membership of the swimming team. Berger
masks the real father's benign weakness.

The first step in Calvin's transformation is when he himself goes to Dr Berger, ostensibly to talk about Conrad, but actually, as it transpires, to talk about himself. This
sequence thus signals the delayed identification of the father with the son, a key component of many 1980s' movies. In his exchange with Berger, Calvin 'talks' (that is, uses
words to convey internalised thoughts and emotions) for the first time. The ability to
talk, to communicate emotionally is a defining feature of many father–son narratives,
and being able to overcome the repressive instinct not to talk indicates that Calvin is
finally equipped to become the father who can help Conrad. Together Calvin and Berger
(like so many 'real' and surrogate parents) comprise the complete, whole father, and
Berger enlightens Calvin, as it is only after visiting Berger that he recognises the twin
needs in himself to reject Beth's repressiveness and to wrestle from Berger the fathering of Conrad.

For all its idealisation of Berger, *Ordinary People* is on Calvin's side, and gradually, as
he begins to take on the effective parenting of Conrad, so the film's style and tone
becomes less dominated by Beth's character and sensibilities. For a large portion of *Ordinary People*, Beth's repressiveness has been echoed by the repressiveness of the film's
style. Within its visual discourse as well, Calvin's position has remained passive. The *mise
en scène* is crisp, harsh and unemotional, particularly when the focus is the Jarrett home.
The unhappy bourgeois home is a Hollywood cliché, characterised by a standardised
series of set pieces and tropes. The family seated for dinner around a formal table so
polished that it literally reflects their unhappiness back at them as they eat, for instance,
is one such signifier of familial discontent, used in many films of the 1950s (*Written on
the Wind*) and various films since *Ordinary People* (*American Beauty*). Another is the resonant use of stairs, the part of any conventional house that links the public reception
spaces with the private, personal and individual bedrooms above.

Although not used in quite the hyperbolic way of 1950s' melodramas (the conclusion
of *Bigger than Life*, for example), the stairs in *Ordinary People* are used symbolically to

compare Calvin with Beth. The strangulated, frigid formality of the Jarrett home mimics Beth's stiffness and the neatness of her appearance. In an early scene rich in irony as well as pathos, Beth and Calvin have returned home after a night at the theatre at which they have enjoyed a naturalistic domestic drama about a superficially happy bourgeois family. The use of the camera and the symbolic value of a staircase are combined to alienate us from Beth and make us more sympathetic to Calvin. Positioned at an obtrusively awkward and unnatural angle on the floor of the upstairs landing (as in *Rebel Without a Cause*, so often the locale for family confrontations and soul-searching) the camera focuses on both parents coming upstairs to bed and upon their differing reactions to seeing, from the light bleeding out from under his bedroom door, that Conrad is still awake. First it frames Beth's feet marching upstairs and across the landing, not missing a step as they stride past Conrad's door. Calvin follows. The parallel shot looks much the same until, responding to his realisation that Conrad is awake, the camera tilts up to show us all of Calvin as he goes towards his son's room. The fragmentation of Beth mirrors her emotional brittleness, while seeing all of Calvin at this juncture humanises him and makes us identify with him.

Beth's gleaming, soulless dining table is used to significant effect later. Upon returning from his visit to Dr Berger, Calvin initiates an argument with Beth that proves the catalyst to the dismantling of their marriage. The film's denouement then begins as Beth wakes up in the night to find Calvin downstairs crying, slumped over her antiseptic table. Tears in *Ordinary People* have taken on a hugely symbolic significance for we know from Calvin's visit to Berger that neither Beth nor Conrad cried at Buck's funeral, Conrad

Calvin and Conrad together after Beth's departure

having only cried since under the tutelage of his psychotherapist. Calvin begins a controlled diatribe that questions the very foundations of his marriage at the end of which Beth goes upstairs to pack and leave, permitting herself one single strangulated yelp of pain before zipping that up as she does her suitcases. David Considine is right to suggest that, in films such as *Kramer vs. Kramer* and *Ordinary People*, the men 'are more together' than the women and that family crisis can best 'be overcome by the father and son, but only when the mother is absent' (1985: 110), but this is rather to presuppose that the father is a figure of resilience and dependency. Calvin is still learning as much about emotional dialogue as Conrad is.

Ordinary People concludes with Calvin and Conrad in the garden on the bleak morning of Beth's departure. Calvin admits his deficiencies as a father and Conrad forgives them. Having started out as a film predicated upon definitive differences, *Ordinary People* closes by emphasising the importance of nuance and flexibility, so when Calvin signals his disappointment in himself as a father, Conrad replies, 'I'm not disappointed – I love you'. This conclusive father–son reconciliation (though somewhat more plausible) is reminiscent of the end of *Love Story*, as Ray Milland says 'I'm sorry', having arrived just in time to be too late for Ali McGraw's death, and Ryan O'Neal interrupts him with the infamous line, 'Love means never having to say you're sorry'. The intrusive shift in camera position during the final scene of *Ordinary People* from conventional close-up to high-angle crane shot, however, signals two things: that father and son are going to be left alone to sort out their relationship and that their closing embrace, far from being a resolution, is a fragile beginning.

The Compromise Father and the Importance of *Fatal Attraction*

The irresolution that characterises the end of *Ordinary People* is symptomatic of distrust in the type of father figure Calvin is. For all his gentleness, Calvin is not a potent figure of masculine identification, and it is this collision between political correctness and what, arguably, men actually wanted, that sealed Hollywood's dismissal of the kindly 'new father' of feminism. Various films appeared from the end of the 70s and beginning of the 80s in which the repressed pre-feminist bad father (imbued with tendencies towards patriarchal domination and violence) violates the 'new father' masquerade, many of them horror films: George Lutz, the seemingly perfect stepfather in *The Amityville Horror* (1979), for example, or Jack Torrance, the more obviously mad father in *The Shining*. George's metamorphosis from new man to aggressive, troubled patriarch is particularly graphic. After the Lutz family (wife Kathy and three children from her previous marriage) have moved into their dream Long Island home, George's façade, like that of their idyllic residence, starts to crack. George and Kathy could afford the house only because its dark history made it cheap: a son killed his family in it the year before, and George's transformation starts as his identification with the murderous son surfaces. His deterioration is rapid and visible; cheerfulness and dependability are replaced by brooding irrationality; black rings appear around his eyes; he is perpetually cold and chops wood obsessively in an attempt to keep warm; he shows signs of impotence (manifestly for the first time); and he becomes a despotic patriarch who tells Kathy her kids need 'a bit of goddam discipline'. Kathy finally stumbles across a newspaper image of the arrested son – he looks like George; her perfect second husband has become the stereotypical mysterious, dangerous stepfather of films such as *The Stepfather* (1987). George's last minute severance of his identification with the brutal son is not convincing. As in *Bigger than Life*, the images of the father on the verge of killing his family (or of almost being sucked into the black satanic slime that slurps around the foundations of his home), are more resonant than the film's actual conclusion, which has George, Kathy and the kids drive away from the haunted house for ever.

What links George Lutz to Calvin Jarrett is a tendency, manifested throughout Hollywood's portrayal of the father at the time, towards compromise, a need to achieve patriarchal equilibrium by rejecting, suppressing or altering extreme paternal archetypes. Despotic fathers such as Jack (Jack Nicholson) in *The Shining*, Allie (Harrison Ford) in *The Mosquito Coast* and even the politically extreme but far more benevolent Al (Judd Hirsch) in *Running on Empty* (1988) are, in the end, killed or rejected. Likewise, Marty McFly in *Back to the Future* ('one of the decade's quintessential films' [Prince 2000: 218]) is willing to take extreme measures to exchange his nerdy dad for a more brashly successful one, even if it means travelling back in time in a makeshift time machine and altering his father's past.

The fathers in *The Shining*, *The Mosquito Coast* and *Running on Empty* take to an unacceptable, even lunatic, extreme the notion of being the 'head of the household', inflicting on a dependent family unit a warped vision of self-sufficiency that is isolating and dangerous. In this, they resemble Ed in *Bigger than Life* or Bull in *The Great Santini*. Narrative factors link *The Shining*, *The Mosquito Coast* and *Running on Empty*. Not only does a father bend a compliant or weak family to his will,[5] but he also takes them away from a familiar environment, forcing them, to varying degrees, to follow the path he has decided upon, even though this leads to death and/or the fragmentation of the family unit. Jack in *The Shining* and Allie in *The Mosquito Coast* both consider themselves visionaries, equipped to wrench their families away from other support networks so all they have to rely upon is them. Jack takes his wife Wendy and son Danny to an isolated Colorado hotel when he accepts the job of winter caretaker; Allie impulsively decides to leave America with his family in order to buy a town (and build an empire) on a remote tropical island. Both men set themselves up as geniuses misunderstood by others, Allie as an inventor and Jack as a writer, and their madness is symptomatic of their delusional self-belief and their creation for themselves of mythic, larger-than-life roles: while Jack becomes the classic horror film monster who threatens the potential normality around him,[6] Allie, in arguing against the words of the Bible and imposing his way of thinking on his townsfolk, establishes himself in direct opposition to God and ruler (and recalls Ed's denunciation of God as 'wrong' at the end of *Bigger than Life*). It is significant also that these fathers are, in diverse ways, anti-establishment: Allie rails against what America has become while Al Pope in *Running on Empty* is a thinly disguised version of one of the Weathermen, the 1960s and 1970s' American terrorists who, pursued by the FBI, went underground to avoid capture. Even in *Running on Empty* in which Sidney Lumet's sympathy with the Weathermen is clear, the father recognises the damaging effect his political commitment has on the rest of the family as he finally lets his eldest son flee the family hideaway and re-enter 'normal' life.

This acknowledgment of the 'normal' sets *Running on Empty* apart from *The Shining* and *The Mosquito Coast*, which have both abandoned any concretised representation of normality, proffering no image of goodness against which the badness of its father figures can be measured. It is this moral disequilibrium that, within the context of the 1980s' predilection for certainty and conservatism, makes these fathers problematic. The underlying fear of *The Shining* and *The Mosquito Coast* is that the mad father could prove unstoppable and in both, the father is almost victorious.

These films' treatment of fatherhood recall Freud's essay 'The Uncanny' (in particular *The Shining*, which Kubrick reputedly was reading while writing the script).[7] Freud defined the uncanny as 'that class of the frightening which leads back to what is known of old and long familiar' (1919: 340) but which has made the crucial transition from being familiar or 'homely' to being frightening. Freud's quest is then to examine what makes this shift possible and 'in what circumstances the familiar can be uncanny or frightening' (340). The uncanny is linked to the repressed, although Freud is at pains to argue that all that is repressed is not uncanny, the important element being that the repressed or other image *recurs* (363), as it is through recurrence that the homely becomes 'unhomely'. One example Freud offers is of a visit he paid to an Italian town. He walked without purpose through the narrow streets and found himself three times back in the same place; as this happened for a third time a feeling overcame Freud 'which I can only describe as uncanny, and I was glad enough to find myself back at the piazza I had left a short while before' (1919: 359). Coincidental repetition transforms an otherwise insignificant location into one that makes Freud uneasy. The relationship between Calvin in *Ordinary People* and a father such as Jack in *The Shining* echoes Freud's findings, especially the idea of recurrence and the notion that the uncanny 'ought to have remained secret and hidden but has come to light' (345). In mimicking or parodying the traditional, hegemonic father figure, Jack recurs as an uncanny rendition of the 'ordinary' Calvin, an altered but recognisable version of the 'good father' that is nevertheless far less benign and far more likely to engender fear in both his fictional family and the spectator. Jack seeks to be the traditional breadwinner (taking the job as caretaker of the Overlook Hotel); he wants to be autocratic leader of his family unit; in declaring himself the undisputed genius of that unit, he also announces his right to order Wendy and Danny around from a position of intellectual as well as monetary and physical superiority. In this he invokes both the traditional father and the contemporary conservative ideal of the family as a self-sufficient island independent of the state. The presence of Jack alongside a positive film such as *Ordinary People*, though, makes us doubt the ability of all traditional fathers like Calvin to see off their uncanny others, a suggestion that would indicate the necessity to repress once more the extremist, authoritarian, demonic father who destabilises our belief in these nice, 'homely' originals.[8]

In an attempt to reverse the uncanny, Hollywood itself not only sought to repress the extreme horror father but also to reconstitute a benevolent but traditional archetype. The stable, strong, old-fashioned father thus became the *sine qua non* of the Reaganite movie about traditional values, because through his resurrection could be buried, with one blow, doubts about both the troubled and troublesome father and feminism. The movement towards ideological consensus emerges in various forms: the softening of Shug Avery's abusive father in Spielberg's screen version of *The Color Purple* (1985), the sanctification of Eliot Ness in *The Untouchables*, the victory of Bud Fox's 'good' honest father over his 'bad' paternal mentor in *Wall Street* and the comparable victory of the middle-class family unit and the unfaithful father at the end of *Fatal Attraction*.

Lynn Segal, in *Slow Motion: Changing Masculinities, Changing Men* (1997), deliberates upon what happened in terms of traditionalism, fatherhood and masculinity in the 1980s. Going against Jeff Hearns' view that the received 'notion of fatherhood must be smashed or more precisely dropped bit by bit into the ocean', Segal proposes a less radical compromise 'because I think that the myth of the good father – the strong and protective father – as well as the actual contribution of the caring father, are too powerful for us to smash and drop' (1997: 57). Segal can sense the dangers of 'reasserting the importance of fatherhood in a context of general male dominance' (57) but she equally can value the pull of the 'strong and protective' father. Segal's equivocation is matched by the ambivalences and binaries that characterise several of Hollywood's 1980s' father movies.

There is, for instance, the good versus bad father pattern present in two Oliver Stone films of the mid-80s: *Platoon* (1986) and *Wall Street*. In *Platoon*, Stone's first Vietnam film, the son figure, Chris Taylor (Charlie Sheen), a fresh 'grunt', is given a stark choice between which of his two superior officers to follow: the benevolent, protective, dope-smoking Sgt Elias (Willem Dafoe) or the crazed war machine Sgt Barnes (Tom Berenger). Stone's films of this period very much mimicked the allegorical structure of the medieval morality play,[9] and (having rejected Barnes as a role model) Chris's final voice-over makes explicit the symbolism of the tussle between Elias and Barnes: they were 'fighting for possession of my soul ... I've felt like a child born of two fathers. Those who made it have an obligation to build again ... to find goodness and meaning in this life'. In *Wall Street*, the adolescent homoeroticism of *Platoon* has been replaced by a less sexual morality play struggle for the soul of over-ambitious Wall Street trader Bud Fox.[10] Bud is again played by Charlie Sheen and the fight here is between his father, union boss

Carl Fox (played with obvious resonance by Martin Sheen, Charlie's father) and his evil mentor, Gordon Gekko (Michael Douglas), a multimillionaire corporate raider. More successfully than Barnes, Gekko wins over the son, blatantly displacing the benevolent father who stands for old-time dignity and honesty. Martin Sheen as Bud's natural father oozes ordinariness – blue work overalls, ugly, functional spectacles and a cigarette lolling perpetually between his lips. He and Bud meet up in a variety of unattractive locales – a sweaty workers' café, an airline hangar and a hospital, following Carl's second heart attack. Conversely, with his slicked, reptilian hair, his fat braces and priapic cigars, Gekko is a 1980s' Mephistopheles, even winning the Faustus-like Bud over with the help of a lovely maiden, Darryl Hannah.

In a discussion of what she perceives to be a relatively new (in the 1980s) development whereby 'Narcissus rivals Oedipus as the dominant metaphor of contemporary psychoanalysis' (Benjamin 1988: 137), psychoanalyst Jessica Benjamin argues that 'Whereas Oedipus represents responsibility and guilt, Narcissus represents self-involvement and denial of reality' (137). Gekko is the self-absorbed, anti-Oedipal narcissist who denies the value of the traditional paternal–filial bond, replacing it with the more generalised buddy relationship between the young man and the older mentor. The temporary elevation of machismo and muscularity (here, viewed metaphorically in terms of Gekko's brutish clout on Wall Street) mirrors the rise of the non-paternal action movie in the 1980s, to be discussed later. Gekko is actually and symbolically positioned as Carl Fox's binary opposite, and the polarised moral codes of the two paternal archetypes converge in a plot involving Gekko's intentions to buy out and liquidate the firm (Blue Star Airlines) where Bud's father has worked for twenty-four years. Asset stripping is here another metaphor for the self-destructive fascination with the bad father; Gekko's lifestyle may be opulent, but the opulence is superficial and transient (in the way that in *Dr Faustus* it is delusional). By contrast, Carl Fox's fidelity to Blue Star, his lack of ostentation and his responsible attitude to fathering signify durability and tradition (Gekko is also a father, but his infant son is more of a trophy baby, wheeled out to impress people before being sent back to the nursery with his nanny). The battle between the two culminates in them being permitted to slug it out metaphorically (as in *Platoon* Barnes and Elias are allowed to do physically). In his willingness to sell himself to Gekko, Bud gives the demi-devil insider information about Blue Star, after which Gekko makes his move on the company, a move Carl Fox, having guessed Gekko's motive, opposes. The confrontation between the two fathers takes place in Bud's grotesquely fashionable apartment, in which his windcheater-clad father and Blue Star colleagues look anomalously sane. Gekko's eventual demise is mooted here in one small gesture – he goes to put down his plate of hors d'oeuvres but misses the tabletop, because the designer table is largely made up of holes. After an argument, Carl Fox storms out, but not before he has intimated, with a deft counter gesture, that he has the mettle to win their battle: Martin Sheen takes his windcheater, rolls it up and manages to put it on in one swift move without even looking at where his sleeves are – a neat working-class Dad trick.

The bad father must be excised before the good father can exert his influence on the son and ensure continuity through the generations. The passing on of wisdom and goodness in *Wall Street* is represented in another ritualistic, restorative father–son bed-side scene. After Carl Fox has left Bud's flat in disgust, Bud rejects his natural father. Carl soon after suffers a heart attack and Bud is summoned to his bedside. Here, the penitent son utters the most clichéd of lines – 'I guess I never told you, I love you, Dad, I love you so much' – while swearing to bring down Gekko and win Blue Star back. The company represents investment in the future as well as the son's belated investment in his father's ideals and love.[11] Carl Fox recovers and, in the final scene of the film, drives Bud to court – where he is due to be admonished for (and cleansed of) his sins. Freud could not think of 'any need in childhood as strong as the need for a father's protec-tion' (1930: 260), but in offering the son protection, the good father also ushers in the return of a conventionalised father–son hierarchy that the narcissism and solipsism of Gekko momentarily challenged.

Bud regresses back into his childhood role as dutiful son, and regression as a means of coming to terms with and accepting the good father is a vital component of several 1980s' Dad movies. Frequently, regression is linked overtly to nostalgia – the period set-tings of *The Untouchables*, the *Indiana Jones* and *Back to the Future* trilogies or *Dead Poets Society* (1989), for example. What is yearned for is a return to 'a more shining and idealistic time than is the present', a tendency that mimicked Reagan's nostalgic rhetoric of the time (Prince 2000: 218). In *Witness* (1985), police officer John Book (Harrison Ford) learns, through immersion in the old-fashioned Amish community, the value of traditional, family-orientated masculinity and in *The Untouchables*, Eliot Ness exempli-fies the importance of nostalgia as a means of idealising the conventional father. It is not, however, always the case that a father such as Ness is viewed as a positive pater-nal archetype. In *Family Fictions: Representations of the Family in 1980s Hollywood Cinema*, Sarah Harwood offers five paradigms of 'paternal failure' (1997: 77) that recur, to her mind, throughout the 1980s. She identifies twin failures in Ness: the 'failure of the patriarch, the failure to uphold the law and the symbolic order' and the failure to protect his family as he pursues Capone (88). Tonally, however, *The Untouchables* does not mark Ness out as a failure: his family is virtuously Christian and united and his wife is supportive of her husband's idealistic desire to 'do some good' as Ness clumsily and pompously characterises his mission when speaking to the press. The overlapping of pri-vate and public personae is crucial to the film's conceptualisation of Ness. The values Ness represents in his fight against organised crime become illustrative of his worth as a father, just as he extends his domestic patriarchal role to the eclectic group of crime-fighting 'untouchables' he assembles, whose very disparateness (the short brainy one, the tough working-class one, the older wiser one) replicates the family unit. Also, Ness's fight against Capone is conceived as a battle on behalf of helpless children: *The Untouchables* opens with a little girl being blown up by a Capone bomb in a Chicago bar, an incident which prompts the appointment of Ness. That Ness's role is to protect children, even as he endangers the lives of his own, is exemplified by the prolonged homage to the Odessa steps sequence in Eisenstein's *The Battleship Potemkin* (1926), in which a baby in a pram is caught in the crossfire. Far from illustrating the father's failure, a sequence such as this (because the baby is ultimately shielded from the 'bad men's' bullets by Ness and his fellow 'untouchable', George Stone) represents the trust universally placed in patriarchal authority. Without the 'untouchables', Brian de Palma posits, Capone would eventually get to both Ness's own family and the larger communal 'family' of innocent Chicago.

Dan Gallagher (Michael Douglas) in *Fatal Attraction* is the most important representative compromise father figure of the 1980s, in what was probably the most notorious Hollywood movie of the decade: men cheered at Glenn Close's death, feminists felt compelled to offer critiques of its portrayal of the professional woman as psychopathic and it spawned a series of 'women from hell' films that continued well into the 1990s. The film's plot is simple: Dan is a seemingly happily married man whose wife Beth (Anne Archer) and daughter Ellen go away one weekend while he stays in New York to work. Over that weekend, Dan has a fling with a work colleague, Alex Forrest (Close) and thinks, come Monday morning, that it is over. Alex, however, pursues him; her pursuit progresses from phone calls to damaging his car, kidnapping Ellen for the afternoon and boiling the family bunny. Alex even manages to get into the Gallagher family home. In a final 'shoot-out', after Dan thinks he has successfully drowned Alex in the bathtub, Alex resurfaces only to be shot by Beth (who is recovering from a car crash suffered while trying to find Ellen, whom Alex had taken to the funfair). Most critical attention has been focused on the portrayal and significance of Alex, the film's she-monster, but here, the focus will be Dan, an equally potent symbol – or symptom – of reactionary 1980s' gender politics. From even the brief synopsis it is clear that Dan is both 'innocent' (in that it is not his fault that the woman he chooses to have an affair with turns out to be psychotic) and entirely weak (it is Beth and not he who kills Alex at the end). As a symbol of the return of patriarchal authority, Dan Gallagher is deeply flawed.

Dan stands for traditionalism: he is a white, middle-class professional breadwinner whose wife does not work; he functions to repress feminist and other calls for the pluralisation of familial structures as he encapsulates the value of the heterosexual nuclear family unit; he is a key figure in reasserting the belief that families need fathers[12] – and fathers, at that, who are heads of their households. During the 1980s, marriage rates started to rise again after years of decline and studies declared the 'family man' to be 'the happiest man' – healthier than his bachelor friends and expected to live longer (see Stearns 1990: 198–201). Stearns posits that the married man's happiness only stems in part from having found 'a woman to do chores and provide emotional support' (201); that men had also increased 'their own active commitment to the family' (201). Susan Faludi, who in *Backlash: The Undeclared War against Women* (1991) mounted one of the most important critiques of *Fatal Attraction*, might argue that this 'commitment' was entirely self-serving.

Faludi outlines in her chapter 'Fatal and Foetal Attractions', how British director and screenwriter James Dearden's original script was altered beyond recognition. In Dearden's script, a writer has a weekend affair while his wife is away; again like Dan, the writer thinks nothing of it; then the woman starts to phone the house, and one time the writer's wife answers the phone; as she says hello, the screen goes black. Dearden's script, as Faludi says, was interested in exploring 'an individual's responsibility for a stranger's suffering' (1991: 146) and the writer becomes the focus of that responsibility and implied guilt. This simple script was turned down by Paramount because 'the man was unsympathetic' (director Adrian Lyne quoted in Faludi 1991: 147) and metamorphosed into *Fatal Attraction*, under the guidance of Lyne, its notoriously misogynistic director, and its producer, Sherry Lansing. Another problem concerning the portrayal of Dan Gallagher was that Michael Douglas made it clear that he was not going to play 'some weak unheroic character' as Dearden recalls (Faludi 1991: 148). So, the script was modified – Dan became nobler as Alex became more deranged; he also became the sole breadwinner as his wife (who in the original was a teacher) became a homemaker. The film's first ending had Alex committing suicide to the strains of *Madame Butterfly* (a

Serenity is restored to the
Gallagher family

recurring leitmotif); however, after the test audience responses proved disappointing (Dearden speculated that 'It was not cathartic' [Faludi 1991: 151]), it was re-shot. The redraft gave the audience a cathartic ending, with its physical battles between Alex, Beth and Dan and the brutally decisive murder of Alex. After the police have been and gone (and one staggering feature of *Fatal Attraction* is that the police are so easily dispatched), Beth and Dan go back into their home. The final shot of the film is a zoom into a family snapshot of them with Ellen. The ideology of this version is far clearer: the strong family is worth preserving and ultimately proves stronger than and superior to the deranged other woman.

Fatal Attraction draws together various tenets of 1980s' conservatism, not only the resurgent belief in 'family values' but also the vilification of the career woman and distrust of the welfare state. Several critics have asked us to read the film 'against the grain', to see the central marriage as unhappy and the careerist she-devil as a positive point of identification, but the film's conservative tenet – that a father is essential to a family's happiness – is hard to dislodge. The central narrative figure upholding this ideological position is obviously Dan, the father and symbol of patriarchal traditionalism. When set against Alex, the madwoman with her Medusa-like tresses and goulish blue eyeliner who lives above a New York meat market in a sterile, minimalist apartment, Dan cannot help but represent normality. His innocence (or perhaps ignorance) represents the solid American institution of marriage, and as Faludi documents, *Fatal Attraction* was credited with 'starting a monogamy trend', 'reinvigorating marriages' and 'slowing the adultery rate' (Faludi 1991: 145); in short for showing men the dangers of transgressing the rules of marriage.

Dan still, however, poses problems. Most importantly, he is totally unremarkable, a New York lawyer who lives with his wife, daughter and dog. His one notable act is to sleep with a woman who is not his wife. Dan's ordinariness, though, is a crucial factor in making him a point of masculine identification and it is stressed in a number of ways. Dan shares with fathers in subsequent 'women from hell' movies (such as *Basic Instinct* [1992], *The Hand that Rocks the Cradle* [1991], *Disclosure* [1994]) the dullness and uniformity of a good upstanding citizen, who dresses in shapeless khaki trousers, check or casual shirts and staid woollens. Additionally, in order to preserve the film's neo-conservatism, Dan must remain innocent in comparison to Alex, but this necessarily entails a certain emasculating passivity. *Fatal Attraction* treads a fine line. It is not because of Dan that Alex is finally killed and his family reunited – but had it been Dan rather than Beth who had fired the fatal shot, he would have been irredeemably guilty. Likewise, Dan, despite being shown elsewhere as an urbane, reasonably savvy guy, when confronted with Alex, becomes naive and helpless, otherwise permanent doubts would have been raised about his underlying honesty and worth. Sex raises particularly problematic issues in *Fatal Attraction*. On the one hand, Dan and Beth's relationship is significantly asexual – not that their marriage is in difficulty, as some have suggested,[13] but that family life (taking the dog for a walk or a wide-awake child) takes priority over sexual intimacy. Convention dictates, as has been discussed earlier, that the Hollywood father (or at least the honourable Hollywood father) has renounced or repressed his sexuality. So, in order for Dan to be recuperable as a good father after his indiscretion, the power and eroticism of the sex needs to have been undermined. Just as Alex is portrayed not as an average career woman but as a hysterical she-devil, so the sex between her and Dan is equally distorted and extreme. As they go from sex in the lift to sex with Alex sitting astride the kitchen sink smearing water on Dan and Dan, with his trousers round his ankles, carrying Alex to the bed, so the act of intercourse becomes a self-conscious performative act that detracts from and hampers our belief in the relationship between the two people performing it.

Fatal Attraction offers a fervent affirmation of the beauty of the ordinary family, although it frequently (as in the sex scenes) veers towards self-parody. At its heart, there is a fundamentally ambivalent attitude towards Dan Gallagher. If the film's ideology is to be sustained, he needs to be credible as the strong patriarchal archetype; however, as Philip Green explains when writing about his dissatisfaction with the film's alternative endings, 'In neither of this film's two versions is the impotent male protagonist left with a type of masculinity that most men would publicly wish to emulate' (1998: 196). For Dan's innocence to be proclaimed, he has to appear weak in the face of the predatory career woman. The inevitable result of these contradictory ideological impulses is that the father or family man as a masculine archetype comes to seem incongruous within the image of hegemonic masculinity offered by Hollywood in the 1980s. As Green suggests, the process of emulation is always key to Hollywood's representation of masculinity; if the father failed to fulfil masculine fantasies, then his most significant counterpart in the 1980s was the action hero. Here again, though, the issue of fatherhood is deeply problematic.

Fatherhood in the Action Film: *Indiana Jones and the Last Crusade, The Terminator, Die Hard*

The action man has seldom proved a successful father, for 'action' signals a representational dependence on the body, physicality and strength, all attributes that the father – the more feminine nurturer, carer – most notably lacks. Macho fathers or fathers preoccupied with their bodies have, within Hollywood's parameters, tended to be deficient paternal role models, as, to cite two late-1950s' examples, Wade in *Home from the Hill* and Raymond in *Bonjour Tristesse* have illustrated. In *Hard Bodies: Hollywood Masculinity in the Reagan Era* (1994), Susan Jeffords suggests parallels between the Reagan/Bush decade and Eisenhower's 1950s, and others have made similar allusions to the similarities between the patriarchal conservatism of the 1950s and the rugged masculinity espoused by Reagan (see Traube 1992: 138). The legitimacy of Jeffords' point of view depends upon her contention that it is impossible to discuss the major films of the 1980s without discussing Reagan, as Reagan was both 'an image of popular culture' and 'an emblem of American national identity' (1994: 6). Linked to this is Jeffords' argument that the films reflected Reagan's conservatism, particularly the action films, as here the 'soft bodies' of the Carter era are conspicuously replaced by the 'hard bodies' of the Reagan era (13). As masculinity becomes 'hard-bodied', so Hollywood becomes action film-centric, and the repeated, significant masculine role models of the decade were Stallone, Schwarzenegger, Gibson, Willis, et al.

With the predominance of the action film – despite the widespread belief that the 'key issue of manhood in the 1980s [was] the relationship between fathers and sons' (Jeffords 1994: 87) – emerged an anti-paternal masculine role model, one that supplanted rather than emulated or proved subservient to the father. In terms of how such images have been interpreted within film theory, the over-emphasis of the body in relation to gender construction has proved crucial, firstly in relation to the representation of women (see Laura Mulvey's 'Visual Pleasure and Narrative Cinema' [1975]) and secondly in relation to cinema's representation of men (see Steve Neale's 'Masculinity as Spectacle' [1983]).[14] Theoretical arguments about gender have traditionally stressed the importance of the body as a gender signifier, so when masculinity came to be discussed in the 1980s and 1990s, Mulvey's terminology was simply reapplied to men. And so, Steven Cohan and Ina Rae Hark, in their Introduction to their edited collection of essays, Screening the Male: Exploring Masculinity in Hollywood Cinema comment that the subsequent essays:

> ... share as a group a concern with issues that film theory has repeatedly linked to the feminine and not the masculine: spectacle, masochism, passivity, masquerade, and, most of all, the body as it signifies gendered, racial, class and generational differences (1993: 3).

This litany of attributes ('masochism, passivity, masquerade') is more usually attached to representations of femininity and, as they are used here, illustrates a central problem in the theorisation of masculinity on the screen. The spectacularisation of the male body concomitantly achieves two mutually dependent and contradictory things. It problematises received notions of masculinity (Cohan and Hark go on to criticise the 'monolithic masculinity produced by a de-contextualised psychoanalysis' [3]) and makes men more interesting subjects for critical appraisal by indicating their flaws, neuroses and performative tendencies.

Such an approach, however, is also frequently mobilised to suggest male strength – and the very hegemonic, dominant masculinity the frailties of men's bodies brought to the surface. So Neale attributes eroticism, narcissism and fetishism to the portrayal of masculinity through the body in cinema, while at the same time arguing, after Mulvey, that male bodies (the physical manifestation of the male ego) remained 'unmarked as objects of erotic display' (1983: 18). Masculinity as spectacle can thereby retain its symbolic strength, Neale asserts, by the linking of that body – however potentially vulnerable and fragmented – to action; action (for example in the Westerns' final shoot-outs or the gladiatorial contests in *Spartacus*) being used as a means of deflecting the erotic look and reflecting instead male potency.

Following on from such arguments, the 1980s' action hero was interpreted using similar terms. Chris Holmlund interprets Stallone's muscles 'as a masquerade of proletarian masculinity' (1993: 214) while Yvonne Tasker remarks that it rapidly became *de rigueur* to talk about men in Hollywood cinema as 'performing the masculine' (1993a: 230) as a prelude to her discussion of *Die Hard*, *Lock Up* and *Tango and Cash*. This emphasis upon the displayed, performative male body serves to repress the relevance and significance of the father – whether literal, idealised or symbolic – for the simple reason that the father's power resides in keeping his phallus (and by extension his phallic body) constitutively veiled. The flaunted presence of the male body in action cinema serves to displace the father, the paternal signifier as the encapsulation of hegemonic masculinity. This male body suggests a masculinity that is not only potent but pre-paternal, still bound up in its own narcissism. Jeffords perceives the relationship between the father and the action hero as quite specific. With reference to Robert Bly's question 'How does [the son] imagine his own life as a man?' when the father is diminished or belittled (as Bly found him to be in the 1980s),[15] Jeffords posits that the son can imagine himself a man through identifying with the film heroes of the time, in particular the white male action heroes (1994: 11).

The problematic position of literal – as opposed to symbolic – fatherhood in the action film is exemplified by *The Terminator* and *Terminator 2: Judgment Day* (*T2*). Repetition, nostalgia and fathering are important elements in both films and in both films the plot revolves around saving the father and son in order to preserve the future. In *The Terminator*, it is the son, John Connor, leader of the human rebel forces fighting the cyborgs in 2029, who sends Kyle Reese back to the pre-war days of 1984 in order to protect his mother Sarah Connor (Linda Hamilton) from the threat of 'the Terminator' (Arnold Schwarzenegger) and ensure that he, John, can be conceived and born. Before he dies, Reese falls in love with Sarah and the result of their brief sexual union is John Connor. As Jeffords observes, John not only selects the person who should protect his mother, he also inadvertently chooses his own father (Jeffords 1994: 248). In this Oedipal scenario there is a direct parallel with *Back to the Future* and that film's similarly futuristic and fantastical desire to enable the son to create or reformulate the father. An extension of this inversion (as it is usually the father who creates the son) is the oddity of seeing the father as younger or less capable. In *The Terminator*, John Connor is invoked as a leader, the hero of the future while his father-to-be Reese is by far the more vulnerable of the two visitors from 2029, contrasted in his frailty with the Terminator, a flesh-coated bodybuilding machine. Likewise in *Back to the Future*, Marty is more knowing and streetwise than his gormless dad.

In keeping with the action film's marginalisation of the father, the action protagonist of *The Terminator* is the cyborg killing machine incapable of feelings (in direct opposition to the father) and whose other mission besides terminating Sarah Connor is to terminate the father figure, Reese. The father's sensibility is eradicated in other respects. Reese, for example, reveals to Sarah that he has learnt to suppress his emotions and not to feel, and when, later, she asks him about her son, he tells her that John chose not talk much about his father. Masculinity in *The Terminator* is predicated upon the repression of emotion and sensitivity (the domain of the father), based as it is on actions rather than words.

Reese and the Terminator enact the polarities of male experience. In *Lethal Weapon*, the cop duo of Danny Glover and Mel Gibson likewise offers a binary opposition of masculinity: Glover is older, a family man and milder; Gibson is younger, single and 'borderline psychotic' (Fuchs 1993: 200). As the series progresses, the two become marked out as not just 'buddies', but more similar; in *Lethal Weapon 4*, for example, during a tense action sequence during which they are nearly petrol torched to death, a mixture of light relief and seriousness is imposed by Glover and Gibson telling each other – as they cower behind their bullet-ridden car – that they are to become a father and a grandfather respectively. The first *Lethal Weapon* opens with two scenes that exemplify the contrasts between the men and their bodies. It is Murtaugh's (Glover's) fiftieth birthday; he looks down at his aging body (half-hidden by his bathtub) as his wife and three kids sing 'Happy Birthday'. In the following scene, Riggs (Gibson) wakes up – alone, dishevelled, living in a trailer. Importantly, his naked body is shown in full and we are given a prolonged glimpse of Gibson's pert buttocks. Within Hollywood's discourse on men, fathers and bodies, it is possible to surmise that Murtaugh, like Kyle Reese, is fatherly, in his attitude to nakedness – and by extension to displays of gratuitous but manly brute force – while Riggs, like the Terminator, is more narcissistic, pre-paternal and more violently manly. In *The Terminator*, both Reese and the Terminator descend to earth in 1984 amidst claps of thunder and shards of lightning, but whereas the latter adopts a bodybuilder's pose, crouching with one knee up on which rests an elbow, showing off his musculature, Reese's position is altogether more vulnerable and foetal.

The vulnerability of the father within the action/adventure film comes to the fore in *Indiana Jones and the Last Crusade*, the last film of the trilogy in which Indiana (Harrison Ford) goes in search of and finds both the Holy Grail and his father, Professor Henry Jones (Sean Connery). Professor Jones has loomed large over the previous two films, but this is the first time he features as a character. Representative of his absence, *Last Crusade* opens with an exchange that explains the difficult relationship between father and son in which the young Indiana (River Phoenix) returns home excited at having snatched a holy treasure from some looters. Henry, the distant father too absorbed in his own work to divert his attention onto his son, is heard but not seen. Indiana follows in his father's footsteps by becoming an archaeologist, an emulation that is more or less explicitly represented as a bid to gain his father's attention. The linking of the father and the Grail in *Last Crusade* is symptomatic of a romantic, nostalgic attitude to both father-hood and masculinity, and the son's symbolic search for his aloof father is the quest for reconciliation. At one point, Indiana's more attentive surrogate father Marcus Brody (Denholm Elliot) muses to Indiana that 'the search for the cup of Christ is the search for the divine in all of us'. It becomes increasingly clear, as also it becomes clear that Indiana's mission first and foremost is to save his captured father, that the 'divine in all of us' is rather sentimentally entwined with the father–son relationship and the handing on from one generation to the next of a masculine ideal.

So, Indiana's quest for the Grail becomes a quest for his father. The latter has had a lasting obsession with finding the Grail and has kept a 'Grail diary' that he sends to Indiana and which, at various points in the story, falls into the hands of the Nazis. Professor Jones is captured and Indiana – or 'Junior', as his father calls him – comes to the rescue, abseiling through a window of a Colditz-like Austrian castle. For the first time in the trilogy, father and son have joined forces and it is the son who, through by now familiar acts of *Boy's Own* derring-do, leads the way to the cup of Christ. *Last Crusade* is overly schematic: the father, via his hand-written diaries, leads the son to both him and the Grail and in so doing forges the hitherto lacking father–son bond. Thus, the 'grail' of masculinity is synonymous with the attainment of a good mutual relationship with the lost father, a further inference crystallised at the end of the film as it becomes apparent that Indiana, when he finds the site where the Grail is kept, and when he chooses 'wisely' as the knight guarding the Grail observes by guessing the correct cup, has fulfilled the destiny of ancient masculinity. With a drink of the elixir of eternal youth Indiana saves his wounded father, but what does Professor Jones tell him to do? Of course, he tells him to let the cup of Christ go – the son's quest for the father now taking priority and now having been satisfactorily completed.

A further generic reconciliation with the father has occurred by the time of *Terminator 2*, as the Terminator T2000 (Schwarzenegger) has changed from killer to protector (Jeffords 1993b: 253) and now functions as surrogate father to John Connor. The lack of and need for a father for John is made explicit, as Sarah Connor, at the beginning of *T2*, is in a high-security psychiatric prison (following a failed attempt to blow up a computer factory) and her son has become a wild boy, brought up by inadequate foster parents and stealing money from cashpoints. It is tempting to interpret *T2* as an allegory for the backlash generation, illustrative of what can go wrong if one's father is dead and one's mother has become too masculine (not through choosing work over domesticity, but through becoming muscled, tenacious and physically aggressive). It is T2000 who now reveals his gentler side and is sent back by the adult John Connor to save his mother and himself as a boy – and so complete the family triad by stepping into Reese's shoes. This is a particularly ill-fitting trio, a symptom of its maladjustedness being that, once again, it is the son who instructs the father, not vice versa. T2000's fatherliness is largely constructed by John Connor: he teaches T2000 how to blend in and sound human, for example, by teaching him street slang like 'no problemo'. T2000 falls in line with John's instructions, having also replaced his menacing catchphrase of *The Terminator,* 'I'll be back' with the more Hispanic and playful 'Hasta la vista, baby'. In keeping with the softening of the tough male that was happening at the end of the 1980s (when Paul Smith sent muscly male models down the catwalk cuddling cute babies), the action hero was letting go of his indestructible hard-bodied image. Of T2000's transformation Susan Jeffords remarks:

> The Terminator offers the ostensible explanation for why men in the 1980s are changing their behavior: they learned that the old ways of violence, rationality, single-mindedness, and goal-orientation ... were destructive, not only for individual men, but for humanity as a whole (1993b: 253).

In response to 'old' masculinity, Jeffords then surmises, men produced a '"new", more internalised man who thinks with his heart rather than with his head – or computer chips' (253). Indeed, the change in T2000 is sufficient to make Sarah Connor confide: 'Of all the would-be fathers who came and went over the years, this thing, this machine was the only one who measured up. In an insane world it was the sanest choice'.

With the generic acceptance of the metamorphosis of the Terminator into kindly surrogate father, certain of the central tenets of action film criticism are laid to rest, for instance Barbara Creed's influential belief that actors such as Schwarzenegger and Stallone began to 'resemble an anthropomorphised phallus, a phallus with muscles if you like' (1987: 65). The rise of this 'exaggerated masculinity', Creed argues, is a 'casualty of the failure of the paternal signifier' (65) – that is that, by extension, the phallic body is the result of the loss or absence of the father. What happens when, in a film such as *Die Hard* (and its two sequels), in which the 'excessive' or hysterically 'over-developed and over-determined body' (Tasker 1993b: 109) is downsized to the more ordinary musculature of Bruce Willis? Willis's character John McClane is immediately characterised as both a father and an action man cop. On his way home to LA for Christmas in an attempt to patch up his rocky marriage to his career-orientated wife Holly Gennaro (Bonnie Bedelia), he gets off the plane clutching an over-size teddy while also wearing a gun. As McClane arrives at the Nakatomi Corporation where Holly works, their building is attacked and sealed off by nebulously defined European terrorists headed by ruthless aesthete Hans Gruber (Alan Rickman). McClane gets embroiled in a fight to the death, ultimately beating off the terrorist threat (with the help of another generically essential black cop buddy) and winning back his girl. In her discussion of *Die Hard,* Tasker legitimately emphasises the film's ironic, performative qualities, and asserts that Willis as McClane offers 'a parody of a classic action movie image' (1993b: 62). Is it simply because we need not take this action hero too seriously that it becomes acceptable for him to be a family man?

Bruce Willis as both atypical action hero and atypical father

McClane is, in most respects, an atypical 1980s' action hero. For one thing, he is artic-ulate. Rather than his body doing the talking as Stallone's body does in *Rambo*,[16] McClane uses words and wit as weapons against Gruber. In fact, their antagonism is grounded in generic atypicality and irony: Gruber's evilness is signalled by his intellec-tuality and his sharp dressing, while McClane's heroism is signalled by his wise-cracking and his shambolic appearance (his trousers, which are too short, give him a childish air and by the end, his vest is grubby and his foot in a makeshift bandage). It is within such a context that *Die Hard* posits fatherhood as oppositional to being 'a man', treating McClane's macho antics (saving the 'towering inferno') rather than his paternal status with heavy irony. Most action heroes are sons in need of fathering. When the father happens to find himself in the position of action hero as McClane does (and his status as accidental hero is crucial to the film's tone), the polarised aspects of masculinity – machismo and fatherhood – become awkwardly synonymous. Important to *Die Hard*'s conceptualisation of McClane is that he is an unsuccessful dad and that the feminist wife who no longer bears his name has chosen a career over marital solidarity. As with many cinematic fathers, McClane finds himself emasculated at the beginning of the film (by the bear, the bare feet and the shortened trousers) and the resuscitation of his action role affords him an opportunity to regain his masculinity. Still, McClane's status as father means that his status as action hero is circumscribed. As Tasker suggests, the action hero McClane is placed perpetually within inverted commas, as when Gruber contemptuously calls him 'Mr Cowboy', after trying and failing to discover his identity (Tasker 1993b: 62). As befits the first of many tongue-in-cheek action films (*Speed* [1994] and *True Lies* [1994] can be cited as later ones), the denouement of *Die Hard* undercuts McClane's action man heroics in favour of heroising the successful reclamation of his familial role.

After Gruber has finally plunged to his death from the top of the Nakatomi building, McClane and Holly are reunited (although the relative unimportance of family status within the action genre is obliquely signalled by the more effusive greeting McClane reserves for fellow police officer, Al Powell). McClane introduces Holly to him as 'Holly Gennaro', but Holly quickly interrupts, giving her name as 'Holly McClane'. This is frequently viewed as indicative of the feminist's capitulation, although the end credits fail to resolve the matter, listing Bedelia's character as 'Holly Gennaro McClane'. What this ending does definitely signal, however, is McClane's resumption of the classic patriarchal role, and this time bereft of self-reflexive irony. On this relationship between hyper-masculinity and fatherhood Robert Griswold quotes a glib remark from best-selling author George Gilder: 'If they [men] cannot be providers, they have to resort to muscle and phallus' (Griswold 1993: 259). Griswold, a little censoriously, then adds: 'And muscle and phallus do not for good social order make' (259). Manifestly, at the end of *Die Hard* what is restored is 'social order' and how it is symbolically achieved is through the restitution of masculinity to the father. This particular conjunction exemplifies Hollywood's relentless tendency towards the romanticisation of the father, and it is over the son that such an idealised figure exerts most influence.

Sons and Their Fathers

As Andy Martin remarks, 'the father wants nothing so much as to be the son' (Martin 2001: 41). This is one masculine imperative that is worked through repeatedly in the romanticised father–son narratives of the 1980s. In *Indiana Jones and the Last Crusade*, the crowning reconciliation of Indiana and Henry Jones comes about because the son learns to love the father – but also the father learns to be like the son. Father narratives in Hollywood are frequently son narratives in disguise, the fathers being viewed from the sons' perspective. In the 1980s there was a particular emphasis on the son and how much he needed the father. In *Wall Street*, Bud Fox finally listens to his sensible, honourable father and discards the ephemeral immorality of Gordon Gekko; in *Back to the Future*, Marty McFly recreates his father in the image not just of himself but of what he himself would like to be; in *Field of Dreams*, Iowa farmer Ray Kinsella hears voices urging him to build a baseball pitch and bring back the ghost of 'Shoeless Joe' Jackson – he follows these instructions, threatens his family's livelihood, and is ultimately reconciled not just with the ghosts of his baseball heroes but with his father. There are two moments when, in the 1980s, the son's need for the father is of peculiar importance: in the films of Tom Cruise (Cruise's repeated portrayal of the son in search of the father continues into the 1990s) and in Peter Weir's emotive schoolboy melodrama, *Dead Poets Society*. What does the quest for the father symbolise? What 'need' does it fulfil? For answers to these questions this discussion will turn for a moment to Robert Bly's *Iron John: A Book about Men*, first published in 1990.

Iron John proved so influential to the 1990s' men's movement because it upheld the twin notions that men were emotional and sensitive and that they needed to re-establish their primal masculinity. These two impulses would at first appear to be contradictory. Popular feminist thinking positioned the sensitive male and his macho counterpart as binary opposites (as indeed the earlier 1980s' action films had done), and Bly's central thesis is that feminism created a type of masculinity that men did not want. He writes that men who subscribed to feminism had lost their identities and the capacity to articulate their needs and desires:

> The 'soft' male was able to say, 'I can feel your pain, and I consider your life as important as mine, and I will take care of you and comfort you'. *But he could not say what he wanted*, and stick by it (my italics; 1990: 4).

For Bly, men's collective troubledness centres on the father, a father who is an amalgam of the actual father and his symbolic ideal. Bly is forever relating the real and specific (the experiences of men's group meetings, for example) to the intangible and metaphoric, hence the distillation of men's troubles to 'There is not enough father' (1990: 92), the staggering inelegance of which is presumably retained to prove the idea's truthfulness.

The quest for the lost father is the central motif of Bly's interpretation of the folk-tale *Iron John*. This fairytale (in Bly's version) tells of a dangerous hairy man who resides in the forest near a castle. He has killed several knights sent by the king to kill him, but one day a fearless knight succeeds in capturing the hairy man, draining the lake where he resides and putting him in a cage. The knight uses buckets to slowly drain the lake of its water and Bly interprets this laborious act as the contemporary man look-ing into his psyche, 'an area no one has visited for a long time' and where his 'ancient hairy man' lurks (6). Bly claims that late 1980s' society had not yet begun this 'buck-eting-out process', but that such a quest for the primal root of masculinity and the welcoming back of man's *nourishing* dark' side was essential (6). The cage where the captured hairy man resides is, Bly intimates on several occasions, feminism or the result of feminism.

Later, the king's eight-year-old son is playing in the courtyard where the hairy man is imprisoned when his golden ball rolls into the cage. He sets about trying to retrieve it. Bly (without irony) suggests that the golden ball represents men's inner masculinity. Men in the 60s, he writes, had wrongly presumed they would find the golden ball in 'the feminine realm' (of 'sensitivity', 'non-aggressiveness' etc. [7–8]), but this is 'not where the ball is' (8). Instead, 'the golden ball lies within the magnetic field of the Wild Man' or the 'deep masculine' (8). What this is, Bly never fully explains, although any reader of *Iron John* instinctively understands this to mean a repressed, primal masculinity. The king's son and the hairy man strike a deal: the boy can have his ball back if he lets the man out of his cage, but first he must get the key to the cage from under his mother's pillow. Bly discusses the Freudian mother–son bond before he recounts the final stage in the boy's journey: opening the cage, being lifted onto the man's shoulders and going off with him into the woods (13–15).

This triumphant moment (when the maternal and the weak paternal are thwarted) is pursued at length by Bly as a strong legitimisation of the need for rites of passage, when a boy is taught to become a man and is brought to the brink of manhood by his male elders. Bly's book proved so influential, perhaps, because it mapped out, using language and imagery that was at once romantic and strident, the need for men to retain their unreconstructed masculine core. Bly's attitude thus legitimated demonstrations of male exclusivity and male aggression (the non-Western rituals he describes, for example, entail separation from women and home, a certain amount of bonding violence – the mingling of blood – and acceptance into an all-male community [1990: 15–16]) and at the heart of it all is the absence in modern Western society of the father. The father, fusing as he does the actual paternal role and the symbolic role of ushering the young man into adult masculinity, becomes the most important masculine figure of all, and his absence, distance or lack becomes Bly's primary cause for concern.

In a film-based article covering not dissimilar territory, Bill Nichols examines those adolescent male characters he calls 'Sons at the brink of manhood'. Examining a sequence of films from the late 1970s/1980s (including *Running on Empty*, *Breaking Away*, *Back to the Future*) Nichols compels his reader to think about the other side of the fundamental masculine dyad – the son. In diagrammatic form Nichols identifies 'the son' to be the 'neutral term' between the male and the female imaginaries, a figure who floats unformed, neutral and presumably asexual between the polarities 'man' and 'woman' (1989: 33). The son, within this formulation, is a third term,[17] a category that still exists outside the normative gender categories (male and female) that created it. Nichols' sons are not-yet-men, they 'may have a penis, but they do not yet possess the phallus' (33). Nichols identifies corporeal identity and change with figurative, metaphorical change as when he observes that in certain films the son is presented 'at that pivotal moment when he attempts to defer, decline or disavow his own relation to and complicity with the law' (35–6), that is, the collective law of the father, the family and the state. In much the same way as Bly has done with myth and anthropological history, Nichols interprets these son movies as rites of passage, as enacting the moment when the son learns separation from the home and becomes a man. Nichols, like Bly, sentimentalises and aggrandises these moments of transition, as for him the son is the idealisation of 'what the male body and male self-consciousness might be', the figure 'arrested and suspended, held in a state where choice, if made, lacks its final burden of consequences (Nichols 1989: 40–1). The son, once again, is what the father – carrying the burden of responsibility and adulthood – would still like to be.

Although Nichols does not discuss the films of Tom Cruise, Cruise fits Nichols' schema, having specialised in playing tortured sons of absent or neglectful fathers. His son persona is often macho but insecure, security coming (alongside the transition to fulfilling adulthood) through reconciliation with a father previously rejected or held too much in awe. There are two paradigmatic Cruise son narratives: in the first, exemplified by *Top Gun*, the son, having felt unworthy, eventually proves himself equal to a dead father he has lived in the shadows of (this relationship is repeated in *A Few Good Men* [1992]); in the second, exemplified by *Rain Man* (1988), Cruise is the son who feels rejected by the father and subsequently, as a defence mechanism, adopts an outwardly swaggering masquerade to hide his vulnerability (posturing later repeated in *Magnolia*). The sons in *Top Gun* and *Rain Man* are simultaneously regressive and mature; they have to both make a psychological return to their childhood lives with their fathers, while also having to make the opposite journey towards maturity and adulthood without the father. In both films the optimum resolution is that the son becomes the father, but the routes taken by the sons are quite different.

In *Top Gun*, the son achieves this resolution through narcissistic identification, the less mature option. Lt Pete Mitchell, nicknamed Maverick (Cruise) is a 'Top Gun' US navy trainee pilot. Maverick is both a brilliant, daring pilot and a dangerous, unruly one. He is good but, unlike his rival, Iceman (Val Kilmer), he has a history and an insecurity that hold him back, namely the death in ambiguous circumstances of his father, also a 'Top Gun' pilot. The official story was that his father had 'screwed up' but, as Mike (a commanding officer who teaches Maverick and flew with his father) reveals, Maverick's father was 'a natural heroic son of a bitch', although the details of the mission on which he died, for security reasons, were hushed up. As Mike remarks, Maverick is 'a lot like he was, only better – and worse'; the son both identifies with the father and (just) remains separate from him. The vulnerability of this position is bound up with narcissism. Until Maverick reaches maturity (in the form of a fuller appropriation of his father), masculinity in *Top Gun* is defined purely through narcissism: pilots strut around the locker rooms, oiled, toned and bare-chested, posing self-consciously; they try to beat each other in the skies and play beach volleyball bare-chested. As film critic Pauline Kael noted 'It's as if masculinity has been redefined as how a young man looks with his clothes half-off' (1986: 117). Like Narcissus, the budding pilots rely on images of themselves or reflections of themselves in others for recognition; like Lacan's infant when he looks in the mirror, the 'Top Gun' pilots recognise this reflection as an image of control.

Maverick loses his immaturity when, through his conversation with Mike, he has his idealised view of his father reinforced. The father in this instance protects the child from reverting to the 'limitless narcissism' (Benjamin 1988: 135) of infancy and, upon learning that his father died not ignominiously but heroically, Maverick finally reaches son utopia: narcissism and Oedipal resolution entwined, as he emulates his father's heroism. He starts to behave in an adult way, congratulating Iceman on getting the Top Gun trophy and helping him rather than striving to outdo him on the army manoeuvres to which they are both, after graduation, assigned. His assimilation of his father's heroism is rounded off by the declaration that his aim – when he could take any mission he wanted – is to become a Top Gun instructor. Trouble is, he is still the narcissist son, for *Top Gun* closes with Tom Cruise being reunited with Charlie (Kelly McGillis), the older woman – or substitute sexual mother.

In *Rain Man*, Cruise plays Charlie Babbitt, who thinks he is an only child until his father dies and leaves his entire estate to a trustee (minus his Buick convertible and prize roses, which he leaves to Charlie). The trustee is the director of a clinic where Charlie's autistic savant brother Raymond (Dustin Hoffman) has lived since their mother's death when Charlie was two. Charlie kidnaps Raymond, wanting to secure half of their father's $3 million inheritance, which he considers to be rightfully his. After a week together, driving from Cincinnati to Los Angeles in the Buick (because Raymond refuses to fly), Charlie grows close to Raymond, *Rain Man* offering an archetypal parable of how present enlightenment can heal the wounds of the past. Although he eventually loses, by the end of *Rain Man*, Charlie has fought to become Raymond's legal guardian. He began as a flashy sports car salesman, a brash talker who wore gleaming suits and whose face did not register pain at the news of his father's death. The source of this detachment is his estrangement from his father, caused by a falling out when he was sixteen. Although it had always been off limits, Charlie had once taken the Buick for an evening out with his friends; his father notified the police that his car had been stolen (knowing that it was Charlie who had taken it) and Charlie got pulled over and put in a cell for two days. His father did not get him out of jail and as retaliation, Charlie, upon his release, left home for good. The father's will is a reciprocal punishment for this desertion, as a letter he leaves with his lawyer attests: he forgives his son for leaving but not for refusing to contact him again, as that 'has left me without a son'.

Through his kidnapping of Raymond, Charlie begins the journey back to his father, travelling in the Buick that caused the rupturing of their relationship and which becomes a fetish object for the father–son bond. The Buick is an equivocal symbol, both liberating and repressive. Its importance is signalled by its omnipresence in the sons' relationship: it is around the Buick, parked outside the clinic, that Charlie and Raymond are reunited and, after Raymond is kidnapped, it becomes a symbol for their lost childhood, the two immature adult sons driving across America in the vehicle so resonant of the father's cruelty. The Buick has been preserved in pristine condition – its clotted cream paintwork, its rounded chrome trims and its luxurious leather seats representing not just the father's sadism (for denying his sons the pleasures of the Buick and also knowledge of each other) but also a comforting lusciousness that suggests what the father should have been.

Through kidnapping Raymond, Charlie also liberates him, as the journey in the Buick enables both sons to re-form childhood memories and purge themselves of the ignorance and resentment that has left them suspended in a state of perpetual immaturity.

Charlie and Raymond drive to Las Vegas in their father's Buick convertible

Through performing the paternal functions Raymond also lacked, Charlie himself attains maturity. As Harwood notes, Raymond's autism is stressed in *Rain Man* as being an inability to communicate and express emotion and so 'a trope which symbolises the failure of the father–son relationship' (1997: 79). As the director of the clinic reminds Charlie, Mr Babbitt's failure as a father had been that he 'had difficulty showing love'. Here, the Tom Cruise son abandons narcissism in favour of assuming the dual paternal role of patriarch and nurturer, and in so doing replaces directly his and Raymond's inadequate father.

What *Iron John* argued with significant popular success appears, on the surface, contradictory. He argued that 'There is not enough father' while simultaneously advocating the necessary separation of boy from parents, in order to ensure successful integration into masculine adulthood. What the Wild Man offered the son – and what the weakened, emasculated post-feminist fathers could no longer offer him – was help with forging this adult identity (Bly argues, for instance, that single mothers, 'even women with the best intentions' suck sons of their identity [17]). Bly would like to see the restoration of 'good fathers' who could, in turn, restore the Wild Man.

Quintessentially of its time, just such a thematic tension drives *Dead Poets Society*. Set in a boys' private school in 1959 (that is, just prior to the era of revolution and change), *Dead Poets Society* centres on the relationship between radical English teacher John Keating (Robin Williams) and his pupils, all of whom have been hitherto oppressed – by their own autocratic fathers, the school establishment, the law and name of the father. Keating is a liberator, freeing – through poetry – the souls (or identities) of his pupils, as the Wild Man does the king's son. Identifying liberation with a fight against conventionality is a favoured Peter Weir theme, recurring in *Witness, Picnic at Hanging*

Rock, *The Mosquito Coast* and *Fearless*, but in *Dead Poets Society* it becomes explicitly linked to masculinity and the fight between fathers and sons.

Keating stands apart from the school, Welton Academy, which employs him and of which he is an alumnus. As a boy, Keating founded the 'Dead Poets Society', a group of pupils who went into the woods at night to read and feel the passion of poetry; when he returns to teach at Welton, his pupils find out about the society and Neil (Robert Sean Leonard), Todd (Ethan Hawke) and others – in their eagerness to emulate Keating – revive it. Each meeting begins with words by Henry Thoreau:

> I went to the woods because I wanted to live deliberately. I wanted to live deep and
> suck out all the marrow of life. To put to rout all that was not life. And not when I die,
> to discover that I had not lived.

Keating's liberation of the oppressed boys is specific. His first lesson entails explaining the maxim 'Carpe Diem' from Robert Herrick's 'To the virgin to make much of time' and from thence he uses poetry to teach his pupils to live life to the full, to unleash their creativity and their sensibility. The boys thrive under his tutelage until they come into direct conflict with the law (or name) of the father, the representative story here being that of Neil Perry who, under Keating's influence, has disobeyed his father's orders by taking the role of Puck in a production of *A Midsummer Night's Dream*. It is not accidental that Neil's transgression is as Puck, the mischievous elf whose final speech ('If we shadows have offended . . .') is Shakespeare's eloquent apologia for naughtiness. Mr Perry, in a vain attempt to re-establish the law of the father, takes his son home after his triumphant performance and punishes him by deciding to take him out of school and to send him to military academy, then medical school. Neil wants to be an actor and his inability to stand up to his father at this point leads him to commit suicide, a death the school (in support of the conventional father) contrives to blame on Keating.

Neil's father – although distraught at his son's death – is, in Bly's terms, the repressive father of the 1950s, the father whose psyche 'lacked some sense of flow' or 'compassion' (Bly 1990: 2). Conversely, Keating – who symbolises the relative freedom of the 1960s – functions as the alternative, enlightened father who lights 'the boys' rites of passage into manhood' (Rutherford 1992: 17). Keating is forever guiding his pupils away from traditionalism; a notable feature of his teaching style, for instance, is that he is perpetually taking the boys away from their desks – and so away from formality, the father's law and repressive instruction. That desks stand for tradition is signalled by details such as Todd being sent a desk set as a birthday present from his parents two years running and Neil finding the revolver with which he shoots himself inside his father's desk (see Hammond 1993). Keating, conversely, teaches outside or makes his pupils stand on a desk to demonstrate the importance of taking a different view of the world. Keating is a hyperbolic character, passionate, unconventional and disapproved of by his colleagues. He is associated more than once with Beethoven's rumbustuous 'Ninth Symphony'.

Hyperbole also infects *Dead Poets Society*'s *mise en scène*, as the film uses excessive style to represent the perennial fight against repressiveness. This fusion of style and meaning is especially clear during Keating's fifth lesson, as he compels Todd Anderson, who is extremely self-conscious of his stammer, to speak. Keating is Todd's ideal father figure. He has guessed that the idea of speaking aloud terrifies Todd and indirectly insinuates that this lack of confidence is the result of painful parental indifference. So, Keating sets out to free the inner voice trapped within Todd's psychosomatic silence. He drags Todd to the front of the class to do (after his favourite poet Walt Whitman) a 'barbaric yawp': to emit a sound that is instinctive, passionate, resonant, but lacking in formal meaning. Goaded by Keating, Todd eventually also emits a stream-of-consciousness description of the picture of Whitman pinned to Keating's classroom wall. His spontaneous poetic outburst is filmed using dizzying circular pans, the camera enveloping Todd just as Keating, his hands capped over Todd's eyes, envelops him, tempting out his 'barbaric yawp'. At the end of Todd's instinctual emission (and there is something orgasmic about how words finally tumble from his mouth and in the way he smiles contently when they stop) Keating, by this time crouched on the floor looking up at his protégé with awe, goes up to Todd and whispers 'Don't you forget this'. The swirling camera and the intimacy between Keating and Todd suggest fusion and reciprocation, and it is here that the good father becomes subsumed into the son. Although Keating is sacked after Neil's suicide, he has helped liberate the sons from the shared burden of their fathers' expectations and has begun to effect their individuation. His love of Romanticism is *Dead Poets Society*'s version of the woodland chest-beatings that Bly persuaded men's groups to participate in, Whitman's 'barbaric yawp' a version of Bly's repressed Wild Man.

The New Father of Late 1980s' Comedies: *Look Who's Talking*, *Three Men and a Baby*

Hollywood endorsed the arrival, in the late 1980s, of the 'new man', an archetype prominently exemplified by a spate of father- and child-centred comedies. *Baby Boom*, *Three Men and a Baby*, its sequel *Three Men and a Little Lady* (1990), *Look Who's Talking* and its sequels, and *Parenthood* have been analysed collectively a number of times as they offer such a coherent message about the state of parenting at the time (Kaplan 1992; Modleski 1988; Matthews 2000). All focus on the 'new man' ideal of the man who actively participates in childcare; they all offer a liberal view of parenting and accept that biological parents are not necessarily the best for the child. But they all also locate such a potentially serious critique within the framework of comedy, a choice of genre that led E. Ann Kaplan to argue that new fatherhood and alternative family structures are, in these films, invariably trivialised (Kaplan 1992: 187–8). Among sociologists and psychologists, the 'new father' was treated with comparable scepticism; although not thought to be 'entirely mythical' (Lamb 1986: 12) he was soon deemed to be 'less prevalent than widely assumed' (Harris and Morgan 1991: 531). As Finch and Morgan concluded, 'A considerable amount of effort on the part of sociologists and journalists ended with relatively few sightings of the New Man' (1991: 65).

Rutherford puts forward a different view, believing that the new man demonstrated a pleasure in being male (see Rutherford 1988). Likewise, the use of comedy in these films could be argued to stem from confidence among men and from a belated recognition that the feminised 'new father' had something to recommend him. As Nicole Matthews observes, several of these comedies, while purporting to be tales of single motherhood, are 'obsessed with the problem of fathers' (2000: 108). The films illustrate a particular sort of obsession with fatherhood, as the father figure (especially the non-biological father) frequently becomes an object of erotic attraction. These films emerged at the same time as the 'new man' and the forcible bonding in advertisements and other media of the toned, virile man and the beautiful child, the most enduring image of this kind being the 1987 *Athena* poster '*L'enfant*', depicting a bare-chested man holding a tiny baby (*Athena*'s best-selling image ever). Whereas the new man ideal of the early 1980s had been a rather worthy figure, his later reincarnation amalgamated sensitivity and sex. Babies became a male fashion accessory; boxer Barry McGuigan was photographed for the cover of the *Observer Magazine* in boxing gloves and a bare torso holding his newborn child and the father's active role in childbirth was featured in the late 1980s' 'The best a man can get' Gillette advertising campaign.

By the latter part of the 1980s fatherhood had become big business. In 1986, *Fathers Magazine* was launched in the US because, as its editor stated, 'fathers were showing a new interest in themselves' (*New York Times* 1986: 34) and a new catalogue 'Me and My Dad' appeared alongside it. That same year, the *New York Times* ran an article on the eve of Father's Day suggesting that 'Signs abound of the new importance being attached to the role of the father', outlining how sales at Tiffany's of 'traditional' Father's Day gifts ('such items as cuff links and tie pins') were 50 per cent up on the year before (*New York Times* 1986: 33). Bloomingdale's ran a series of ads in the run-up to Father's Day around the theme of 'The joys of fatherhood' and Hallmark confirmed an increase in the number of Father's Day cards being sent in America (*New York Times* 1986: 34). 'Fatherhood is fashionable' (Franks 1984: 103).

However, the treatment of the child as fashion accessory and its father as a narcissist preoccupied with grooming and showing off his physique displayed an ambivalent attitude to fathering. For, although the late 1980s' comedies concentrate on and promote domestic diversity (only in *Parenthood* are the fathers the biological ones; in the other comedies the biological fathers flee or, as in *Baby Boom*, have died), they still make a joke out of fathering. Thus babysitter and future stepfather John Travolta makes a fool of himself dancing to 'Walking on Sunshine' to entertain baby Mikey in *Look Who's Talk-*

ing and, in the same film a baby friend pokes fun at new man paternity as, to a bemused Mikey (who 'talks' with the voice of Bruce Willis), she defines a Dad as 'you know, the big men types that hang around the mummies. That's a Daddy'. Dads are now much better than they once were, but it is hard to banish from one's mind Sarah Connor's relief that in T2000 she had alighted upon the best Dad she could for her son. All the comedy dads are likewise imperfect but they will do – and they are certainly better than the philandering, absent dads they replace.

In *Three Men and a Baby* (a remake of Colinne Serreau's successful French original *Three Men and a Cradle*) three men – Jack (Ted Danson), Michael (Steve Guttenberg) and Peter (Tom Selleck) – share a bachelor shag-pad. One day, they are compelled to change their lifestyle when a baby girl, Mary (Jack's biological child from a short-lived relationship) is left by her mother on their doorstep. After the initial trauma, all three men relish their paternal responsibilities and are distraught when Mary's mother Sylvia returns to claim her baby back. However, Sylvia finds she cannot cope as a single mother so both she and Mary move into the men's apartment, thus creating a convenient four-some that is sorted out in the sequel film *Three Men and a Little Lady* as Peter (the most instinctive father) and Sylvia marry.

Three Men and a Baby, despite being a light comedy, has been the subject of con-siderable negative feminist attention, the most sustained attack coming from Tania Modleski who, just after its release, wrote an article accusing the film of being 'pae-dophilic' and its use of baby Mary's nakedness as 'shockingly voyeuristic' (1988: 71–2). Later, Vicky Lebeau argued that the film invokes 'the father-as-pervert' (Lebeau 1992: 245). The issue here is one of tone. Hollywood in the 1980s, even when it is ostensibly criticising individual fathers, was pro-fathers and paternity, and, as in *Kramer vs. Kramer*

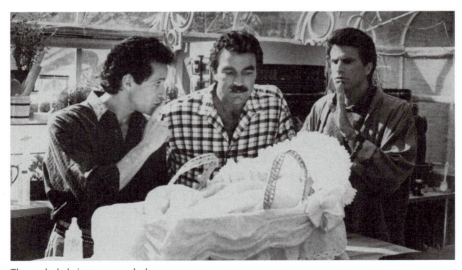

Three dads bring up one baby

eight years earlier, *Three Men and a Baby* wants its audience to delight in the intimate bond between father and child made possible by the mother's convenient exclusion (in both instances, to continue or restart a career). In so doing, Hollywood also proposes that men as well as women can learn to nurture and that women are just as capable of leaving their children as men are, both mainstays of the 1970s' women's liberation agenda. Modleski continues to valorise the role of the biological mother just as she admonishes *Three Men and a Baby*'s portrayal of men; in this she brings to the surface an uncomfortable truth: that women wanted to have careers and independence without relinquishing to men primary care of their children. There is plenty to suggest that women were compelled to juggle careers and childcare because men and fathers were simply reluctant to take on much of the domestic burden, but equally there is evidence to suggest that women would rather keep up this juggling act than hand over the nurturing to those few men willing to take on the responsibility. So, Modleski argues that *Three Men* 'reveals men's desire to usurp women's procreative function' (70) as well as demonstrating men's anxieties about their minimal role in procreation (69–70).

In response to this, it is equally valid to suggest that the men's assumption of the nurturing role is indicative of the relative lack of importance of the biological bond between parent and child. Such an attitude (that parenthood is learnt rather than innate) becomes increasingly important in these late 1980s' Hollywood comedies, all of which feature a child missing its natural father (in *Three Men*, only for a short time) and which glorify his non-biological counterpart. The biological father is made into the butt of jokes (in *Little Lady*, there is a brief exchange between Sylvia's mother and Jack: 'Oh look, it's the biological one'; 'Mom'; 'Why, when you say it, does that sound such a frightening word?') and is often seen to have less of a claim to 'his' child than the alternative father who demonstrates better nurturing skills. So, Jack in *Little Lady*, is happy to hand over the paternal role to Peter, because it was Peter who had become the main father within the communal home. Similarly in *Baby Boom*, J. C.'s (non-biological) daughter acquires dishy and homely Sam Shephard as a father and in *Look Who's Talking*, Mikey's natural father (George Segal) is unfavourably compared to James (Travolta).

Allied to this is the contention that women are not naturally predisposed to nurturing. In *Baby Boom*, J. C., like the trio in *Three Men and a Baby*, cannot – despite her Ivy League education – figure out how to put on a nappy. Similarly, in both *Three Men* films, while all the women fail to mix careers with parenthood, the men manage to do so with relative ease. As Elizabeth Traube comments, *Three Men and a Baby* was 'the movie that showed us what fun mothering can be when it's done by the right men' (1992: 145). In this and other fathering comedies there lurks a positive motivation for this exaltation of the paternal role, centring on the masculine desire to assert an alternative, not too serious model of fathering, one that, in short, is pre-Oedipal and emphasises fun.

It is largely because the child in *Three Men* is a daughter and not a son that Modleski reads the film as a neurotic Oedipal portrayal of the fathers' collective use of Mary – 'an adequate object of sexual desire for three aging bachelors' (1988: 71) – as the fetish object through which to deflect their fears of castration (74). It seems imprudently hysterical to propose that all acts of parenting performed by a father for a daughter are perverse; as Foucault warns in *The History of Sexuality*, the articulation of sex creates perversity where before there was none. Both *Three Men* films are pedantically Foucauldian on the subject of sex, stressing (and so bringing into the realm of discourse) the importance of Mary's four parents' sexual activity and their heterosexuality, while maintaining a decent distance between parenthood and sex, as their house rule dictates that partners cannot stay overnight.

The commodification of masculinity and fatherhood in the late 1980s' media suggested that erotic interest had alighted upon the body of the father. Modleski finds obscenity in the shower sequence between Jack and Mary in *Three Men and a Baby*, but perhaps the real surprise is the sequence's sexualisation of the father's body. Danson singing to, washing and cuddling his (biological) daughter is very similar in appeal to the *Athena* poster. In both instances, the object of eroticisation is not the naked child but the naked man, the underlying intention of this juxtaposition between the idealised male body and a baby being to make the former into the object of desire. It becomes apparent that the image of a father (particularly a butch one) on his own with a baby fulfils a potent female fantasy, as consolidated by the montage sequence in which the three fathers take Mary to the park and find themselves surrounded by numerous attentive women. Conversely, in *Look Who's Talking*, Molly (Kirstie Alley) only finds men ogling her when she is out *without* her baby son. From John Ford's *Three Godfathers* (1948) (on which *Three Men and a Baby* is loosely based) to more recent romantic comedies such as *Sleepless in Seattle* or *One Fine Day*, the father alone with his child is the focus of both comedy and desire.

Jonathan Rutherford argues that 'New Man is an expression of the repressed body of masculinity', but that masculinity continued to disavow men's potential for passivity, which 'strips him of his masculine power' (1988: 32). Kaplan remarks that 'The 1980s became increasingly the decade for fantasies of the Father as nurturer' (1992: 184). The decade concluded ambivalently, with the rejection of aggressive Reaganite masculinity, but with new men and fathers still reluctant to relinquish patriarchal control. The end of the 'backlash' era saw some relaxation of hard gender divisions and the emergence of a more tolerant attitude to parenting and families, and popular comedies such as *Parenthood* and *Uncle Buck* celebrated both 'male domesticity and female independence' (Traube 1992: 146). Glorification of male domesticity is at the heart of *Parenthood* – 'or *Fatherhood* as it might have been more aptly named' (Matthews 2000: 105). *Parenthood* opens with a flashback in which Gill (Steve Martin) recalls how his own far from progressive father Frank (Jason Robards) used to take him to baseball games as a birthday treat, only to pay an attendant to sit with him. Gill (he looks like a boy but talks as Steve Martin) tells the bemused attendant: 'I swore things would be different with my kids. It's my dream – strong, happy, confident kids'. As in *Dead Poets Society*, there is an intense desire to prove that the new man of the late 1980s is mark-edly better at fathering than his own father had been. In *Parenthood*, though, Frank acknowledges his failings as a father and recognises that Gill is more successful than he was. When, for example, his youngest child Larry (Tom Hulce) goes to Frank for $26,000 to clear his gambling debts, Frank asks Gill for advice. Gill is a traditional dad but he exemplifies the late 1980s' notion of 'updated paternalism' (Stearns 1990: 246) or sen-sitive patriarchy, as it could be termed. Frank likewise becomes an 'updated patriarch'. Assured that Frank will cancel his debts, Larry flees, and leaves behind his son Cool to be looked after by Frank and his wife. Frank thereby gets a second stab at fatherhood.

Parenthood's mission is to bury the spectre of the bad father and to suggest a posi-tive future for fatherhood. It is full of reformed fathers and it also has its fair share of troubled sons who have suffered at their neglectful hands. As one of these, Tod (Keanu Reeves), remarks: 'You need a license to buy a dog or buy a car, hell you need a license to catch a fish, but they'll let any butt-reaming asshole be a father.'

Parenthood ends on a maternity ward: Gill's sister Helen has just had a daughter and is surrounded by her extensive family. The emphasis here is on the joys of fatherhood: Gill is changing his fourth child's nappy, Nathan is about to become a father again, Tod is a dad and Cool is happy with his grandparents. As the announcement comes that both mother and baby are doing fine, Frank, the reformed paterfamilias, takes down the 'No Smoking' sign and gives all the fathers present a fat cigar. His overruling of the hospital regulations brings *Parenthood* to a close with a mixture of traditionalism and the relaxation and pluralisation of the father's role. Although the 1980s was a conser-vative decade, with the emergence of Masculinity Studies in the 1990s, the diversification of the father's image that was coming to the fore by the end of it would continue to be in evidence in Hollywood.

Notes

1. See Interview with Carter in *New York Times*, 19 June 1977.
2. Representative Marge Roukema's Father's Day Speech, 16 June 1983, *New York Times* 1983.
3. See Coontz, who argues that, despite increasing divorce rates, fathers in the 1980s stayed more involved with their children (Coontz 2000: 1).
4. The original screenplay for *Ordinary People* contained a flashback that does not appear in the final film that showed Beth, who knew that one of her sons had survived the accident but not which one, showing relief as she thinks it is Buck who survived.
5. In *Running on Empty*, although Al's wife was equally politically active in the 1970s, she says, in a conversation with her father, that had it been up to her, she would have given herself up to the authorities for the sake of her two sons.

5

The Next Best Thing: Men in Crisis and the Pluralisation of Fatherhood in the 1990s and 2000s

Hollywood has produced an enormous number of father-centred films recently, but variety as well as quantity sets this final period apart. It is notoriously difficult to offer an overview of what is contemporary or comes from the very recent past and so finding homogeneity and consistency among the films made between 1990 and the present was never going to be possible. However, it does seem, even taking this into account, that the final period to be discussed in this book offers a diversity of representations of the father that, consequently, suggests the fragmentation – or at least the dissipation – of the traditional paternal role model that has hitherto underpinned Hollywood's preoccupation with the father.

The diversity and quantity of recent American father films is linked to the dominant idea concerning contemporary masculinity: that men are in 'crisis'. A film that captured this post-feminist mood and has produced a surprisingly ample amount of scholarly discussion is Joel Schumacher's *Falling Down* (1992). It tells the story of the last day in the life of an 'average white male', redundant defence worker Bill Foster (known as D-Fens, his car's number plate) who, stuck in traffic on the LA freeway, abandons his car, announcing, 'I'm going home'. 'Home' is a fantasy location, a utopian end to a troubled journey, for what D-Fens means by 'home' is the house he used to share with his ex-wife Elizabeth and his daughter Adele, and from which a court order now bars him. D-Fens crosses Los Angeles to get 'home', going through both deprived and privileged neighbourhoods and killing several people (largely from racial minorities) before being killed himself by Prendergast (Robert Duvall), the cop who has been trailing him. D-Fens is played by Michael Douglas who, with films such as *Fatal Attraction* and more recently *Traffic*, has come to epitomise the modern Hollywood father: sometimes weak but usually morally upstanding.

Falling Down is notable for showing the average white family man as social victim. In one of the best articles written on the film, Carol Clover charts the ambivalent press response to the film (Clover 1993: 138–9) before proposing a reading of *Falling Down* that centres on its reconfiguration of 'The Average White Male': the 'guy everybody is mad at and wants compensation from' and who 'theoretically owns the world but in practice, in this account, not only has no turf of his own but has been closed out of the turf of others' (143–4).[1] This reversal is underscored by Schumacher's visual emphasis of D-Fens' alienation from the 'ordinary' or 'average'; a quotidian detail such as a woman applying lipstick becomes, in the opening sequence a lurid, distorted close-up in D-Fens' wing-mirror. The ordinary no longer makes sense. Having arrived at the uncomfortable realisation that he, the purported backbone of post-Industrial society, is expendable, D-Fens, a latter day 'man in the grey flannel suit', rebels. D-Fens's motive, as his journey 'home' attests, is to recapture that which he has lost, namely a masculinity predicated upon professional and domestic security. Alongside losing his job, being rejected and feared by his family and being mocked and patronised by most of those he eventually kills – from Chicano gang members to gentlemen golfers in hats and lurid slacks, D-Fens mourns the loss of his masculine identity. So he resorts to performing an elaborate masquerade, an ironic rendition of the breadwinner father he used to be, replacing the signifiers of this old existence (a breast pocket full of pens, an empty briefcase) with the spoils of war acquired during his murder spree (a baseball bat, a knife, a gun, a missile launcher).

Pinning its social critique to masculinity is what made *Falling Down* resonate with an early 1990s' audience, and it exemplified the convincing arguments Susan Faludi proposes in *Stiffed: The Betrayal of the Modern Man* for the 'crisis' in masculinity. Faludi argues that after the victory in World War II, through the Cold War and the space race, an idea(l) of masculinity was formed in which men became the masters of the universe, the conquering heroes and in which fathers bequeathed to their sons a sense of certainty and purpose. However, when that image was, in the latter half of the twentieth century, quashed, men discovered they had nothing to put in its place, so, Faludi concludes, both fathers and sons were 'buffeted by the collapse of society's promise' and modern-day America proved to be a society 'deeded by the fathers, inhabited by the sons, but belonging in the end to neither' (47). Men, she concluded, had no idea how to 'mobilize for their own – or their society's – liberation' once feminism had precipitated them into crisis (41). This image of flailing men who belatedly discovered that society had changed around them and who no longer knew what their role in life was, is encapsulated in D-Fens' journey towards a lost manhood he once thought he owned. *Falling Down* ends (after D-Fens' death) with old home-movie images playing on the family television; D-Fens had put these on when he had finally got 'home' – reminders of a lost, but happier time.

D-Fens' nostalgic over-identification with a traditional image of masculinity is thus shown in the film never to have existed. In *The Way We Never Were: American Families and the Nostalgia Trap* (2000), Coontz attests that, while women in the 1980s and 90s increasingly wanted to stay at home, by 1988 only 25 per cent of all families (compared with 44 per cent in 1975) conformed to the traditional division of labour between a breadwinner father and a housewife mother (1992: 18). This shift in familial demographics is what some experts (see Volling and Belsky 1991) have argued was the catalyst for the increased interest, through the 1990s, in understanding men and fatherhood. The recent Gender Studies emphasis upon masculinity is thereby not merely a theoretical concern, but has its roots in socio-political change. Although *Falling Down* expresses many of the key concerns of 1990s' Masculinity Studies, it is anomalous in one key respect, namely that its protagonist does not conform to the middle-class, sensitive 'new father' model its volumes promote.[2] It is in relation to class that a marked diversion can be identified between the ideal masculinity proposed by theory and the more realistic images identified by sociology and history. Pleck and Pleck, for instance, suggest that the 'new father' is the 1990s' ideal but not the norm and that it is middle-class fathers who more frequently uphold the new age ideals while working-class dads more often abide by traditional gender roles, but 'engage in considerable sharing of housework and childcare out of necessity' (Pleck and Pleck 1997: 35).

An important facet of 1990s' masculinity studies was the pervasive attempt to carve out a niche for fathers, but the persistent identification of this paternal identity with sensitivity and nurturing led to an adverse reaction in some quarters to the over-determined requirements of feminism. Burgess in *Fatherhood Reclaimed* mentions the US National Fatherhood Initiative, which argued that to be proper fathers, fathers must perform different tasks to mothers, that rather than be nurturers, they should 'contain emotions and be decisive' (1997: 27). This sounds suspiciously like the 1950s' notion of companionate marriage, although the National Fatherhood Initiative argued that they did not want to revert to such past models. Such confusion about what it meant in the 1990s to 'be a man' led, for example, to a significant rearguard action (greatly indebted to Robert Bly) against feminism with the publication of a series of steadfastly traditional masculinist books such as David Thomas's *Not Guilty: In Defence of the Modern Man* (1993), Geoff Dench's *The Frog Prince and the Problem of Men* (1994) and Neil Lyndon's *No More Sex War: The Failure of Feminism* (1992). All of these to some degree argue that the women's liberation movement was to blame for the disintegration of masculinity and family values. Dench argues, for example, that

> Perhaps the fundamental weakness of feminist analysis, from which many mistakes flow, is to fail to see that men may need the status of the main provider role to give them a sufficient reason to become fully involved, and stay involved, in the longer-term draggy business of family life (1994: 16).

This justification for patriarchy is given voice by both Thomas and Lyndon, Thomas protesting that, far from the patriarchal male being an omnipotent authoritarian ogre, he was probably a decent bloke we should all welcome back:

> Consider your father. He may be alive, he may be dead. He may have been a decent man who did his best, or he may have been a monster. But did he look to you like an all-powerful patriarch? Did he seem to be someone who was getting any great personal benefit from all this male power that we hear so much about? What was in it for him? (1993: 9).

The 'crisis' in masculinity emerged from the unresolved ambiguities of how men and fathers were being and might want to be defined. This 'crisis', however, was also regenerative, for in the 1990s, masculinity and fatherhood became topics for discussion, as they never had been before. One early writer signalled his annoyance at the lack, in the early 1990s, of 'a history of fatherhood, a silence which I regard as a sign of a more systematic pathology in our understanding of what being a man and being a father entail' (Laqueur 1992: 155). This desire to talk about men spawned a wide variety of studies, some vituperative moans such as those of Thomas and Dench, quoted above. The aggressive reaction to feminism voiced in such books epitomised a particular moment in the early 1990s, although a similar masculinist conservatism pervades Francis Fukuyama's *The Great Disruption: Human Nature and the Reconstitution of Social Order* (1999b) and the various books to have followed in the footsteps of Robert Bly's *Iron John* (discussed in the last chapter). Among the more significant are: Guy Corneau's *Absent Fathers, Lost Sons: The Search for Masculine Identity* (1991), Steve Biddulph's *Manhood: An Action Plan for Saving Men's Lives* (1998), David Blankenhorn's *Fatherless America: Confronting Our Most Urgent Social Problem* (1996). The converse perspective is offered by the many examinations of men that consider masculinity as an adjunct to, a result (in the 1990s) of feminism, a liberal intellectual tendency that links Faludi's *Stiffed*, Coontz's *The Way We Really Are: Coming to Terms with America's Changing Families* (1997), Lynn Segal's *Slow Motion: Changing Masculinities, Changing Men* (1997), Rosalind Coward's *Sacred Cows: Is Feminism Relevant to the New Millennium?* (1999), and, as a representative of 'new man' writing, Anthony Clare's *On Men: Masculinity in Crisis* (2000). Recurrent concerns run through these, in particular: the replacement of 'masculinity' with its plural 'masculinities'; the equation of modern masculinity with 'fragility'; the belief that men and not women were to be understood as the more socially constructed gender; the notion that men's greatest battles were now the internal rather than the external ones.

The importance of the shift from the singular term 'masculinity' to the plural 'masculinities' is important to Coward and Clare, for example, because the term itself opens up 'not just uncertainties but also possibilities and freedoms. Men can now invent themselves, as women did at the birth of feminism, in all their roles as fathers, husbands, lovers, workers' (Coward 1999: 95). Clare (from his psychiatrist's perspective) then observes that men had not, until recently, been taught 'what it means to be a man, a son, a brother, a lover, a dad' (Clare 2000: 1). Such pluralist identifications of what it means to 'be a man', however, carried with them insinuations of fragmentation and fragility. At the outset of *Absent Fathers, Lost Sons*, Corneau, a Jungian analyst, states that in his book he wants 'to talk about the things we began to open up and explore together [at a men's workshop], especially the fragility of masculine identity' (1991: 3). Later, Blankenhorn wrote the highly influential *Fatherless America*, whose thesis is that the widespread absence of fathers is America's most urgent current social problem.

Blankenhorn bemoans contemporary society's refusal to celebrate his archetype of the 'Good Family Man', instead making him the 'principal casualty of today's weakened father script' (1996: 5). 'Fragility' thus positively comes to connote sensitivity, but it also implies the undermining of traditional masculinity, a battle that Fukuyama and others argue was a direct result of the social revolutions of the 60s and 70s. These are the years that Fukuyama termed the 'great disruption', because they undermined fatherhood and dislodged the ideal of the traditional family.

Fukuyama also proposed that the fragmentation of modern masculinity was made possible at the time of the 'great disruption' by the fact that the role of the father 'is socially constructed to a greater degree than the role of mother, and tends therefore to be a much more fragile bond' (Fukuyama 1999a). With his diagnosis that masculinity and fatherhood are socially constructed to a greater degree than femininity and mother- hood, Fukuyama echoed much of the other writing about masculinity in the 1990s, which sought to reverse Simone de Beauvoir's feminist dictum 'one is not born a woman, rather one becomes one'. Corneau, for instance, states that 'Woman is, Man is made' (1991: 14), basing his claim on biology – that, 'as far as sexual identity is concerned' women simply 'are' by virtue of menstruation, while men have to learn and acquire their identity (14); likewise to Blankenhorn, 'fatherhood, much more than motherhood, is a cultural invention' because women are better than men at fusing the biological and social dimensions of their parental role, musing wistfully, 'Is she feeding or bonding? We can hardly separate the two . . .' (1996: 3). Fatherhood became viewed as a process of personal development, the vehicle for teaching a man how to feel. Because of the need in the 1990s to equate masculinity with feelings and emotional articulacy, it became apparent why the male whose very role is defined by nurturing, sensitivity and expressiveness, became so central to these discussions. Emotions become particularly fraught and convoluted around fathers and fathering. Corneau concludes his introduc- tion with the suggestion that 'the role of the sons, now, is to break through the silence [of masculinity]' (1991: 5), the silence not just of the physically absent father but also of the 'spiritual and emotional absence' (13) of the traditional father. Corneau is still talk- ing about the symbolic father, but his concerns are echoed in the work of, for example, Steve Biddulph, an Australian family therapist who, in the 1990s, produced a series of popular practical manuals outlining how to be a good father. Biddulph puts into prac- tice what Corneau, Blankenhorn and others discussed in more theoretical terms and his argument rests on his belief that 'a *father has to be there*' (1998: 109), the physical pres- ence of the father fulfilling a boy's '*biological need*' for 'several hours of one-to-one contact *per day*' with their Dad (113).

The articulate, caring father emerged, through these 'crisis' books, as the most val- ued male archetype. However, as Coward suggests, the 1990s, in assuming 'the psychological need for men to be involved with their children' (154), in turn cemented the importance of the need for male role models, a move that reflects a fundamental ambivalence within the men's movement: men were radicalised to the extent that they were more in touch with their feelings, but they were also regressing into essentialism that was, at heart, rooted in tradition as they began to 'think of masculinity as something which needs to be passed from man to man, from father to son' (155).

Fathers in Hollywood at the time pursued a similarly fragmentary trail, the films encapsulating the same intermingling of radicalism and traditionalism and, taken as a whole, providing few certainties. It is no more the case, as Susan Jeffords believed in 1993, that the 'warrior/cop' of the 1980s was replaced by the 'more sensitive, nurturing, protective family men of the nineties' (1993a: 200; 197) than it is true to suggest, as Coward does, that, once heroism ceased to be 'a male certainty', the 90s signalled that the 'really heroic struggle is now about facing inner obstacles, owning up to emotions in order to become a less repressed person' (1999: 110). This is only one aspect of how masculinity and fatherhood has shifted in recent years; Jeffords pins her argument on films such as *Regarding Henry* and Coward cites the film *Fly Away Home* (1996) and Nick Hornby's novel *About a Boy*. Just as there have been numerous melodramas and romantic comedies, so the 1990s also produced a variety of father movies: old-fashioned, traditional Hollywood father narratives, films that finally examine Black masculinity and fatherhood, genre movies in which the father is traditional but weak, films that centre on gay fatherhood, several comedies and a notable sequence of films, released around the millennium, in which fathers cause tragedy and the implosion of the family unit. As we come closer to the present day, there is less consistency than ever in Hollywood's depiction of the father.

Traditional Hollywood Father Narratives

Despite fundamental changes to how masculinity was now perceived, the traditional Hollywood father far from disappeared. Films that continued to idealise the traditional father included *Backdraft*, *A Few Good Men*, Robert Redford's *A River Runs through It* and *Quiz Show*, *Legends of the Fall*, *Apollo 13* (1995) and *Gladiator*. These films are traditional in two ways: they are ideologically conservative in their portrayals of masculinity and fatherhood and they demonstrate a nostalgic adherence to Hollywood generic orthodoxy, self-consciously reviving older Hollywood genres such as the Western, the epic, the father–son melodrama, the men in crisis movie. Such formal conventionalism is tied to the need to work through (and there is more than a waft of therapy about several of these films) a troubled, 'fragile' father–son relationship, which, as past chapters have demonstrated, has been how Hollywood, concomitantly, has so frequently 'worked through' its anxieties about masculinity and masculine genealogy in general. These films demonstrate a tonal consistency and sustain the ideal of an omniscient, guiding father; they are also characterised by a notable lack of irony or cynicism. Faludi has, for example, highlighted the inherent bathos of the 1960s' race to the moon, how it promised 'a mission to manhood' but 'turned out to be a place not much worth conquering' (1999: 26; 28) while *Apollo 13* persists in retaining the notion of space as a locus for men to prove their manhood. Jack Swigert's successful locking of one phallic component of the space ship to another vulval part is just one example of man's conquest of space re-assuming its virility. The near fatal crisis for which the Apollo 13 mission is remembered (a faulty oxygen tank that necessitates its dangerous but ultimately triumphant early return to Earth) tests the crew's masculinity, explicitly in relation to fatherhood and patriarchy. The central juxtaposition of *Apollo 13* through which the crisis is enacted and resolved is between a series of active, heroic men (the crew in conjunction with the NASA control centre) and the passive, anxious women and children who can only watch the news and wait. This faithful rendition of Apollo 13's story[3] thus serves as a modern reminder of the value of the nuclear family – by the mid-1990s, a familial model in as much trouble as the spacecraft.[4]

The inherent conservatism of such films conforms to the thesis propounded by Fukuyama, as he contends that the decline of nuclear families in the West since the 1960s had 'strongly negative effects' on most aspects of life (1999b: 115). *Apollo 13* is set in the 1960s but offers a retrogressive, traditional masculine ideal. The other films under discussion are also (except *A Few Good Men*, which, with its Cold War atmosphere, feels old-fashioned) set in the past, indicating a shared nostalgic desire to return to older values. Fukuyama's concept of social order is predicated upon the centrality of the father and the social decline his demotion precipitates is 'measurable in statistics on crime, fatherless children, reduced educational outcomes and opportunities, broken trust and the like' (5). Order thereby becomes dependent upon the preservation of patriarchal lineage, a generational, symbolic and temporal stability that also lies at the heart of these 'traditional' films. Both *Quiz Show* and *A Few Good Men* centre on a white, privileged son whose future hegemony is directly dependent upon the eminence of his father. Both sons have followed their fathers into the family profession: Charles van Doren (Ralph Fiennes) has become a literature professor while Daniel Kaffee (Tom Cruise) has become a naval lawyer. As they seek to emulate the father or seek his approval, both sons also learn the value of what their fathers stood for and that such a value system should be preserved. In *Quiz Show*, this validation is achieved negatively as Charles's cheating on the TV quiz show 'Twenty-One' reveals him to be inadequate in comparison to his father, while Daniel's unexpected legal triumph at the end of *A Few Good Men* shows him to be his father's natural successor.

In *Backdraft* and *Gladiator*, the father's legacy and the preservation of patriarchal succession is paramount to the sons' understanding of what it is to be a man. In *Backdraft*, 'manliness' is metaphorically enacted as fire-fighting. Again, the father's profession is now the sons', fire representing the mystery of unruly, primal masculinity. The narrative trajectory is the sons' indirect pursuit of their dead hero father; the sons (Stephen and Brian McCaffrey) are immature, demonstrably unformed until they have reached a point of reconciliation with him. In the opening flashback the young Brian (later played by William Baldwin) sees his father die after saving a child from a blaze. Brian is then immortalised on the cover of *Life* magazine, a shell-shocked boy clutching his father's helmet. The continuity between father and son is represented through the casting of Kurt Russell as both the father and the elder brother Stephen, although this casting also in part ensures that both sons remain two-dimensional reincarnations of their father until the end, when Stephen reaches a point of identification with his father through his own death in a fire and Brian conquers his fear of becoming his father by no longer running from his desire to remain a fireman.

For a film that is essentially a straightforward fable of sons emulating their father, *Backdraft* pursues a strangely convoluted plot about tracking down the arsonist who has started a series of fatal fires. At one point, Brian leaves active fire service to join the forensic investigation. In not being able to solve the arson case, Brian and his boss (played by Robert de Niro) offer another metaphoric enactment of the oblique father–son relationship, as at the root of both the forensic investigation and the son's search for the father lies an intuitive understanding of fire. As de Niro (one of several father figures) tells Brian, a fire 'is a living thing ... the only way to kill it is to love it a little', thus echoing Freud's belief in the son's compunction to both kill the father and to learn to love him as he strives for independence and maturity. Stephen dies never having reached this point of separation, while Brian, with his intellectual as well as emotional understanding of fires and fathers, has. The younger son's contentment is exemplified by *Backdraft*'s finale: following Stephen's funeral (the whole of Chicago, it seems, turned out) the final shot of Brian's face, in a fire engine on his way to a fire, shows him as contented, at peace. This is followed by a swooping crane shot careering along a straight, long road at the end of which is the fire. Brian, this image suggests, has finally conquered his fear of his father and masculinity.

In *Gladiator*, to occupy the position of father means becoming the omnipotent patriarch: being a father, ruling the army, ruling the Roman Empire. In these terms, after he has led the Romans to victory in Germania, Maximus (Russell Crowe) is bequeathed both the role of father and the phallus by the reigning emperor, Marcus Aurelius (Richard Harris) when he ('the son I never had') is asked to become the Protector of Rome and to make her a republic again. This act would mean breaking the dictatorial, patrilineal rule of the Caesars, but to be a good father necessitates also being able to release Rome/the child from subservience. Either side of his exchange with Maximus, Caesar has encounters with his two children, in which he (a dying man who, like many recent Hollywood fathers, wants to belatedly make amends for his neglectful fathering) admits to having been an imperfect father. As Marcus assures his son Commodus: 'Your fault as a son is my failure as a father'. The parricide that follows immediately after (and the subsequent murder of Maximus's family) ensures, however, that Rome is not entrusted to its natural father Maximus, but to its imperfect son Commodus.

But *Gladiator*, even more than *Spartacus*, which it recalls, journeys towards the only masculine ending it wants: the re-emergence of the good father as saviour of Rome. Commodus had ordered Maximus's assassination, but Maximus escapes (in a narrative move that, if any further pointers were needed, echoes the story of Oedipus). Maximus, like Spartacus, becomes the leader of the slaves and a triumphant gladiator. As Maximus wins yet another gladiatorial contest, Commodus descends into the arena of the Coliseum to greet the unknown warrior. Maximus is reluctant to reveal his identity, but when he does, he spells, through the invocation of himself as Rome's perfect father, the end of Commodus's corrupt and sterile dictatorship:

> My name is Maximus Decemus Meridius. Commander of the Armies of the North, General of the Felix Legions. Loyal servant of the true Emperor, Marcus Aurelius, father to a murdered son, husband to a murdered wife, and I will have my vengeance in this life or the next.

As the actor uttering this resolute defence of the good patriarch, Crowe is perfect; just the sort of dad (part boot-boy, part protector) you would want to call to your defence.

This is a different image of paternal masculinity to that found in several other genre movies in the 1990s, films in which similarly patriarchal males are, if not disempowered, then undermined. This occurs in several thrillers, a traditionally masculine genre. The weakened father recurs in such genre films as Curtis Hanson's *The Hand that Rocks the Cradle* and *The River Wild* (1994), *Disclosure* and *Don't Say a Word* (2001). The significant feature shared by the fathers in these films is ambiguity. They are not simply killed off as the hapless heroes of noirs were; they are often victorious, but such victories are equivocally achieved. The fathers here are not saved in the way that Dan Gallagher was

'My name is Maximus Decemus Meridius . . . father to a murdered son, husband to a murdered wife, and I will have my vengeance in this life or the next'

at the end of *Fatal Attraction*; instead, their attempted recuperations are, as Philip Green remarks about the end of *The River Wild*, acts of unconvincing desperation (1998: 85). In *The River Wild*, Tom (David Strathairn) is a workaholic father distanced from his family; he is also coded as a wimp: clumsy, with tense shoulders and fearful eyes cowering behind flimsy wire-rimmed spectacles. As with *Backdraft*, *The River Wild* is about taming the elements, in this instance perilous river rapids; but unlike *Backdraft* or *Apollo 13*, here it is Tom's wife Gail (Meryl Streep) who steers the family to safety and kills the crazy murderer Wade (Kevin Bacon) in pursuit of them. Tom's role is ambiguous for, although he does help save his wife and son Rourke (Rourke proudly tells a Ranger at the end of the film that while his mother guided the boat through the rapids 'all by herself' his father 'saved our lives'), in doing so he adopts the conventional feminine role by leaving the macho stuff to Gail while he uses intuition and guile. In all these genre films, the threat to the family is ultimately dispatched with the assistance of the fathers, but the fathers are seldom the ones to strike the final blow. In *Disclosure*, the father starts sexual harassment proceedings against a female boss, but she is finally trapped not by him but by the hacking abilities of the son of another colleague; in *The Hand that Rocks the Cradle*, the killer nanny is pushed onto the family's white picket fence by the gardener; one exception is *Don't Say a Word* in which the father eventually kills the villain himself. Unlike the triumphantly traditional father films, these examples convey a sense of masculine muddle and loss; the father who might expect to regain generic supremacy by the end, finds his position irretrievably compromised.

The Father in New Black Cinema

Rowena Chapman and Jonathan Rutherford prophesied that 'masculinity will be shorn of its hierarchical power and will become simply one identity among others' (1988: 11). Although not overtly stated, the term 'masculinity' is here being applied to the White, heterosexual male, for it is he who has been forced to change and lose some of his hierarchical power. Alternative types of masculinity – Black or gay, for example – are set apart from the dominant critical discourse on gender and identity. Whiteness is automatically considered to be an attribute of the traditional father. In the early 1990s, the resurgence of Black American film-making that became known as 'new Black cinema' foregrounded issues of masculinity, fatherhood and race. The majority of these films also dealt with, as Manthia Diawara indicates, the manifestly traditional subject of the boy's transition from childhood to adulthood (1993: 20). What further characterises – and then complicates – any discussion of films such as *Boyz n the Hood* and *Deep Cover* (1992) is that they are not merely rites-of-passage movies, but also social realist texts that engage overtly with contemporary social issues of Black masculinity. Diawara observes after teaching these films that his students' connection with the films indicated that 'Clearly, there is something in the narrative of films like *Boyz n the Hood* and *Straight out of Brooklyn* (1991) that links them, to put it in Aristotelian terms, to existent reality in Black communities' (1993: 24). The 'new Black cinema' films, are, however, fraught with anomalies; for example, within their exploration of contemporary racial and community issues, they offer depressingly regressive images of Black masculinity and fatherhood. *Boyz n the Hood, Deep Cover* and *Jungle Fever* (1991), the three films discussed here, offer stereotypical, polarised images of African-American masculinity: the good male characterised by articulacy, a propensity to study and the successful pursuit of a profession and the bad male who drops out of education and enters an often fatal life of crime and drugs. In these films, the definitive factor determining which group a boy will fall into is his father: whether he is present, attentive and a good role model or whether he is absent, criminal and a bad role model.

Since the publication in 1965 of the controversial Moynihan report into the Black American family, the community's main 'problem' has been perceived to be its lack of good fathers: 'Everyday observation suggests that many whites stereotypically perceive of black fathers as inner-city, hypermasculine males who are financially irresponsible and uninvolved in their children's lives' (Marsiglio 1995: 4–5). This view of modern African-American fathers was first cemented in the report that Senator Daniel Patrick Moynihan, then Assistant Secretary of Labor and Director of the Office of Policy Planning and Research, produced for President Lyndon Johnson entitled 'The Negro Family: A Case for National Action', although the interest of most researchers since its publication has focused on its supposed demonisation of the Black single mother.[5] What Moynihan actually said was that a multitude of social problems could be linked to the proliferation, in African-American communities, of single-parent families headed by women, but that the *cause* of such problems was the widespread absence of fathers. Moynihan was the first person to spell out the direct correlation between the instability of the African-American family and the father's unemployment. Although 'higher family incomes are unmistakeably associated with greater family stability' in White as well as Black families, what, according to Moynihan, set Black families apart was that, whereas 'White children without fathers at least perceive all about them the pattern of men working', Black children did not, so 'Negro children without fathers flounder – and fail' (Rainwater and Yancey 1967: 21/67; 35/81).[6] Moynihan stated that there were almost three times as many Black fatherless families as there were White (36/82), a statistic he then linked to the under-achievement of Black children at an educational level (36–7/82–3) and their far greater implication in inner-city crime (38/84). Amid all this, Moynihan then praises the Black youths who did succeed, because they needed 'the something extra' that could carry them over 'the worst obstacles' (35/81).

Have things changed that much since 1965? The underpinning issue determining the success or otherwise of the Black father is still socio-economic. In one study from 1986, statistics revealed that in the sixteen- to nineteen-year-old age range, 43 per cent of Black males were unemployed, as opposed to 17 per cent of Whites, while in 1984, 33 per cent of Black families and only 10 per cent of White families were below the poverty level. As one analyst of these statistics surmises, 'These constantly high unemployment and underemployment levels mean that many Black fathers cannot adequately fulfil a provider's role in the family, which in turn may seriously influence their ability to fulfil other roles related to the rearing of their children' (McAdoo 1988: 81). As another socio-logical study of fatherhood in the 1990s concludes, 'Working-class men were as likely to emphasize the nurturing dimensions of fathering as middle-class men' (Cohen 1993:19). The difference that makes all the difference is money.

Deep Cover tackles the negative attitude that dominates the majority of discussions of Black fathering.[7] It centres on the story of Stevens (Laurence Fishburne) a police offi-cer who goes undercover in order to infiltrate a South American-led drug ring. Stevens (pseudonym John Hall) is, at the beginning, teetotal and has never tried drugs. He becomes acquainted with corrupt attorney David Jason (Jeff Goldblum), masquerades as a successful crack dealer and becomes Jason's partner. After a spell of experimenta-tion with drugs and alcohol, Stevens reverts to teetotalism, finally killing Jason. He also exposes the leader of the drug cartel, an outwardly respectable South American poli-tician. His exoneration is not complete, however, as at the very end he is still in possession of $11 million of drug money, unable to decide what to do with it.

The motivating factor in Stevens' story is his father. *Deep Cover* opens with a flash-back, narrated by Fishburne, to 'Cleveland, 1972'. He tells us 'My father was a junkie', as his crazy-eyed dad turns towards his young son in the passenger seat of his car and implores him 'never to do this shit'. He then takes a revolver from the glove compart-ment and holds up a liquor store. Having witnessed his father come out with the money, the young Stevens then sees him shot in the back and die in front of him. As in *Road to Perdition* (2002), the scene in which a son sees his corrupted father killed becomes the defining moment of the son's life because in this act are compressed so many things: loss of his father, disillusionment and fear for his own life. Stevens' rejection of his father's example ostensibly establishes a sense of moral certainty. However, tensions reside in Stevens and, while an undercover cop, he discovers that right and wrong are mutable terms. Throughout his stint as a drug dealer, Stevens evokes his father, most explicitly when, after having shot a rival dealer, he has a flashback to his father's death. For the Black male, *Deep Cover* seems to be saying, the blurring of the distinction between good and bad is endemic. So, when doing the work he is supposed to do as an undercover cop, Stevens muses 'I was supposed to be making a difference. Here I was selling drugs to kids and pregnant women . . . I was good at it . . . Being a cop was never this easy.' Later, just before quitting his job and tasting his first drink, he remarks, 'I ain't nothing but a drug dealer pretending to be a cop'. The status of the voice-over in *Deep Cover* is intriguing. Here, as Stevens talks of the inversion that has made him more dealer than cop, he talks in the present, as if, bereft of fatherly influence, he must

Furious teaches Tre to fish

be his own conscience and moral guide. Elsewhere, the narrator's voice is retrospective. As with the moral ambiguity running through the film, the slipperiness of Stevens' persona (that we get to know him as he is pretending to be someone completely different) enacts the plight of the fatherless, directionless Black male. Even at the very end of the film as Stevens is preparing, it would seem, to adopt the son of the dead crack-addicted mother who lived across the hall from him, he cannot decide whether to keep or to relinquish his drug money, asking us 'What would you do?'.

Markedly unlike Stevens, Tre in *Boyz n the Hood* is fully able to distinguish good from bad, basically because he is brought up by an exemplary father, Furious Styles (Fishburne again). Diawara comments that 'to be a man is to be responsible for the Black community' (1993: 24). Furious personifies this notion of the father as protector and community provider and Singleton, who was only twenty-three when he directed *Boyz*, has said that the character is modelled on his own 'awesome' father (Singleton 1991: 13). *Boyz* tells a parabolic tale of life in South Central Los Angeles: Tre, who initially lives with his mother Reva, goes to live with Furious because, in Reva's words, 'I can't teach him to be a man'. He passes his late childhood, adolescence and early adulthood with his father, until he leaves for college. Furious is a strict, conventional father who works hard to maintain the racial integrity of his community. Tre turns out well – good at school, monogamous, drug- and crime-free, very different from his friends across the street, Ricky and Doughboy, who have been brought up by their single mother, Brenda and are both murdered in a gangland feud.

The root cause, *Boyz* suggests, for the statistic that functions as a prelude to the film (that one in twenty Black males will be murdered, most of them by other Black males) is a lack of fathering. In his fathering of Tre – and the extended community – Furious enacts the part of the traditional father of psychoanalysis by separating his son from his mother and guiding him to manhood. Inevitably, Singleton's idealisation of Furious has been criticised for its conservatism and limitations. Rinaldo Walcott argues that Singleton's vision of masculinity is emphatically patriarchal and heterosexist (1992: 71; 73). Michele Wallace, adopting a similar tone, accuses *Boyz* of engaging in 'opaque cultural analysis' and of presenting too straightforward a formula: 'The boys who don't have fathers fail. The boys who do have fathers succeed. And the success of such a movie at the box office reflects its power to confirm hegemonic family values' (1992: 125). Neatly echoing the contradictory responses to the Moynihan Report, most critics of *Boyz* view as problematic the twinning of its message that 'black men must raise black boys if they are to become healthy black men' (Dyson 1992: 19) with its vilification of Black women and mothers.

In place of one stereotype – the stud Black male of *Shaft* – *Boyz* has inserted another, that conforms just as much to White popular iconography. Ideologically, personally, sexually, Furious is an archetypal (White) Hollywood father. He is in a stable economic position, he is held in high regard by his community, he has gone beyond needing sex

(sex in *Boyz* is perennially associated with immaturity and irresponsibility) and he views fatherhood as a vocation. A role model might be Atticus Finch. There is one scene in which Furious's coalescence with the archetypal Hollywood father image is at its most overt – when, not long after he has come to live with him, he takes Tre fishing. The juxtaposition of sport and a significant man-to-man chat is a generic father–son bonding moment. Here, the exchange, coming just prior to a '7 Years Later' gap in the narrative during which time Tre effectively grows up, marks the beginning of Tre's departure from boyhood (actually, between the fishing scene and the '7 Years Later' intertitle there is a brief sequence in which Doughboy is arrested – what happens, *Boyz* is telling us, if there is no dutiful father around). Furious begins by asking Tre 'Are you a leader or a follower?' He then tells Tre about sex and how he came to be a father at seventeen, making sure that Tre understands the difference between sex and fathering when he says: 'Any fool with a dick can make a baby, but only a real man can raise his children'. The way Furious talks about his own immaturity when he became a father indicates that such knowledge is learnt, not innate, adding further weight to the need for sons to be taught, as Furious is teaching Tre, to become 'real men'. That we are not supposed to doubt Furious as a role model is signalled by the sequence's closing moments: father and son on the waterfront, the camera looking up at Furious and the whole scene imbued with a soft, golden light: a vision of real manliness.

The next time we see Tre (now played by Cuba Gooding Jr) is at a party to welcome Doughboy home from prison. He is about to sit his college exams and, unlike Doughboy, he has become respectable and dutiful. When discussing *Boyz*, Paula Massood, one of the few critics to highlight the contradictions of Furious's fatherly instruction of Tre, comments that Furious's 'influence over Tre is tenuous' (2003: 161). Whereas Furious the separatist has chosen to remain in and help his own community, he has, ironically, given Tre the tools to escape the same. As Massood concludes:

> Thus, while *Boyz* explores the limits placed on residents of the hood, its solutions actually replicate the problems that first contributed to the conditions under investigation – the demonization of the black mother and the flight of the black middle classes from the inner city (2003: 161).

But Tre and Furious are, the film would like us to believe, different. Reva may have used her education to escape in this way (the last time she appears, she meets Furious in a swanky [White] restaurant), but Furious has instilled in his son different values, namely belief (albeit dubious) in the importance of the Black patriarch.

The essential problem of what the good African-American father's role should be is exemplified by Spike Lee's *Jungle Fever*, in which there are various, quite different fathers (a feature that in fact sets it apart from the more youth-orientated new Black films). At its core is Flipper Purify (Wesley Snipes), a young, professional father, much as one imagines Tre will become. Around Flipper, there are three older-generation fathers, his own (the Good Reverend Doctor Purify, a lay Baptist preacher) and two unreconstructed, macho Italian-American fathers – the dad of Angie Tucci (Annabella Sciorra), the temp with whom Flipper has an affair, and the marginally less tyrannical but equally controlling father of Paulie (John Turturro), Angie's sweet but goofy fiancé. *Jungle Fever* uses these older fathers to represent what, for differing reasons, Flipper does not want to become. All three older fathers are, in their own ways, brutal role models. The Reverend Doctor uses his religiousness to mask an unforgiving censoriousness, while the two Italian-American fathers simply attack their children if they disobey orders, Spike Lee's attitude to Italian-Americans, both here and in *Do the Right Thing* (1989), bordering on racism. Angie's father, a loud-mouthed slob flanked by two Neanderthal sons, beats Angie with a belt when he learns of her affair with Flipper (ashamed of being the 'father of a nigger-lover') while Paulie's father Lou (Anthony Quinn) forces his way into the bathroom in which Paulie, having been left by Angie, is crying – not to comfort him but to slap him around the head for snivelling over 'a bit of skirt'.

Older-generation fathers in *Jungle Fever* – Black or White – are the signifiers for traditionalist intolerance, commonly manifested as racial hatred. Both the Reverend Doctor and Paulie's father are openly racist when it comes to their sons' choices of partner. The Reverend Doctor invites Flipper and Angie for dinner simply to admonish them; he delivers a mini sermon and then departs from the table with the line: 'Excuse me, I don't eat with whoremongers'. Lou tells Paulie 'I'll put your balls right through your throat' as his son prepares for a date with a Black woman. This is the generation of fathers to whom Flipper is compared. Flipper has not sold out; like Furious, he still lives in a Black neighbourhood (Harlem), although he lives in one of its few gentrified streets and personifies the successful Black male around whom liberal Whites feel comfortable. Flipper is compromised by this duality; he is restoring faith in African-American fatherhood and making amends for what Michele Wallace (1992) calls the Reverend Doctor's 'criminally bad fathering' (126) (the Reverend Doctor eventually kills his other son Gator, a crack addict he cannot control). Flipper is also, though, the male character who has most obviously consumed the values of the White community.

Flipper is a crucially mixed and flawed father. He does his share of childcare, and it is he and not his wife who regularly accompanies their daughter Ming to school; he is a successful and ambitious architect in an otherwise White firm; he lives the life of a 1990s, *New York Times*-reading yuppie and, in his garishly coloured suits, looks like one too. The problem with *Jungle Fever* remains that the good (or at least better) young Black father remains not only traditional in his gender outlook but embedded within specifically Black phallocentrism. bell hooks surmises that 'Perhaps black folks cling to the fantasy that phallocentrism and patriarchy will provide a way out of the havoc and wreckage wreaked by racist genocidal assault', but counters this with the thought that 'This way of thinking means that black people do not have to envision creative strategies for confronting and resisting white supremacy and internalised racism' (1992: 101–2). This is the issue that hovers over these portrayals of the Black father: that subscription to the hegemonic patriarchal norm is the only way out of the cycle of drugs, violence and death that otherwise awaits the contemporary Black male.

Fathers and Romance

A different problematisation of the traditional father takes place in numerous and diverse romantic comedies. The notion of the father as romantic hero is not new, especially the widowed or surrogate father (*Gentleman's Agreement*, *The Search*, *The Courtship of Eddie's Father*). What has changed is the way in which new romances such as *Sleepless in Seattle*, *The American President* (1994) and *One Fine Day* configure desire and romanticise the father himself. Conversely, representing the increased acceptance of non-conformist familial arrangements, two recent romantic comedies have appeared in which gay men take on the role of father to the children of their best friends: *The Object of My Affection* (1996) and John Schlesinger's last film *The Next Best Thing* (2000). Alongside these there are other interpretations of the fatherly romance, the most interesting being 'epiphany movies' such as *Regarding Henry*, *What Women Want* (2001) and *The Family Man* (2000) in which a symbolic brush with death or a freak accident persuades hitherto awful men to become good fathers. There has also been the revival of the quasi-homoerotic father–son romance with Clint Eastwood's *A Perfect World* and several other instances where bonding with a child (invariably within this homosocial context a boy) proves the catalyst to a male character's romantic success with a woman, as happens, in very different circumstances, in both *Jerry Maguire* (1996) and *Big Daddy* (1999).

As has been perennially the case, positive portrayals of fatherhood conventionally deeroticise the father, which is why here the father is most frequently the object of affection as opposed to straightforward desire – not that sex does not feature, but it is subsumed into other more important emotions or events. The romantic finales of these films reiterate the value of parenting over the allure of sex. In *One Fine Day*, after a day of flirting and sparring with each other, divorced father George Clooney comes to visit divorced mother Michelle Pfeiffer; after a short kiss, she retires to the bathroom to freshen up 'so I feel a little more like a woman and not a dead mommy', but when (after a prolonged toilette sequence) she returns, Clooney is asleep on the sofa, so she joins him. The child plays a crucial part in this equivocal romantic/erotic framework as the father's gentle phallus, an essential mediator between the father's power within the patriarchal paradigm and the necessary repression, for romantic purposes, of such symbolic potency. The child can function as the mechanism through which the father recuperates his lost power, as occurs at the end of *The River Wild*, but in the romantic comedies the child serves the dual purpose of affirming the father's capacity for romance.

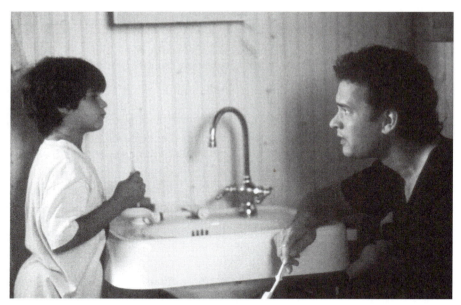

Jonah asks Sam if he would have sex with his new wife

Sleepless in Seattle exemplifies the classical generic imperatives of Hollywood romantic comedies as reconfigured in the 1990s. Sam Baldwin (Tom Hanks) is a widower with an eight-year-old son Jonah. Eighteen months after his mother's death, Jonah calls a radio phone-in, confiding in 'Dr Marsha' that his father 'needs a new wife'. Annie (Meg Ryan) is listening and, despite being newly engaged, instantly falls in love with Sam. Of the 2,000 letters Sam receives after the show, Jonah picks out Annie's and finally engineers a meeting between them, which is how the film concludes. *Sleepless in Seattle* is self-consciously old-fashioned; it repeatedly cites *An Affair to Remember*, the 1957 Leo McCary melodrama and its soundtrack comprises nostalgic songs that promote a traditional ideological message ('As Time goes by', 'Somewhere over the Rainbow', 'Stand by Your Man').[8] Its central premise – that a son actively tries to find his father a new wife – is that of *The Courtship of Eddie's Father*, and there are other similarities between Sam and Minnelli's Tom Corbett, such as Sam's reluctance to talk to Jonah about the emotive issue of his mother's death. Although the woman Sam is currently working for (he is an architect) says gushingly, having heard him on the radio, 'It's so nice when a man can express his feelings', the dynamics of the phone-in scene – Sam and Jonah talking on different telephones through an interlocutor – send out contradictory signals.

The most sustained expression of *Sleepless in Seattle*'s old-fashionedness is its obsessive reaffirmation of sexual difference (in her DVD 'Director's Commentary', Ephron says that 'One of the things this movie is about is that difference between men and women'). *An Affair to Remember* is repeatedly evoked not just as a romantic prototype but as a 'chick's movie', and by association, *Sleepless* encodes itself as a 'chick's movie', a gender attachment further emphasised by the handling of the radio phone-in. Sam's long eulogy to his wife Maggie is genuinely moving and it moves every female who hears it: Annie, the waitresses in the roadside café where she breaks her journey, Sam's client and her mother, the 2,000 women who write to Sam and the few who get a chance to call the show direct and ask for his address.

Although, as Annie's best friend Becky warns, Sam could be 'really sick' and although, as Sam tells Jonah as he is trying to get his dad to meet Annie,

> There's no way we're going on a plane to meet a woman who could be some crazy sick lunatic. Didn't you see *Fatal Attraction*? . . . It scared the shit out of me, it scared the shit out of every man in America.

Sleepless utilises its traditionalism to suppress any potential perversity. An essential component of this struggle is the absurdity of Sam's anachronistic innocence about dating matters. As he tells his colleague and friend (played by Rob Reiner), the last time he was 'out there' was at the time of Jimmy Carter, in 1978 (just the mention of Carter, the famously chaste President who nevertheless admitted to having 'lusted in his heart', conjures an image of chastity). In the same conversation he reveals that he would not feel comfortable about letting a woman pay for dinner and seems alarmed at the prospect of women doing the asking out. Conformist gender politics pervade other contemporaneous heterosexual romantic comedies. In *The American President*, as similarly widowed father President Andrew Shepherd (Michael Douglas) has trouble ordering flowers for Sydney Wade (Annette Bening) or inviting her on a date, he mutters 'it used to be easier'. The hyper-traditional father of romantic comedy is there to affirm the regressive basis for even contemporary heterosexual romance. The situations he finds himself in are modern and potentially threatening (Annie, who effectively stalks Sam, is not so far removed from Alex in *Fatal Attraction*) although they are sanitised and romanticised by the father's residual old-fashionedness. As Rob Reiner advises Sam before he asks a woman out on a date: 'Think Cary Grant'.

From the multiple contrivances of *Sleepless in Seattle*, one is led to infer what a strain it is to impersonate such an image of masculinity. The strain of becoming a good father is even more strenuously evoked in the 'epiphany romances', as the protagonists of *Regarding Henry* or *What Women Want* have to be nearly killed in order to metamorphose into worthwhile, nurturing dads. In *Regarding Henry*, Henry Turner (Harrison Ford) is shot in the head by a man robbing his local liquor store and loses his ability to speak, read or even to recognise his family. Such a tabula rasa approach to unwanted masculinity is most convenient, and as one critic remarked, Henry, once he has undergone his transformation, is 'never held accountable' for his previous life (Fuqua 1996: 30). Nick Marshall (Mel Gibson) in *What Women Want* is likewise transformed from misogynist into sensitive new man when he electrocutes himself in the bathroom while experimenting, for a new ad campaign, with women's beauty products. After their road to Damascus accidents, both Henry and Nick become better lovers and vastly improved fathers. If only making a man into a good father were this simple.

Regarding Henry is the story of Henry's rehabilitation. On the surface this entails learning how to speak, read and walk again, but underneath it means rehabilitating himself into fatherhood. Before getting shot in the head, we see Henry being a father only briefly as he goes into his daughter Rachel's bedroom specifically to reprimand, to lay down the law. To the old Henry, fathering is a peripheral concern; he is unkind, distant and, as the family's maid later reminds him, always too busy to sit and have breakfast with his family. After the accident, Henry regressed to infancy; his rehabilitation is then gauged by how successfully he can 'grow up' and become a different man, and the reconstruction of his relationship with Rachel becomes central to this. It is Rachel who teaches Henry to read and with whom he bakes cookies; it is for Rachel that Henry buys a puppy (she had previously not been allowed to have a pet) and it is to preserve this newfound father–daughter bond that Henry takes Rachel out of boarding school at the end of the film. After having told his wife Sarah, 'I want us to be a family', Henry justifies his actions to Rachel's headmistress thus: 'I missed her first eleven years, I don't want to miss any more'. With the discovery of his fatherly instincts, Henry heals both himself and his family; but like the wound to the head, the slavish simplicity of this conclusion barely masks the problems it so optimistically seeks to repress: Henry has become an admirable father by chance.

The role of chance in *Regarding Henry* or the hysterical reflexivity of *Sleepless in Seattle* cause anxiety and convey the residual implausibility of the films' idealised images of fatherhood. Anxieties are also repressed in *A Perfect World*, but here, the source of romance is the surrogate father, Butch Haynes (Kevin Costner), a boy's attachment to whom threatens both traditional fatherhood and family relations. Haynes is both an escaped convict and a gentle father figure to the little boy Philip, whom he kidnaps while on the run. Philip's father has left home and his mother is a strict Jehovah's Witness, so Haynes functions as the fun parent he has not had – he takes him 'trick or treating' and lets him ride on the roof of his stolen car. *A Perfect World* recalls earlier films such as *The Search* (discussed in Chapter 1) and the 1950s' British film *Hunted*, whose story it very closely resembles; like *The Search* and *Hunted* (the former starring Montgomery Clift as the surrogate father, the latter Dirk Bogarde), *A Perfect World* establishes a father–son romance that puts on trial 'the audience's anxieties about close relations between men and boys' (Simpson 1994), an anxiety generated by the indirect sexualisation of the father–son romance, as the earlier casting of Clift and Bogarde accentuated. Haynes' name 'Butch' affirms his heterosexuality, but certain factors exist to make his relationship with Philip ambiguous, most significantly the love that Philip manifestly feels for Haynes and which recalls the homosocial bond between 'Jim' and

Steve in *The Search* or Robbie and Chris (Bogarde) in *Hunted*. The child's love for the surrogate father both threatens the stability of the son's relationship with his family and initiates him into the adult world of love and attraction. As in *Dead Poets Society*, this dual threat to the family and to heterosexuality must be suppressed. In several of these surrogate father films, the sons are unhappy at home (the most extreme example is *Hunted*, in which Robbie witnesses Chris commit a murder while on the run from an adoptive father who beats him). The surrogate fathers offer them temporary happiness before the boys are returned to their less than perfect homes.

The necessary generic curtailment of the father–son romance stems from the need to repress the threat it poses to heterosexual stability. In *The Bronx Tale* (1993), for example, in which the rivalry between Calogero's father and his surrogate father figure, Mafia boss Sonny, is manifestly asexual, the surrogate – once dead – can even be eulogised by the father. In *A Perfect World*, there is one scene that explicitly confirms the reasons for Haynes having to be exorcised at the end. While driving, Haynes tells Philip to change out of his grimy clothes into the Casper the Friendly Ghost costume he has just stolen, but Philip is too embarrassed to undress in front of him. Haynes asks 'Are you embarrassed because I might see your pecker?' and Philip replies 'It's puny'. Haynes guesses that it was the other convict (whom he has since shot) who told Philip this and, as the good father figure, sets out to repair the damage inflicted by this comment. Haynes says, 'Let me see' and, while still driving leans over and looks down at Philip's groin, remarking 'Hell no, Philip. Good size for a boy your age'. Pride sweeps over Philip's face. It is frequently the role of the surrogate father in films to instruct a boy in the ways of the world, and as Peter Lehman argues about this scene, Haynes 'fulfils both literal and symbolic functions of the absent father' by making Philip feel good about his penis (Lehman 1998: 132). In this sense, this formative scene is not entirely different from the lessons in streetwise-ness offered by the surrogate fathers in either *The Bronx Tale* or *Big Daddy*, for instance. However, the formation of male subjectivity around the penis is problematic because it fails to mount an argument against the centrality of the penis to cultural iconography. The equation of masculinity with sexuality both here and in Haynes' later attempt to get laid with a waitress, mark him out – as much as his violence does – as an unsuitable father. As at the end of *The Search*, the capitulation to heterosexual conformity is necessitated for a number of reasons.

The illicit combination of needing to be nurtured and desiring the nurturer is crystallised but also sanitised in two films in which the father is gay, *The Object of My Affection* and *The Next Best Thing*, both of which provide a satisfactory (and asexual) solution to the anxieties derived from such a combination. In both films a woman's gay best friend agrees to help her bring up her child; while in *The Object of My Affection* the gay friend George (Paul Rudd) knows he is not the baby's biological father, in *The Next Best Thing*, Robert (Rupert Everett) thinks that he is, until an acrimonious custody battle with his son Sam's mother, Abby (Madonna), instead reveals that her ex-boyfriend

Kevin is. The gay father is the ideal solution to the conundrum of the romantic father: he offers the possibility of a child without the sex. Writing about the emergence of the gay best friend in Hollywood, Baz Dreisinger draws a parallel between the 'safe eroticism' displayed in films such as *My Best Friend's Wedding* (1997) (Rupert Everett again as Julia Roberts' gay best friend) and 1990s' self-help books which stress the idea that, for women, non-sexual communication is as important as sexual rapport (2000). The incarnation of this ideal is the gay father. The gay father is also the logical symbolic conclusion to this book's continued discussion of fathering and sexuality, that because the notion of the sexual father has proved so problematic to Hollywood, the father's eroticism has had to be repressed – or, as is possible with the gay father, displaced onto another object of desire beyond the family unit. It is this displacement that allows, for instance, Robert to prove the more attentive, traditionally maternal parent in *The Next Best Thing*. It is also this displacement that opens up the possibility of the gay father as a better romantic alternative to the straight one. Steve Neale identifies as one of the archetypal figures of new romantic comedy 'the wrong partner', a man – like Annie's fiancé in *Sleepless in Seattle* – who the heroine is on the verge of marrying before the unexpected arrival of the right man, whom she subsequently falls for (Neale 1992: 290).[9] In both *The Object of My Affection* and *The Next Best Thing*, an inversion takes place as the gay friend proves the 'right partner' while the 'wrong partner' is the child's biological father, an inversion that manifestly suggests that romantic perfection should be disentangled from sex.

Although George in *The Object of My Affection* and Robert in *The Next Best Thing* are not gay fathers from within an exclusively gay relationship (this scenario in Hollywood is reserved for a broader comedy such as *The Birdcage*), their domestic presence challenges the equilibrium of the traditional family structure. British psychoanalyst Sebastian Kraemer has observed that (in Rosalind Coward's words) 'he has never met a child from a single-parent family who did not wish he or she was part of an ordinary two-parent family' (Coward 1999: 158). The use of the word 'ordinary' here betrays a narrowly heterosexist vision of parenting that, one can reasonably securely surmise, does not encompass gay dads and their best friends. What is pleasing about the two – albeit intensely flawed – gay romantic comedies is their heterodoxy, that they endeavour to find a romantic alternative to the traditional heterosexuality of the nuclear family. Coontz goes against much orthodox thinking on the family that still endorses the nuclear family when she argues that 'holding onto tradition sets families back ... not because we've changed too much but because we haven't changed enough' (1997: 109). In her anti-nostalgia Coontz goes on to suggest that the traditional nuclear family system 'no longer meets the needs of today's families. Now, as then, clinging to old values and behaviors merely prolongs the period of transition and stress, preventing us from making needed adjustments in our lives and institutions' (1997: 114–15). Within the pluralisation and greater democratisation of familial relationships, the gay father presents an alternative, radical model that both exemplifies the now widespread belief that 'men have the same capacity for nurturing as women' (Silverstein 1996: 20) and mounts an offensive against such a nurturer being the traditional heterosexual father.

The Object of My Affection and The Next Best Thing posit alternative views of the gay father. In the first, sexuality complicates and ultimately destroys the potential domestic bliss of George's relationship with Nina (Jennifer Aniston), to the extent that one critic has argued that the The Object of My Affection comes close to reinforcing the 'traditional homophobic view' that gay parents are too 'unstable and hedonistic' to be effective parents (Keller 2002: 161–2). The Next Best Thing is more schematic and scheming in its support of Robert's rights as a parent, to the extent that, after Abby becomes engaged to another man and decides she wants custody of Sam (to give him an 'ordinary' family), the Black female judge speaks eloquently against the laws that prevent her from granting joint custody to Robert. In the end, Abby relents, allowing Sam time with Robert and admitting, when dropping Sam off, that she misses their past relationship. Amy Aronson and Michael Kimmel argue that it is gay men like George and Robert who have combined the old Hollywood feminine role of changing a bad man into a good man through love and the contemporary role of persuading women to 'realize the errors of their ways and to come back to the home' (2001: 47). They also note that these gay men do not have sex, so being gay has come to signal domesticity, commitment, an ability to talk to women and help them through crises and sexual abstinence. This abstinence is crucial to the films' promotion of their gay fathers as perfect parents.

What the union between a mother and a gay father specifically offers is a domestic 'third term'. Marjorie Garber uses the 'third term' to demarcate the critical domain of the cross-dresser, who, she argues, exists outside traditional gender boundaries and who should not be subsumed into either (1993: 10–17). The gay man, in forming a trio with a close female friend and a child, creates just such a 'third term', one that likewise should not be subsumed into and understood as being either heterosexual marriage or a gay relationship. At the end of The Next Best Thing, Robert confesses to Abby 'I miss us', suggesting that what he misses is just this 'third term' – the ambiguous, not-quite-sexual relationship he shared with Abby while they lived together bringing up Sam. Sexual desire complicates the 'third term'. Aronson and Kimmel offer an over-simplified analysis of The Object of My Affection when commenting that Nina realises that what she needs 'is a husband and father for her child – someone with whom she won't have sex!' (2001: 48). In fact, Nina does want sex with George and gets increasingly miserable as her feelings are not reciprocated. More essential to these 'third term' movies than simple sexual abstinence is the sublimation of sexual desire, the replacement of it by an ambiguous relationship between the romantic protagonists, an almost sexual rapport that is then echoed by the 'third term's' unconventional parental set-up, a domestic situation that mimics a heterosexual marriage but remains distinct from it. In both The

Molly is accompanied home by the most important members of her extended family –
mother Nina and nearly surrogate father George, her gay drama teacher

Object of My Affection and *The Next Best Thing*, there is a scene in which the mutual
attraction of the 'third term' couple comes out. In the former it is when Nina and George
are on her bed (a recurrent location for their almost sexual chats) and start to embark
on sex, only for George's ex to phone and interrupt them. In *The Next Best Thing*, it is
when Robert and Abby get drunk and wake up to find they have slept together. *The
Birdcage* contains another version when the gay father Armand meets up with the
estranged mother of the son he has raised with his boyfriend Albert. She starts to unbut-
ton his shirt, only to be interrupted.

Important to how the 'safe eroticism' of these films is played out is the fact that the
women initiate sexual contact; the gay men's desire is channelled into fatherhood. In
both *The Object of My Affection* and *The Next Best Thing*, there is a scene in which the
gay man, having been approached by their best friend to become the father of her
unborn child, chances upon an idyllic (heterosexual) father–son scene that persuades
him to agree. George in *The Object of My Affection* walks past a father teaching his son
how to pitch in baseball and is so entranced by this masculine ritual that when he returns
home he accepts Nina's offer, cooing 'I could be the guy who says "Goodnight"'. In
The Next Best Thing, Robert's conversion happens at the airport as he is waiting for his
parents and glances over at all the men with kids in the passenger lounge. Despite such
idyllic beginnings, things do not work out for the 'third term' trios as sex gets in the
way, but the unconventional family remains their shared romantic ideal. Robert is re-
introduced into Sam's life at the end of *The Next Best Thing*, while Nina's daughter
Molly, at the end of *The Object of My Affection*, has a utopian extended family who, in
the concluding scene, all attend her school play (directed by George): Nina, her new

partner, Louis (a Black policeman), her sister, brother-in-law and niece, a gay friend and George's new partner, Paul. Molly merrily lists all her 'friends' to George as he carries her home and this romanticisation of the alternative family offers the final affirmation of the romantic value of the 'third term' partnership.

Fathers in Comedies

This endorsement of unconventionality in the father and the fragmentation of the traditional paternal role model are characteristics that persist into broader Hollywood comedies of the 90s. With the exception of Charles Shyer's 1991 remake of *Father of the Bride* and its sequel, the father-centred comedies of the 1990s have championed the alternative pluralist vision of parenthood portrayed in the gay romances. *Father of the Bride* represents the traditional father image, although with problematic results, as the obsessive paternalistic attention George Banks (Steve Martin) pays to his daughter Annie's imminent nuptials and the jealousy he displays towards her fiancé Brian border on the incestuous. The hyper-conformity of Annie's elaborate white wedding (as with Minnelli's original, the film comprises little else but the preparations for it) has trouble masking the connotations of Annie telling George that she fell for Brian because 'he's like you, dad', or the equally uncomfortable insinuations of George's flustered reminder to the engaged couple as they go out for the evening to 'fasten your condoms'. She is looking for a version of her father and he automatically links his daughter to sex. In this context (in the sequel, *Father of the Bride 2* [1995], both Annie and George's wife Nina become pregnant), George's desperate search for Annie after the wedding to give her a farewell kiss acquires lurid connotations.

Other 1990s' comedies invert the expectations of traditional father films such as *Backdraft*, voicing a preference for the unconventional father. In films such as *Mrs Doubtfire* (1993), *Father's Day* (1997) *The Birdcage* (all starring Robin Williams as a father) or *Big Daddy*, the unconventional father model consistently fares better than his more ordinary counterpart, and the straight (heterosexual, conventional) man/father becomes the butt of gags and the object of ridicule. In *Father's Day*, Scott's father Bob has to exchange his regulation Chinos and sweater for grubby overalls when a lorry backs into the chemical lavatory he is using and sends it tumbling down a hill; in *Mrs Doubtfire*, divorced father Daniel Hillard, while disguised as his family's nanny, wastes no opportunity to crack small penis jokes at the expense of his ex-wife's new beau Stuart (played to good parodic effect by Pierce Brosnan); in *The Birdcage*, the only way that ultra conservative politician Kevin Keeley (Gene Hackman) can escape the marauding hoards of journalists lying in wait for him at Armand's drag club is to dress in drag himself.

Although these father comedies positively endorse alternative models of fatherhood, their alternativeness is symbiotically bonded to the traditional models they profess to have refuted. *Big Daddy* is exemplary in this respect. Adam Sandler plays Sonny, a 'loser' (his girlfriend leaves him, he is without a job, even his Dad tells him he is inept) who by chance becomes the foster father to his absent flatmate's son, Julian. In a manner reminiscent of Jerry Lewis in 1950s' comedies such as *Rock-a-Bye Baby*, Sandler's parenting is based on incompetence and 'bad' fathering: he allows Julian to watch inappropriate television and eat junk food, he teaches him to urinate in the street and to trip skateboarders up in Central Park. But, by the time he is fighting a custody battle for Julian everyone, including his own previously sceptical father, vouch for him as a good parent; the incompetent, zany father has been utterly recuperated. In an ending that again echoes *Rock-a-Bye Baby*, the court awards custody of Julian to his natural father Kevin (who in the postscript is also shown to be a reformed man) while Sonny finds true love and is rewarded for his previous good parenting with a baby of his own.

The interrelationship between unconventionality and competence is complicated in *Mrs Doubtfire* and *The Birdcage*, as the unconventional fathers are also the most competent. *The Birdcage* (a remake of the French comedy *La Cage aux Folles* [1978]) revolves around the engagement of Val Goldman, son of Armand (Robin Williams) and his drag queen partner Albert, and Barbara Keeley, the daughter of a parodically conservative senator and co-founder of the 'Coalition for Moral Order'. Val asks Armand and Albert to disguise the fact that they are gay for the duration of the imminent visit by Keeley and his family. Their flat is overhauled to look 'straight', Armand tracks down Val's mother so that they can pretend to be a 'normal' family for the evening, and Albert is taught not to act so camp. Inevitably these plans backfire: Armand rebels against his son's fascism and asks the temperamental Albert to stay, Albert dresses up as Mrs Goldman (although in another nod to fascism, Val has also requested that his family pretend they are not Jewish so they change their name to 'Coldman') and Val's mother arrives anyway, half way through the evening. In addition to all this, Senator Keeley is involved in a scandal of his own, hoping that the marriage of his daughter will deflect attention from the recent death of his Coalition partner while in bed with a Black under-age prostitute.

The tensions in the film are exemplified by the differences between the two fathers. Keeley's blinkered conservatism makes him incapable of discerning the multiple dissemblances being practised upon him, failing to comprehend that South Beach is a gay resort, just as he fails to notice that Mrs Goldman is a middle-aged man in drag – indeed, he takes a particular liking to Mrs Goldman, believing her to be a fine, old-fashioned, small-town girl of traditional morals. When, finally, the masks slip as Val's mother arrives and Keeley asks 'How many mothers does your Val have?', Val claims Albert as his mother and takes his wig off for him. It is left to Mrs Keeley to explain what is going on.

That it is so hard to impersonate the straight father – and that this impersonation and the straight father are represented so negatively – is illustrated by Armand, who demonstrates that the 'natural' fathering model in *The Birdcage* is the gay one. When he first arrives home to tell his father about his engagement, Val assures Armand that he has been 'an incredible role model', adding that he is 'the only guy in my fraternity who doesn't come from a broken home'. *The Birdcage* repeatedly reaffirms Armand's value as a father, often as a means of validating homosexuality itself and of confirming Armand's naturalness over the falsity of the heterosexual characters. When Val bitchily runs his finger down his father's cheek to reveal how much foundation he is wearing and tells Armand to make himself a 'little less obvious', Armand replies 'at least I know who I am'. In this and other comedies such surety is seldom afforded the straight fathers. There is an archetypal Robin Williams sequence in *Father's Day* when his character Dale, having been told (fraudulently, as it transpires) that he is the biological father of a teenage son he did not know existed, performs quick cameos of assorted Dads he might or might not like to resemble, from new age to straight to excessively camp. Fatherhood – or at least 'ordinary', heterosexual fatherhood – is, these comedies suggest, performative.

As it was at the end of *The Object of My Affection*, a utopian vision of the alternative family is glimpsed at the end of *The Birdcage* as Senator Keeley, his wife and daughter are compelled to join in as the whole drag club sings 'We Are Family'. The alternative family model is also endorsed by *Mrs Doubtfire*, in which Williams plays another unconventional father, a distraught divorcé who disguises himself as a British nanny, Euphiginia Doubtfire, in order to be able to see more of his children. *Mrs Doubtfire* offers a heartfelt defence of fatherhood. When in court for his second custody hearing (following the revelation that he is Mrs Doubtfire), Daniel's justification for his cross-dressing is his addiction to his children: 'I can't live without air, and I can't live without them'. The judge remains unmoved and decides that this is simply another good performance, granting custody again to his ex-wife. Mrs Doubtfire has been, on a literal level, a performance, but through his impersonation of a nanny, Daniel became a better, less chaotic father. He learnt to cook (cooking often functioning as a gauge of a Hollywood father's success), his children started to do better at school and, through becoming her confidante, he and his ex-wife Miranda reach a point of rapprochement.

A parallel with the gay father films is that here, once again, the repression of traditional masculinity/heterosexuality improves the father, so that even when Daniel's two eldest children discover that under the prosthetics and pearls lurks Dad, they want to maintain the masquerade. The moment of revelation could be traumatic, as Daniel's son Chris comes into the bathroom to find Mrs Doubtfire urinating standing up. He runs to his older sister Lydia who is about to call 911 until Daniel lowers his voice and his children recognise him. While Lydia is happy to hug 'Dad', Chris keeps his distance (as Daniel understands, 'it's a guy thing'). This potentially transgressive exchange functions, though, as a stabilising moment when father and children are reunited, again reflecting the instability of 'ordinary' fatherhood. The end of *Mrs Doubtfire* substantiates this as Miranda admits that everyone was happier when 'Mrs Doubtfire' was around. Good fatherhood is so difficult to attain that desperate measures, such as inventing a strange Scottish nanny, are needed to preserve it. Daniel – this time as himself – is once more hired to look after his children after school. He has not, though, abandoned Mrs Doubt-

conducted by the present Sheriff, Sam Deeds (Chris Cooper), who, in turn, is the son of the much loved and mourned Sheriff Buddy Deeds (Matthew McConaughey). The search for evidence about Wade's death leads Sam to his own father, whose deification by the Texan town in which he lives (at one point Sam has to unveil a statue of Buddy – his arm around his son) comes in the way of a tranquil father–son relationship. Sam discovers that Buddy helped cover up Wade's murder and make the body disappear, and that the whole town colluded in the repression of this knowledge. The search for this truth then leads Sam to the even more suppressed truth that Buddy had an affair with Mercedes, mother of Pilar, Sam's childhood sweetheart and the woman with whom he is now in love. So literal and figurative searches in *Lone Star* coalesce, etching out another of the borderlines that preoccupy the film.[10] Sam's crossing of the borderlines between truth and fiction about his father and between permitted and illicit sex make *Lone Star* remarkable, for the discovery of evidence that besmirches the memory of Buddy Deeds – and is considered by all townsfolk to be a brutal violation – is the lesser transgression that then enables Sam to accept and decide to continue his own incestuous relationship with Pilar. In electing to continue their incestuous relationship (Pilar can no longer have children, so there will be no offspring), Buddy's two children expunge the memory of their hitherto idealised father.

In Paul Thomas Anderson's *Magnolia* the structuring of the narrative itself becomes the metaphor for the tortuous searches which, this time, the fathers undertake in their attempts to be reunited with their estranged children before their deaths. *Magnolia* (like *Happiness*) evolves via a kaleidoscopic, non-linear series of intertwined stories in which all the father–children relationships are linked to a kids' television quiz show. The two principal fathers are television executive Earl Partridge (Jason Robards) and quiz show host Jimmy Gator (Philip Baker Hall), whose show *What Do Kids Know?* is produced by Earl's company. Both fathers are dying of cancer (a secondary metaphor for the destructiveness of the father's reluctance to relinquish the phallus) and both want resolution with their children before they die, Earl because he feels guilt at having abandoned his first wife and son Frank T. J. Mackey (Tom Cruise), thereby leaving Frank to look after his mother as she died of cancer, and Jimmy because he thinks he may have sexually abused his daughter Claudia (Melora Walters). The third father is the pushy dad of *What Do Kids Know?* prodigy Stanley. The very fragmentariness of *Magnolia*'s narrative – and that the tentacles of each narrative thread reach back to problems with the father – emphasises the father's omniscience and his extended symbolic presence, although the searches remain incomplete and closure is not secured as it was, in such a bold way, in *Lone Star*.

Affliction, directed and written by Paul Schrader, can be twinned with *Lone Star*, containing as it does a similarly tortured father–son relationship (although a far more violent and obsessive one) that the son seeks unconsciously to resolve through embarking upon a tangential criminal investigation. In *Affliction*, the father Glen Whitehouse (James

Coburn) is still alive, loathed by his son Wade (Nick Nolte) and abandoned by his other children Rolfe (Willem Dafoe) and Lina. Wade is the police officer in a small New Hampshire town, a divorced father whose daughter Jill is frightened of him but who fantasises about mounting a custody battle to win her back from her mother. Wade fantasises too that his friend and colleague Jack will be found guilty of the murder of Twombley, a rich businessman killed while hunting deer. Here, the search for evidence comes to represent Wade's worsening relationship with his family and his encroaching derangement. Throughout, there are flashbacks to Glen's brutality towards his sons and wife. This is a family whose interactions with each other are founded on violence. Wade is abandoned, in the end, by everyone; he drives away Jill and his girlfriend Margie (Sissy Spacek) and loses his job. He lives with Glen and father and son fight for the last time. Their cycle of beatings and taunts comes to an end as Wade kills his father and sets fire to his body, then killing Jack and leaving town, never to be heard of again. As the more measured Rolfe explains in his concluding voice-over:

Our stories – Wade's and mine – describe the lives of boys and men for thousands of years. Boys who were beaten up by their fathers, whose capacity for love was crippled almost at birth, men whose best hope for connection with other human beings lay in detachment, as if life were over. It's how we keep, in turn, from destroying our own children and terrorising the women who have the misfortune to love us, how we absent us from the tradition of male violence, how we decline the seduction of revenge.

Schrader comments that men like Wade 'have this kind of bad blood, the kind of male violence, bred in the bone, passed down from father to son' (Quart 1998: 13).

Affliction offers a deeply pessimistic vision of a father's brutalising effect on his sons. It is one of many films in which the father's negative influence is bifurcated – between the son who stays nearby and, though against his will, becomes like the father and the son who escapes identification with the father by going far away, thus physically and psychologically detaching himself. The coldness of Rolfe's voice-over as he tells his family's history and charts Wade's decline, is symptomatic of this distance. Rolfe's detachment affords him an awareness Wade lacks; whereas Rolfe says of Wade's story that everyone knows the facts, but 'facts do not make history', Wade cannot see beyond the 'facts', he can never stand back and understand how parabolic, how stereotypical and avoidable his downfall is. Wade's literalness is exemplified by his (symbolic) toothache. As he gets consumed by his hatred for Glen, his obsession with winning Jill back and the death of Twombley, he fails to get a tooth that is troubling him fixed. Finally, he takes a swig of Glen's liquor and pulls it himself with a pair of pliers. His personal, emotional degeneration has been matched by physical discomfort, and after this abrupt, horrific scene, an expression of clarity and relief overwhelms Wade's face as if now he knows what to do. In fact, what happens is that Wade hurtles even more quickly to the fatal showdown with Glen. This is clarity of sorts, but Rolfe's voice-over just after the tooth-pulling is significant: he remarks that Wade 'lived on the edge of his emotions' and that he had 'no perspective to retreat to, even in a crisis'. Wade is too like Glen and too little protected by him. Because he cannot recognise this but can only feel the alleviation of his physical pain, the cycle of violence is not terminated. This lack of closure, echoed by the doubts over what happens to Wade at the end, suggests that this male cycle is continual and the son's severance from the bad father incomplete. This is the metaphoric force of the bleak, snowy landscape that dominates the screen; it has no contours, no definitions and no edges, just like Wade's chaotic emotions.

The 'affliction' at the film's core directly relates to Glen. Wade is plagued by a flashback to a childhood memory of himself and Rolfe being forced by Glen, despite harsh weather conditions, to shovel snow. One son pleads to go back inside, at which Glen roars 'What are you, a quitter?'. Later, Rolfe explains the impact of this defining moment and casts doubt on Wade's recollection of it by suggesting that he (Rolfe) was not actually there, an absence that explains how he was never 'afflicted by that man's (Glen's) violence'. Like the children in *Magnolia*, Wade is incapable of burying the father's curse. Once more the expressionless landscape seems to equate with this inability: the snow only temporarily covers something up. Wade, unlike Sam Deeds in *Lone Star*, cannot get beyond his relationship with his father, a traumatic lack of detachment reflected in the film's use of flashback. Whereas the recollections of the past in the latter help to resolve the tensions in the present – and their restorative collusion with the present is indicated neatly by the stylistic elision between the two times, the camera panning seamlessly from past to present[11] – Wade's memories of Glen's brutality are frenzied and uncontainable snatches of jerky and roughly hewn home movies, scars on the psyche as opposed to tempered reflections. These images invade Wade's thoughts; they do not evolve like his fantasies about Twombley, engineered, it seems, by his unconscious to make himself feel important, to give his life some machismo and purpose. Glen denies Wade this power. He taunts his son both in the present and in flashbacks that capture him, on grainy home movie footage, from low angles looming over his children. As Wade becomes more obsessively deranged about the murder of Twombley and fixated upon a conspiracy theory, as his life starts to conclusively fall apart, so, predictably, he comes to resemble Glen. In the end, during father and son's fight to the death, Wade effectively kills himself, disappearing just after he has killed his father. The prelude to this final battle has been another of Glen's taunts. As Margie leaves, taking Jill with her (Wade's inability to stop the cycle of male violence is such that he has thrown his daughter to the ground and made her nose bleed), Glen comes out and, seeing Wade sprawled in the snow, tells him 'I know you ... You're my blood, you're a goddam piece of my heart'. Wade refutes this and Glen tells his son 'I love you', more as a challenge than an admission. After Glen has hit him over the head, Wade pushes his father over, accidentally killing him. As if registering that, in doing away with Glen, he is disposing of himself, Wade feels his dead father's face then, as if blind, runs his hands over his own. Freud asserted that parricide was 'the principal and primal crime of humanity as well as of the individual' (1928: 448). Hollywood has used, particularly in Westerns, either parricide or the father's slaying of his son as a last desperate sign that the two cannot be reconciled. Wade's ritualised execution of Glen (he carries his body to a table and then sets him alight, the family barn becoming a funeral pyre) is as much an expression of unresolved dependency as hatred.

These millennial films depict an often inelegant, desperate litany of abuse. In *Happiness*, the main father figure, Dr Bill Maplewood (Dylan Baker) is a paedophile who rapes two eleven-year-old boys and is eventually abandoned by his family; in *American Beauty*, Lester Burnham (Kevin Spacey) becomes obsessed with his teenage daughter's best friend, although he stops short of having sex with her; in *Magnolia*, as mentioned above, there are various manifestations of child abuse and neglect. These films, from the point of view of the damaged child, offer explicit, angry, intricate critiques of fatherhood. Only in Sam Mendes' *American Beauty* is the father in any way redeemed, and here only through martyrdom as Lester is shot by his ludicrous caricature of a neighbour Frank Fitts (Chris Cooper), a repressed homosexual ex-US Marine who collects Nazi memorabilia. The emphasis in these films is upon the wounded child, blighted by their upbringing and the fathers who have caused irreparable damage. The conglomeration of emotions around this central idea is evident: the damaged child in *Affliction*; the search for the father in *Magnolia*; the abandonment of the father in *Lone Star*, *Happiness* and *American Beauty* (in which the two 'wounded children' Jane Burnham and Ricky Fitts leave the trauma and chaos of their respective families for a new life together).

Happiness and *American Beauty* are thematically very similar. Both focus overtly upon paedophilia and display a pervasive preoccupation with sex in general, in particular alternative sexual practices. But whereas *Happiness* has been frequently condemned for its obscenity and ugliness, *American Beauty* was applauded and festooned with awards. Why? While the latter offers a sanitised, safe image of fatherhood and sexuality, the former does not shy away from perversity and trauma. In a comparison of *Happiness* and *American Beauty*, Casey McKittrick examines the films' relative treatment of paedophilia and the reception they received, looking in particular at the comments and reviews received on the IMDB (International Movie Database) website. A major difference (identified by several of the IMDB correspondents) between the two central fathers is that while Bill's sexual compulsions are identified as pathological (see McKittrick 2001: 9), Lester's are contextualised within the framework of the film's over-arching subject, Lester's midlife 'crisis'. So Lester's desire for Angela sits alongside his rebellion against conformity and his desire to recapture his youth (he quits his job, takes up smoking dope and stands up to his wife Carolyn).

Bill's perversity does not perform an additional narrative function and so remains perverse. He tries (after returning home having committed his second rape) to confide in his bovine wife Trish, telling her as she is half asleep that he is sick. Before sliding into unconsciousness, Trish advises him to 'take some time off'. *American Beauty* treats Lester quite differently. Although Lester harbours illegal desires (Angela is still under-age), *American Beauty* is not 'about' them, for these sexual longings are merely symptoms of – and in some ways a metaphor for – his middle-aged malaise. It is symptomatic of this distancing of Lester's perversity that his sexual fantasies are visually stylised and non-naturalistic. Conversely, the rapes in *Happiness* are signalled by harsher, more severe cuts to black. Lester falls for Angela during a cheerleaders' routine in the break of a school basketball match. From this point on his fantasies feature luscious red rose petals (those of the 'American Beauty' variety) emerging from Angela's opened sweater or camouflaging her naked body. Their colour is suggestive of sexual maturity and adult femininity, but the petals are also vehicles of disavowal. That they both stand for Lester's lust and deny access to Angela's pubescent body means that the audience never has to confront the raw obscenity of the sexual situation. There is one scene when the awkwardness of this disavowal becomes strained, as Lester fantasises about entering an imaginary bathroom as Angela is in the tub. Her body is hidden by petals and Lester inserts his hand into the water, thereby penetrating the layer of petals, an act that insinuates the deflowering of Angela. But here the fantasy is cut short, a judiciously timid edit signalling a moment of self-censorship and metaphorical coitus interruptus. When finally Lester is on the verge of having sex with Angela, it is the sight of her actual body that makes him rethink. She lies on his sofa, willingly unbuttoning her shirt (in much the same way as, in his fantasy, she had willingly undone her sweater), and tells Lester she is still a virgin. This signal of sexual immaturity seems to bring Lester to his senses, prompting him to enshroud Angela's body once more and to offer her a sandwich. He belatedly remembers his fatherly duty towards a girl who is the same age as his daughter.

Just such a boundary between fatherly duty and depravity has been eroded in *Happiness*, and in its amorality there is also a diminished sense of the difference between good and evil. In *American Beauty*, Lester is easily contrasted with Frank Fitts, not only the man who kills Lester (after Lester has sensitively repelled his homosexual advances) but a punitive, repressive father to Ricky. In *Happiness*, the fathers that surround Bill Maplewood are also flawed. The father of Johnny, the first boy Bill rapes, for instance, is worried that his son is displaying homosexual tendencies and muses to Bill, while at a school baseball game, that he might enlist the services of a hooker to help him (he is eleven years old) over his problem. Although after Bill has raped the man's son the same father phones Bill and tells him 'You're a dead man', *Happiness* offers little sense of a normative, safe image of fatherhood. In fact, what *Happiness* constructs is a mosaic of sexual perversity that renders perversity 'normal' – simply by virtue of its prevalence.

In *Happiness*, as in *Magnolia*, the father is the font of all neurosis, although in Todd Solondz's film this is worked through as shared perversity as opposed to shared hysteria. In 'The Sexual Aberrations', Freud offered a polemical paradigm for understanding human sexuality. He imposed a binary opposition between 'normal' and 'abnormal' sexualities. The latter category is large and unwieldy, encompassing everything not included in the former – which, in turn, is intentionally and provocatively limited, as what Freud terms 'normal' is only heterosexual, penetrative sex. What is 'normal' thus invariably centres on the father. Just as Freud set up this contentious polemic, so in *Happiness*, 'normality' is hard to come by. Its narrative encompasses Allen (Philip Seymour Hoffman) who calls women up at random and talks dirty to them as he masturbates, Trish Maplewood who, despite ostensible fecundity and happiness, is frigid and never remembers having had sex with Bill, and Allen's neighbour Christina who has killed and dismembered the apartment block's porter and who confesses on a date with Allen: 'I'm a passionate woman, but I hate sex'. Everyone in *Happiness* is dysfunctional.

The clearest expression of this inversion is the series of three father–son chats between Bill and his eldest son Billy, eleven years old and beginning to think about sex. The instructive conversation between father and child is a longstanding cinematic convention. Unlike comparable exchanges between Atticus and his daughter Scout in *To Kill a Mockingbird*, however, or Ted Kramer's attempt to explain to his son Billy why his mother left home in *Kramer vs. Kramer*, the chats between Bill and Billy Maplewood are traumatic. The source of trauma (for the audience, if not until the final conversation for Billy) is the subject of these father–son chats: masturbation, penis size and paedophilia. The perversity of the scenes is heightened by the contradictory, violent juxtaposition of sexual explicitness and their benign, saccharine tone and visual style. *Happiness* makes extraordinary use, particularly in relation to Bill Maplewood, of the middle-of-the-road, whether this be decor, music, clothes or conventionalised narrative scenarios. It is important that Bill and Billy's chats are ostensibly as 'normal' as possible: they take place

Father and son conclude their chat about masturbation

in the bedroom or on the sofa, Bill's tone (as befits the psychiatrist he is) is honeyed, calm and warm, and neither father nor son talk as if their situation is bizarre.

These graphic conversations forego the comforts of euphemism, so in the first chat Billy begins by asking 'What does "come" mean?'. Bill gives the bed a paternal, welcoming pat and proceeds to give an elaborate clinical explanation of orgasm and ejaculation. Billy confides in his Dad that he has not yet experienced orgasm, to which Bill responds by offering to show him some good masturbatory techniques. Billy declines the offer, they hug, Bill assures his son 'You're normal' and the scene ends with him giving Billy's upper arm a manly punch. The second father–son chat follows a similar pattern, the topic this time being penis size. Billy – like Philip in *A Perfect World* – appears worried about the length of his penis, a schoolfriend having boasted that his was eleven inches long. Bill assures Billy that it is not length but width that matters, as this makes things 'a little more intense'. Billy again fails to grasp the full implications of what he is being told. In both these sequences there is a specific juxtaposition (reminiscent of Luis Buñuel's surreal comedies) between extreme subject matter and an exaggeratedly unexceptional visual style and conversational tone. Also significant is the narrative placement of these sequences: the first takes place very soon after Bill has been masturbating in the back of his car over the image of a pubescent boy adorning the cover of a teen magazine; the second, after Bill has raped Billy's friend Johnny. Both scenes then end with Bill asking Billy an inappropriate, bizarre question that transgresses the boundaries of taste and humour. While the first scene concludes with Billy declining his father's offer to help him masturbate successfully, the second ends with Billy turning down a similar offer from Bill to measure his penis. The cause of our laughter here is twofold: disbelief at a father talking to his pre-pubescent son in these terms and shock at Bill, a paedophile and a psychiatrist, not acknowledging the inappropriateness of such a conversation.

The final father–son exchange comes just after 'Serial Rapist Pervert' has been daubed across the Maplewoods' neat suburban home (again the humour generated by the surreally normal chat is contextualised by coming after a harsh reminder of Bill's true perversity). Billy wants to know if the allegations about his father are true. Bill explains that he 'touched' the boys, 'fondled them' and 'made love' to them. The pattern established by the previous conversations is reversed, as here it is Billy who poses the transgressive question when he asks Bill 'What was it like?' His father is a serial paedophile rapist and the boy wants to know what the sex was like? This, the penultimate scene of the film, builds to a fine crescendo as the conversation about the paedophile rape continues:

BILL: 'It was great'

BILLY: 'Would you do it again?'

BILL: 'Yes'

By this point both are in tears and the words are spoken slowly, deliberately. Then, Billy again takes an already transgressive conversation into more extreme, obscene territory when he asks his Dad 'Would you ever fuck me?' Bill says he would not, and as Billy cries beside him, he explains 'I'd jerk off instead'. His son becomes overwhelmed by uncontrollable sobs. It is here that one has to wonder whether or not the actor playing Billy received counselling for these scenes. During this conversation the two actors are not together in shot (and so the boy might not have been exposed to the full meaning of the exchange), although Billy still has to ask things like 'Would you fuck me?'.

This scene, like the two rape scenes, concludes with a cut to black – the black having been used to signal that sex has taken place. Its use here is even more terrifying as it suggests the father's sexual interest in his own son. This is the logical, perverse end to these father–son dialogues: that the paedophile has consciously repressed his incestuous instincts towards his son and that these criminal longings are finally made explicit. However, despite the extremity of the conclusion to the Bill and Billy dialogues, *Happiness* in its entirety ends with Billy finally masturbating to orgasm while ogling a sunbathing woman and bursting in on his extended family to announce to them 'I came'. Billy is as blighted by his paternal legacy as Wade is in *Affliction*. Like *Affliction*, *Happiness* has no stabilising or normative image of contented, conventional patriarchy. Not only has Billy finally come but this triumph has been preceded by the family dog licking Trish rapaciously on the lips. The omnipresence of perversity is the exorcised father's ultimate bequest.

The issue of sons being inextricably bound to their fathers' guilt recalls Freud and the violence, anxiety and traumatic irresolution of the Oedipus complex. While the sexual revolution and the men's movement implied that we had gone beyond Freud, the tortured, destructive father–child relationships in *Affliction*, *Happiness*, *American Beauty* and *Magnolia* suggest that a return to Freud, as a means of explicating the sexualised power relations between the generations, is inevitable. The son's attempts to rebel against the dominant father or his realisation that he will necessarily become the father he has loathed to destruction are there in all these films, recalling both Freud's writings on the Oedipus complex and 'Totem and Taboo' and the primal struggles of earlier Hollywood movies such as *House of Strangers*, *Broken Lance* or *The Big Country*. Thus these more modern father–son relationships conform to patterns previously established by Hollywood: the pietà of the father holding the dying son or vice versa or a reconciliation at the sick father's bedside. The dominant model of psychoanalysis has also proved to be the dominant (though not exclusive) model of Hollywood's representation of the father. For all its formal newness and radicalism, Anderson's *Magnolia* exemplifies this recapitulation, offering yet further renditions of the Oedipal narrative. As previously identified, the film's story is constructed around the father's omnipotence, in the form of Earl Partridge's extended television empire and his extended dominance of the film's various narrative strands and it is in the characterisation of Earl's son, Frank T. J. Mackey, that the son's imprisonment within an Oedipal relationship is most clearly manifested.

Frank has consciously repressed links to his father, who left home when he was a teenager, by changing his name and maintaining the fiction that he is dead. In Frank's reinvention of himself we see Freud's 'Family Romances', the creation of a fantasy family by the child eager to free himself (or herself) from real familial bonds. However, for Freud the rebellious child's imaginative hostility towards the father in particular is based upon a contradictory impulse to exalt and continue to idealise him. He concocts a 'family romance', which he recounts to his interviewer: a 'true rages to riches story' in which his mother is still alive, but his father is dead, a death that he appears upset by. Mackey runs a highly successful business, tutoring more timid men in how to dominate women and become sexually successful. His programme is entitled 'Seduce and Destroy'. The first time we see Mackey he comes on stage to rapturous applause accompanied by the soundtrack of *2001: A Space Odyssey*, his arms outstretched in a Christ-like pose. Dressed in tight black leather trousers, his hair pulled back into a ponytail, Mackey starts to speak, telling his audience to 'Respect the cock, tame the cunt'. He exemplifies the belief that the 1990s' 'crisis' of masculinity was prompted by fear of female domination and a need for men to reassert control. His language and gestures are crude and extreme, he celebrates and puts on show the male body and he is fixated upon the importance of the penis. This exhibitionism betrays Frank's need to repress the centrality of his own father to how he understands and perceives himself, hence the fictionalisation of his past (and the denial of a far more positive real family history in which he was the dutiful son who cared for his dying mother).

The interview (interspersed throughout the film and intercut with the other narratives) takes place in the interval of a 'Seduce and Destroy' lecture. Frank arrives backstage and strips off down to his underpants. He poses and performs backflips for a bemused and amused Black female interviewer, thrusting out in front of him his bulging briefs and assuring her that he could pick up any 'sweet little honey' on the street in one second. Mackey gets dressed and sits down, legs astride, his chest peeking through an unbuttoned suede shirt. He starts to pant like a dog on heat and is only pacified by his interviewer, in ironically maternal tones, urging him to 'calm down, be a good boy'. Frank is the monster that the men's movement created, desperate to regain the lost 'wild man' within, believing its recapture to be the force that can assuage his dual fear of the father and women. The overvaluation of the penis is inextricably linked to Frank's imaginative destruction of Earl, the awesome father; while emphasising his own possession of the penis, the son's hysterical performances of hyper-masculinity fail to mask the realisation that the power of the phallus eludes him. Because of his estrangement from Earl, Frank only knows his father's omnipotence – his continued possession of phallic power via his television empire, his promiscuity, the hold he has over his own self-image. Frank has not witnessed Earl's physical deterioration to the prostrate dying man he is for the entirety of the film.

Like other traumatised sons in these millennial films, Frank both wants to assert his independence from his father and finds himself being brought back to him. Whereas the search for the father in *Lone Star* was executed via the investigation into the murder of Sheriff Wade, and whereas in *Affliction*, Wade's return to his father is (self-destructively) self-imposed, in *Magnolia*, the search for the father is engineered not by Frank, Earl's actual son, but by his nurse Phil (Philip Seymour Hoffman), a surrogate son, caring for the dying Earl as Frank had cared for his mother. Earl has talked to Phil of his desire to be reconciled with his son before he dies and running alongside Frank Mackey's interview is Phil's telephone call to the 'Seduce and Destroy' offices in search of him. In the film's most moving speech Phil tells one of Frank's minions:

> I know this sounds silly, and I know that I might sound ridiculous, like this is the scene in the movie where the guy's trying to get hold of the long lost son, you know. But this is that scene, this is that scene. And I think they have those scenes in movies because they're true, you know, because they really happen. And you've got to believe me, this is really happening, because see, this is the scene in the movie when you help me out.

The pain of this scene (Earl, barely conscious, is lying in bed in the open-plan room from where Phil is making his call) is accentuated by being intercut specifically with Frank's fabrication of a 'rags to riches' story. The reflexivity of both constructed scenarios – the parallels between the movies and real life, the creation of a clichéd life history – is an appropriate place to conclude this discussion of 1990s' Hollywood fathers: there is little sense any more of what differentiates myth from what the father can really be or can achieve; the fiction is as powerful and thus as valid as the reality. Perhaps the power of the father is best understood through the movies, through the Oedipal scenarios, through the hyperbolic, poetic words of Robert Bly, for otherwise the search for him, the son's individuation from him, his emulation of him should not matter so much because all he is is a frail, muddled old man.

The muddle of the actual father–son relationship is replicated in *Magnolia* as Frank is finally tracked down (through protective layers of minders) and comes to visit Earl, who is by now comatose on liquid morphine. This bedside scenario (a vital reconciliatory generic exchange between father and son) has been replicated in films discussed throughout this book. Here, it functions atypically as Frank does not come to Earl's side immediately remorseful and seeking rapprochement. Instead, he arrives at Earl's side, calls him a 'cock-sucker' and tells him 'I'm not gonna cry for you . . . I hope it hurts'. He is then left to weep and repeat (to a virtual corpse) his hitherto repressed plea to Earl not to go away again. Earl regains consciousness for one last time, looks at Frank and expels his last breath. The final 'scene in the movie' when the dying father is reconciled with his

Frank finally comes to the bedside of his dying father, Earl

son never quite happens, although Frank, the voice-over informs us, does go to visit Earl's second wife, Linda as she is recovering from a suicide attempt and Jimmy is reconciled with Claudia. What is the tone at the end of *Magnolia*? As bedside scenarios multiply, the voice-over maintains the necessity of healing, coming to terms with the past ('We may be through with the past, but the past ain't through with us') and Claudia, for the first time in the film, is shown smiling as Jimmy sits by her bedside talking soothingly to her. Stanley the quiz show boy, faces a bleaker future with his father. He goes into his father, who is still in bed (the repetition of beds here compels us to take these concluding scenes as a trio) and asks 'Dad, will you be nicer to me?' His dad's reply is gruff: 'Go back to bed'. To the end, *Magnolia* remains equivocal about the good father's existence.

This most recent period has offered a pluralisation of the father's image within American cinema, but there remains a fundamental ambivalence towards what to do with the authoritarian, traditional father. Much of 1990s' Hollywood dispenses with him, but ultimately it seems to protest that the traditional father is what we want. Contemporary American cinema acknowledges the validity of alternative paternal models, nevertheless it still feels – often quite urgently – the lack of a strong, conventional father. This conservatism continues to manifest itself in films as diverse as *Far from Heaven*, *Catch Me If You Can* and *Road to Perdition* (all 2002), all of which bind the father's failure to their unconventionality. Although Hollywood's disillusionment with the father is painfully widespread, within these scenarios of loss lie its ultimate masculine melodrama: just out of reach for these flawed fathers lies the perfected image they aspire to but know they cannot match. It is this disparity between the real and the symbolic father that Hollywood finds impossible to resolve, perpetually hoping instead to effect their coalescence.

Notes

1. Other discussions of *Falling Down* include: Jude Davies 'Gender, Ethnicity and Cultural Crisis in *Falling Down* and *Groundhog Day*', *Screen*, 36: 3, Summer 1995: 214–33; Chapter 1 'White Masculinity as Paternity' in Jude Davies and Carol R. Smith 1997; and John Gabriel 'What Do You Do When Minority Means You? *Falling Down* and the Construction of "Whiteness"', *Screen*, 37: 2, Summer 1996: 129–51.

2. For a discussion of working-class fathers in Hollywood in the 1970s see Chapter 3.

3. Cf. Susan K. Opt 'American Frontier Myth and the Flight of Apollo 13', *Film and History*, 26: 1–4, 1996, 40–51.

4. For a discussion of conservatism, contemporary politics and *Apollo 13*, see Martin Walker 'Apollo and Newt', *Sight and Sound*, 5: 9, September 1995, 6–8.

5. For a critical discussion of Moynihan, see Ruth Feldstein 'Pathologies and Mystiques: Revising Motherhood and Liberalism in the 1960s', in *Motherhood in Black and White: Race and Sex in American Liberalism, 1930–1965*, Ithaca, NY and London: Cornell University Press, 2000. For a discussion that argues that Moynihan has been widely misinterpreted, see Sara McLanahan and Gary Sandefur *Growing up with a Single Parent: What Hurts, What Helps*, Cambridge MA: Harvard University Press, 1994: p. 7.

6. The authors introduced and then reproduced the Moynihan report in its entirety. The page numbers here refer to the page numbers of the original (the first digits) and those of the later edition (the second digits).

7. See Michael E. Connor 'Some Parenting Attitudes of Young Black Fathers', in Robert A. Lewis and Robert E. Salt (eds), *Men in Families*, London and Beverly Hills, CA: Sage, 1986: 159–68.

8. For a discussion of the film's soundtrack, see Ian Garwood 'Must You Remember This? Orchestrating the "Standard" Pop Song in *Sleepless in Seattle*', *Screen*, 41: 3, Autumn 2000: 282–98.

9. This is a reversal of the pattern established in earlier melodramas, in which the heroine frequently ends up marrying not her great love but a make-do admirer whom she does not love but who can offer her security. This pattern is discussed in Chapter 1.

10. See John Gibbs *Mise-en-Scène: Film Style and Interpretation* (London: Wallflower Press, 2002): 27–38 for a discussion of this element of *Lone Star*.

11. Ibid.

Bibliography

Abramovitch, Henry (1997) 'Images of the "Father" in Psychology and Religion', in Michael E. Lamb (ed.), *The Role of the Father in Child Development*, 3rd edn, New York: John Wiley: 19–32.

Adler, Alfred (1931) *What Life Could Mean to You*, Oxford: Oneworld Publications, [1938].

Agee, James (1958) *Agee on Film*, New York: McDowell, Oblensky Inc.

Anshen, Ruth Nanda (1949) 'The Family in Transition', in Ruth Nanda Anshen (ed.), *The Family: Its Function and Destiny*, New York: Harper.

Aronson, Amy and Kimmel, Michael (2001) 'The Saviors and the Saved: Masculine Redemption in Contemporary Films', in Peter Lehman (ed.), *Masculinity: Bodies, Movies, Culture*, New York and London: Routledge: 43–50.

Babington, Bruce and Evans, Peter (1990) 'All That Heaven Allowed: Another Look at Sirkian Irony', *Movie*, 34/35, Winter: 48–58.

Baker, M. Joyce (1980) *Images of Women in Film: The War Years, 1941–1945*, Ann Arbor, Michigan: University Microfilms International.

Beebe, John (ed.) (1989) *Aspects of the Masculine*, London: Ark Paperbacks.

Behlmer, Rudy (ed.) (1972) *Memo from David O. Selznick*, New York: Viking Press.

Bell, Daniel (1960) *The End of Ideology: On the Exhaustion of Political Ideas in the Fifties*, Glencoe, IL: Free Press of Glencoe.

Benedek, Therese (1949) 'The Emotional Structure of the Family', in Ruth Nanda Anshen (ed.), *The Family: Its Function and Destiny*, New York: Harper.

—(1970) 'Fatherhood and Providing', in E. James Anthony and Therese Benedek (eds), *Parenthood: Its Psychology and Psychopathology*, Boston, MA: Little, Brown.

Benedict, Ruth (1949) 'The Family: Genus Americanum', in Ruth Nanda Anshen (ed.), *The Family: Its Function and Destiny*, New York: Harper.

Benjamin, Jessica (1988) *The Bonds of Love: Psychoanalysis, Feminism and the Problem of Domination*, London: Virago.

Bergstrom, Janet (1979) 'Alternation, Segmentation, Hypnosis. Interview with Raymond Bellour', *Camera Obscura*, 3–4, pp. 71–103.

'Berkeley Men's Center Manifesto' (1974) in Joseph H. Pleck and Jack Sawyer (eds), *Men and Masculinity*, Englewood Cliffs, NJ: Prentice-Hall: 173–4.

Bernard, J. (1981) 'The Good Provider Role: Its Rise and Fall', *American Psychologist*, 36: 1–12.

Biddulph, Steve (1998) *Manhood: An Action Plan for Saving Men's Lives*, Stroud, Glos.: Hawthorn Press.

Biskind, Peter (1974) 'Rebel without a Cause: Nicholas Ray in the Fifties', *Film Quarterly*, 28: 1, Fall, 32–8 .

—(1983) *Seeing Is Believing: How Hollywood Taught Us to Stop Worrying and Love the Fifties*, New York: Pantheon Books.

Bitsch, Charles (1985) 'Interview with Nicholas Ray', in Jim Hillier (ed.), *Cahiers du Cinéma, the 1950s: Neo-realism, Hollywood, New Wave*, London: Routledge and Kegan Paul.

Blankenhorn, David (1996) *Fatherless America: Confronting Our Most Urgent Social Problem*, New York and London: HarperCollins.

Bly, Robert (1990) *Iron John: A Book about Men*, Shaftsbury: Element Books.

Bowie, Malcolm (1991) *Lacan*, London: HarperCollins.

Bowlby, John (1969) *Attachment and Loss, Volume I: Attachment*, London: Hogarth Press.

Bradshaw, Jan (1982) 'Now What Are They up to? Men in the "Men's Movement"!', in Scarlet Friedman and Elizabeth Sarah (eds), *On the Problem of Men: Two Feminist Conferences*, London: Women's Press.

Brenton, Myron (1967) *The American Male*, London: Allen and Unwin.

Britton, Andrew (1976) 'American Cinema in the '70s: *Jaws*', *Movie*, 23: 27–32.

—(1986) 'Blissing Out: The Politics of Reaganite Entertainment', *Movie*, 31/32: 1–42.

Bronstein, Phyllis (1988) 'Marital and Parenting Roles in Transition: An Overview', in Phyllis Bronstein and Carolyn Pape Cowan (eds), *Fatherhood Today: Men's Changing Role in the Family*, New York: John Wiley: 3–10.

Brooks, Gary R. and Gilbert, Lucia Albino (1995) 'Men in Families: Old Constraints, New Possibilities', in Ronald F. Levant and William S. Pollack (eds), *A New Psychology of Men*, New York: Basic Books.

Burgess, Adrienne (1997) *Fatherhood Reclaimed: The Making of the Modern Father*, London: Vermillion.

Byron, Stuart and Rubin, Martin L. (1972) 'Elia Kazan Interview', *Movie*, 19, Winter: 6–13.

Campbell, Beatrix (1996) 'Good Riddance to the Patriarch', *Guardian*, 15 April.

Caputi, Jane E. (1978) '*Jaws* as Patriarchal Myth', *Journal of Popular Film and Television*, 6: 4: 305–26.

Chambers, Deborah (2001) *Representing the Family*, London: Sage.

Chapman, Rowena and Rutherford, Jonathan (1988) 'The Forward March of Men Halted', in Rowena Chapman and Jonathan Rutherford (eds), *Male Order: Unwrapping Masculinity*, London: Lawrence and Wishart: 9–18.

Chenoune, Farid (1993) *A History of Men's Fashion*, Paris: Flammarion.

Chodorow, Helen (1978) *The Reproduction of Mothering: Psychoanalysis and the Sociology of Gender*, Berkeley and Los Angeles: University of California Press.

Clare, Anthony (2000) *On Men: Masculinity in Crisis*, London: Chatto and Windus.

Clinebell, Charlotte Holt (1977) 'Happiness Is a Warm Father: Some Characteristics and

Implications of Liberated Fathering', in Edward V. Stein (ed.), *Fathering: Fact or Fable?*, Nashville, TN: Abingdon, 160–90.

Clover, Carol (1993) *'Falling Down* and the Rise of the Average White Male', in Pam Cook and Philip Dodd (eds), *Women and Film: A Sight and Sound Reader*, London: Scarlett Press: 138–47.

Cohan, Steven (1997) *Masked Men: Masculinity and the Movies in the Fifties*, Bloomington and Indianapolis: Indiana University Press.

Cohan, Steven and Hark, Ina Rae (1993) 'Introduction', in Cohan and Hark (eds), *Screening the Male: Exploring Masculinities in Hollywood Cinema*, London and New York: Routledge: 1–8.

Cohen, Theodore F. (1993) 'What Do Fathers Provide? Reconsidering the Economic and Nurturing Dimensions of Men as Parents', in Jane C. Hood (ed.), *Men, Work and Family*, Newbury Park, CA: Sage: 1–22.

Connor, Michael E, (1986) 'Some Parenting Attitudes of Young Black Fathers', in Robert A. Lewis and Robert E. Salt (eds), *Men in Families*, London and Beverly Hills, CA: Sage: 159–68.

Considine, David (1985) *The Cinema of Adolescence*, Jefferson, NC and London: McFarland.

Cook, David A. (2000) *Lost Illusions: American Cinema in the Shadow of Watergate and Vietnam, 1970–1979*, New York: Charles Scribner's Sons.

Cook, Pam (1998) 'Duplicity in *Mildred Pierce*', in E. Ann Kaplan (ed.), *Women in Film Noir* (new edn), London: BFI.

Coontz, Stephanie (1997) *The Way We Really Are: Coming to Terms with America's Changing Families*, New York: Basic Books.

—(2000) *The Way We Never Were: American Families and the Nostalgia Trap* (new edn), New York: Basic Books.

Coote, Anna and Campbell, Beatrix (1982) *Sweet Freedom: The Struggle for Women's Liberation*, London: Pan Books.

Corneau, Guy (1991) *Absent Fathers, Lost Sons: The Search for Masculine Identity* (trans. Larry Shouldice), Boston, MA and London: Shambhala.

Coward, Rosalind (1999) *Sacred Cows: Is Feminism Relevant to the New Millennium?*, London: HarperCollins.

Coyne, Michael (1998) *The Crowded Prairie: American National Identity in the Hollywood Western*, London and New York: I. B. Tauris.

Craik, Jennifer (1993) *The Face of Fashion: Cultural Studies in Fashion*, London and New York: Routledge.

Creed, Barbara (1987) 'From Here to Modernity: Feminism and Postmodernism', *Screen*, 28: 2, Spring: 47–67.

—(1998) 'Film and Psychoanalysis', in John Hill and Pamela Church Gibson (eds), *The Oxford Guide to Film Studies*, Oxford: Oxford University Press: 77–90.

Davies, Jude (1995) 'Gender, Ethnicity and Cultural Crisis in *Falling Down* and *Groundhog Day*,' *Screen*, 36: 3, Summer: 214–33.

Davies, Jude and Smith, Carol R. (1997) *Gender, Ethnicity and Sexuality in Contemporary American Cinema*, Edinburgh: Keele University Press.

de Beauvoir, Simone (1949) *The Second Sex*, London: Picador [1988].

Demos, John (1986) *Past, Present and Personal: The Family and the Life Course of American History*, New York and Oxford: Oxford University Press.

Dench, Geoff (1994) *The Frog Prince and the Problem of Men*, London: Neanderthal Books.

Deutsch, Helene (1968) *Selected Problems of Adolescence: With Special Emphasis on Group Formation*, London: Hogarth Press.

Diawara, Manthia (1993) 'Black American Cinema: The New Realism', in Manthia Diawara (ed.), *Black American Cinema*, New York and London: Routledge: 3–25.

Doane, Mary Ann (1987) *The Desire to Desire: The Woman's Film of the 1940s*, London: Macmillan

Donnelly, Denise and Finkelhor, David (1992) 'Does Equality in Custody Arrangement Improve the Parent–Child Relationship?', *Journal of Marriage and the Family*, November, 54: 4: 837–45.

Dreisinger, Baz (2000) 'The Queen in Shining Armor: Safe Eroticism and the Gay Friend', *Journal of Popular Film and Television*, Spring: 2–11.

Dye, Phil (1998) *The Father Lode: A New Look at Becoming and Being a Dad*, St Leonards, NSW: Allen and Unwin.

Dyer, Richard (1985) 'Male Sexuality in the Media', in Andy Metcalf and Martin Humphries (eds), *The Sexuality of Men*, London: Pluto Press: 28–43.

Dyson, Michael Eric (1992) 'Out of the Ghetto', *Sight and Sound*, 2: 6, June: 18–21.

Edwards, Tim (1997) *Men in the Mirror: Men's Fashion, Masculinity and Consumer Society*, London: Cassell.

Ehrenreich, Barbara (1983) *The Hearts of Men: American Dreams and the Flight from Commitment*, New York: Pluto Press.

Elliot, Anthony (1994) *Psychoanalytic Theory: An Introduction*, Oxford: Blackwell.

Erikson, Erik (1950) *Childhood and Society*, Harmondsworth: Penguin [1965].

Evening Standard (1949) Review of *The Search*, 27 October.

Evening Star (1951) Review of *Teresa*, 19 April.

Faludi, Susan (1991) *Backlash: The Undeclared War against Women*, London: Chatto and Windus.

—(1999) *Stiffed: The Betrayal of the Modern Man*, London: Chatto and Windus.

Fassbinder, Rainer Werner (1975) 'Fassbinder on Sirk', *Film Comment*, November–December, 11: 6: 22–4.

Finch, Janet and Morgan, David (1991) 'Marriage in the 1980s: A New Sense of Realism?', in Dave Clark (ed.), *Marriage, Domestic Life and Social Change: Writings for Jacqueline Burgoyne (1944–1988)*, London and New York: Routledge: 55–80.

Flügel, J. C. (1930) *The Psychology of Clothes*, London: Hogarth Press.

Foucault, Michel (1984) *The History of Sexuality: An Introduction*, Harmondsworth: Peregrine Books [1976].

Franks, Helen (1984) *Goodbye Tarzan: Men after Feminism*, London: Allen and Unwin.

Freud, Sigmund (1905a) 'Fragment of an Analysis of a Case of Hysteria ('Dora')', *Case Histories I: Penguin Freud Library, vol. 8*, ed. Angela Richards, London: Penguin [1990].

—(1905b) 'Transformations of Puberty', *Three Essays on the Theory of Sexuality, On Sexuality: Penguin Freud Library, vol. 7*, ed. Angela Richards, London: Penguin [1991].

—(1905c) 'The Sexual Aberrations', *Three Essays on the Theory of Sexuality, On Sexuality: Penguin Freud Library, vol. 7*, ed. Angela Richards, London: Penguin [1991].

—(1909a) 'Family Romances', *On Sexuality: Penguin Freud Library, vol. 7*, ed. Angela Richards, London: Penguin [1991].

—(1909b) 'Notes upon a Case of Obsessional Neurosis (The 'Rat Man')', *Case Histories II: Penguin Freud Library, vol. 9*, ed. Angela Richards, London: Penguin [1991].

—(1913) 'Totem and Taboo: Some Points of Agreement between the Mental Lives of Savages and Neurotics', *The Origins of Religion: Penguin Freud Library, vol. 13*, ed. Albert Dickson, London: Penguin [1990].

—(1914) 'On Narcissism: An Introduction', *On Metapsychology: Penguin Freud Library, vol. 11*, ed. Angela Richards, London: Penguin [1991].

—(1918) 'From the History of an Infantile Neurosis (The 'Wolf Man')', *Case Histories II: Penguin Freud Library, vol. 9*, ed. Angela Richards, London: Penguin [1991].

—(1919) 'The Uncanny', *Art and Literature: Penguin Freud Library, vol. 14*, ed. Albert Dickson, London: Penguin [1990].

—(1921) 'Group Psychology', *Civilization, Society and Religion: Penguin Freud Library, vol. 12*, ed. Albert Dickson, London: Penguin [1991].

—(1923) 'The Ego and the Id', *On Metapsychology: Penguin Freud Library, vol. 11*, ed. Angela Richards, London: Penguin [1991].

—(1924) 'The Dissolution of the Oedipus Complex', *On Sexuality: Penguin Freud Library, vol. 7*, ed. Angela Richards, London: Penguin [1991].

—(1928) 'Dostoevsky and Parricide', *Art and Literature: Penguin Freud Library, vol. 14*, ed. Albert Dickson, London: Penguin [1990].

—(1930) 'Civilisation and Its Discontents', *Civilization, Society and Religion: Penguin Freud Library, vol. 12*, ed. Albert Dickson, London: Penguin [1991].

—(1931) 'Female Sexuality', *On Sexuality: Penguin Freud Library, vol. 7*, ed. Angela Richards, London: Penguin [1991].

—(1939) 'Moses and Monotheism', *The Origins of Religion: Penguin Freud Library, vol. 13*, ed. Albert Dickson, London: Penguin [1990].

Friedan, Betty (1963) *The Feminine Mystique*, London: Penguin [1992].

—(1981) *The Second Stage*, Cambridge MA: Harvard University Press [1998].

Fuchs, Cynthia J. (1993) 'The Buddy Politic', in Steven Cohan and Ina Rae Hark (eds), *Screening the Male: Exploring Masculinities in Hollywood Cinema*, London and New York: Routledge: 194–210.

Fukuyama, Francis (1999a) 'A Man's Place', *Sunday Telegraph*, 20 June.

—(1999b) *The Great Disruption: Human Nature and the Reconstitution of Social Order*, London: Profile Books.

Fuqua, Joy van (1996) ' "Can You Feel It, Joe?": Male Melodrama and the Feeling Man', *The Velvet Light Trap*, 35, Autumn: 28–38.

Fussell, Paul (1989) *Wartime*, Oxford: Oxford University Press.

Gallafent, Edward (1990) 'The Adventures of Rafe Hunnicut', *Movie*, 34/35, Winter: 70–81.

Garber, Marjorie (1993) *Vested Interests: Cross-Dressing and Cultural Anxiety*, London: Penguin.

Garwood, Ian (2000) 'Must You Remember This? Orchestrating the "Standard" Pop Song in *Sleepless in Seattle*', *Screen*, 41: 3: Autumn: 282–98.

George, Victor and Wilding, Paul (1972) *Motherless Families*, London and Boston, MA: Routledge and Kegan Paul.

Gibbs, John (2002) *Mise-en-Scène: Film Style and Interpretation*, London: Wallflower Press: 27–38.

Gilmore, David G. (1990) *Manhood in the Making: Cultural Concepts of Masculinity*, New Haven, CT and London: Yale University Press.

Glancy, H. Mark (2000) 'Dreaming of Christmas: Hollywood and the Second World War', *Christmas at the Movies: Images of Christmas in American, British and European Cinema*, London and New York: I. B. Tauris: 59–76.

Grant, Barry Keith (1998) 'Rich and Strange: The Yuppie Horror Film', in Steve Neale and Murray Smith (eds), *Contemporary Hollywood Cinema*, London and New York: Routledge.

Green, Maureen (1976) *Fathering*, New York: McGraw-Hill.

Green, Philip (1998) *Cracks in the Pedestal: Ideology and Gender in Hollywood*, Amherst: University of Massachusetts Press.

Green, Richard (1987) *The 'Sissy Boy Syndrome' and the Development of Homosexuality*, New Haven, CT and London: Yale University Press.

Greenfield, Barbara (1985) 'The Archetypal Masculine: Its Manifestation in Myth, and its Significance for Women', *The Father: Contemporary Jungian Perspectives*, London: Free Association Books.

Greer, Germaine (1970) *The Female Eunuch*, London: Flamingo [1993].

Griswold, Robert L. (1993) *Fatherhood in America: A History*, New York: Basic Books.

Hacker, Helen (1957) 'The New Burdens of Masculinity', *Marriage and Family Living*, 19: 3, August: 227–33.

Hall, Calvin S. and Nordby, Vernon J. (1973) *A Primer in Jungian Psychology*, New York: Mentor.

Halliday, Jon (ed.) (1997) *Sirk on Sirk: Conversations with Jon Halliday*, London: Faber.

Hammond, Mike (1993) 'The Historical and Hysterical: Melodrama, War and Masculinity in *Dead Poets Society*', in Pat Kirkham and Janet Thumim (eds), *You Tarzan: Masculinity, Movies and Men*, London: Lawrence and Wishart, 52–64.

Handler Spitz, Ellen (1992) 'Carpe diem, carpe mortem: Reflections on *Dead Poets Society*', *Post Script*, 11: 3, Summer: 19–31.

Harris, Kathleen Mullan and Morgan, S. Philip (1991) 'Fathers, Sons and Daughters: Differential Paternal Involvement in Parenting', *Journal of Marriage and Family*, 53: 3, August: 531–44.

Harvey, John (1995) *Men in Black*, London: Reaktion.

Harwood, Sarah (1997) *Family Fictions: Representations of the Family in 1980s Hollywood Cinema*, London: Macmillan.

Herald (1949) Review of *The Search* by Paul Holt.

Hill, Reuben (1945) 'The Returning Father and His Family', *Marriage and Family Living*, Spring: 31–4 .

Hillier, Jim (1972) '*East of Eden*', *Movie*, 19, Winter: 22–3.

Hoile, Christopher (1984) 'The Uncanny and the Fairy Tale in Kubrick's *The Shining*', *Film/Literature Quarterly*, 12: 1: 5–12.

Hollander, Anne (1994) *Sex and Suits: The Evolution of Modern Dress*, New York and Tokyo: Kodansha International.

Holman, Richard L. (1997) 'The Everyman Movie, Circa 1991', *Journal of Popular Film and Television*, 25: 1, Spring: 21–30.

Holmlund, Chris (1993) 'Masculinity as Multiple Masquerade: The "Mature" Stallone and the Stallone Clone', in Steve Cohan and Ina Rae Hark (eds), *Screening the Male: Exploring Masculinities in Hollywood Cinema*, London and New York: Routledge: 213–29.

hooks, bell (1992) *Black Looks: Race and Representation*, London: Turnaround.

Horkheimer, Max (1949) 'Authoritarianism and the Family Today', in Ruth Nanda Anshen (ed.), *The Family: Its Function and Destiny*, New York: Harper.

Horrocks, Roger (1995) *Male Myths and Icons: Masculinity in Popular Culture*, London: Macmillan.

Jameson, Fredric (1990) 'Reification and Utopia in Mass Culture (1979)', *Signatures of the Visible*, London and New York: Routledge: 9–34.

Jeffords, Susan (1993a) 'The Big Switch: Hollywood Masculinity in the Nineties', in Jim Collins, Hilary Radner and Ava Preacher Collins (eds), *Film Theory Goes to the Movies*, London: Routledge: 196–208.

—(1993b) 'Can Masculinity be Terminated?', in Steven Cohan and Ina Rae Hark (eds), *Screening the Male: Exploring Masculinities in Hollywood Cinema*, London and New York: Routledge: 245–62.

—(1994) *Hard Bodies: Hollywood Masculinity in the Reagan Era*, New Brunswick, NJ: Rutgers University Press.

Jermyn, Deborah (1996) 'Rereading the Bitches from Hell: A Feminist Appropriation of the Female Psychopath', *Screen*, 37: 3, Autumn: 251–67.

Jung, C. G. (1949) 'The Significance of the Father in the Destiny of the Individual', in John Beebe (ed.), *Aspects of the Masculine*, London: Ark Paperbacks [1993].

Kael, Pauline (1986) 'The Current Cinema: Brutes', *Village Voice*, 31, 26 May: 114–17.

Kaplan, E. Ann (1992) *Motherhood and Representation: The Mother in Popular Culture and Melodrama*, London and New York: Routledge.

Keeler, Greg (1981) '*The Shining*: Ted Kramer Has a Nightmare', *Journal of Popular Film and Television*, 8: 4, Winter: 2–8.

Kehr, Dave (1983) 'The New Male Melodrama', *American Film*, 8: 6, April: 43–7.

Keller, James R. (2002) *Queer (Un)Friendy Film and Television*, Jefferson, NC: McFarland and Co.

Kinsey, Alfred C., Pomeroy, Wardell B. and Martin, Clyde E. (1948) *Sexual Behavior in the Human Male*, Philadelphia, PA and London: W. B. Saunders.

Kitses, Jim (1969) *Horizons West*, London: BFI.

Klein, Melanie (1997) *The Psychoanalysis of Children*, London: Vintage [1932].

Krämer, Peter (1998) 'Would You Take Your Child to See This Film? The Cultural and Social Work of the Family-Adventure Movie', in Steve Neale and Murray Smith (eds), *Contemporary Hollywood Cinema*, London and New York: Routledge: 294–311.

LaRossa, Ralph, Gordon, Betty Anne, Wilson, Ronald Jay, Bairan, Annette and Jaret, Charles (1991) 'The Fluctuating Image of the 20th Century American Father', *Journal of Marriage and the Family*, 53, November: 987–97.

Lacan, Jacques (1977) 'On a Question Preliminary to Any Possible Treatment of Psychosis', in *Ecrits: A Selection*, London and New York: Routledge [1955–6].

—(1993) 'The Highway and the Signifier "Being a Father" ', in *The Psychoses: The Seminar of Jacques Lacan, Book III, 1955–1956*, ed. Jacques-Alain Miller, London and New York: Routledge [1956].

—(1977) 'The Signification of the Phallus', in *Ecrits: A Selection*, ed. Alan Sheridan, London and New York: Routledge [1958].

Ladies' Home Journal (1958a) 'What Makes a Child Aggressive?', by Benjamin Spock, April, 48.

Ladies' Home Journal (1958b) 'Should Mothers of Young Children Work?', November.

Laing, R. D. (1971) *The Politics of the Family and Other Essays*, London: Tavistock.

Lamb, Michael E. (1986) 'The Changing Role of Fathers', in Michael E. Lamb (ed.), *The Father's Role: Applied Perspectives*, New York: John Wiley.

Laqueur, Thomas W. (1992) 'The Facts of Fatherhood', in Barrie Thorne and Marilyn Yalom (eds), *Rethinking the Family: Some Feminist Questions*, revised edn, Boston, MA: Northeastern University Press: 155–75.

Lasch, Christopher (1977) *Haven in a Heartless World: The Family Besieged*, New York: Basic Books.

Lawrence, Amy (1991) *Echo and Narcissus: Women's Voices in Classical Hollywood Cinema*, Berkeley and Los Angeles: University of California Press.

Lebeau, Vicky (1992) 'Daddy's Cinema: Femininity and Mass Spectatorship', *Screen*, 33: 3, Autumn: 244–58.

Lehman, Peter (1993) *Running Scared*, Philadelphia: Temple University Press.

—(1998) 'In an Imperfect World, Men with Small Penises Are Unforgiven', *Men and Masculinities*, 1: 2, October: 123–37.

Lightning, Robert K. (1999) 'A Domestic Trilogy', *CineAction!*, 50, September: 32–42.

Lundberg, Ferdinand and Farnham, Marynia (1947) *Modern Woman: The Lost Sex*, New York and London: Harper.

Lyndon, Neil (1992) *No More Sex War: The Failures of Feminism*, London: Sinclair- Stevenson.

Lynes, Russell (1953) *A Surfeit of Honey*, New York: Harper.

Lynn, David B. (1974) *The Father: His Role in Child Development*, Belmont, CA: Wadsworth.

Lyons, Donald (1995) 'Family Values', *Film Comment*, 31: 1, January: 78–81.

McAdoo, John Lewis (1988) 'Changing Perspectives on the Role of the Black Father', in Phyllis Bronstein and Carolyn Pape Cowan (eds), *Fatherhood Today: Men's Changing Role in the Family*, New York: John Wiley: 79–92.

McCall's (1946a) 'Now You Have a Man' by Marynia Farnham, February 1946: 18, 126, 128, 130, 133.

McCall's (1946b) 'Is Your Child Your Own?' by Jacques Bacal and Louise Sloane, August 1946: 25, 50, 52.

McCall's (1946c) 'Marriage Is Like This' by Jonathan Daniels, October 1946: 18–20, 64, 66, 68, 70.

McCall's (1961) 'Hold Your Man and Stay Human' by George Starbuck Galbraith, May 1961: 118–19, 168.

McKittrick, Casey (2001) ' "I Laughed and Cringed at the Same Time": Shaping Pedophilic Discourse around *American Beauty* and *Happiness*', *The Velvet Light Trap*, 47, Spring: 3–14.

McLanahan, Sara and Sandefor, Gary (1994) *Growing Up with a Single Parent: What Hurts, What Helps*, Cambridge, MA: Harvard University Press.

Maltby, Richard (2003) *Hollywood Cinema* (2nd edn), Oxford: Blackwell.

Marsiglio, William (1995) 'Fatherhood Scholarship: An Overview and Agenda for the Future', in William Marsiglio (ed.), *Fatherhood: Contemporary Theory, Research and Social Policy*, Sage: London: 1–20.

Martin, Andy (2001) 'Sins of the Fathers', *Tate Magazine*, Summer: 38–41.

Massood, Paula J. (2003) *Black City Cinema: African American Urban Experiences in Film*, Philadelphia, PA: Temple University Press.

Matthews, Nicole (2000) *Comic Politics: Gender in Hollywood Comedy after the New Right*, Manchester: Manchester University Press.

May, Martha (1997) 'From Cads to Dads: The Unwed Father in American Films', *Journal of Popular Film and Television*, 25: 1, Spring: 2–8.

Mellen, Joan (1977) *Big Bad Wolves: Masculinity in the American Film*, London: Elm Tree Books.

Middleton, Peter (1992) *The Inward Gaze: Masculinity and Subjectivity in Modern Culture*, London and New York: Routledge.

Millett, Kate (1970) *Sexual Politics*, London: Virago, 1983.

Mitchell, Juliet (1971) *Woman's Estate*, Harmondsworth: Penguin.

—(1974) *Psychoanalysis and Feminism*, London: Penguin, 1982.

Modleski, Tania (1988) 'Three Men and Baby M', *Camera Obscura*, 17: 68–81.

Moi, Toril (1985) *Sexual/Textual Politics: Feminist Literary Theory*, London and New York: Routledge.

Monaco, Paul (2001) *The Sixties: 1960–1969*, New York: Charles Scribner's Sons.

Mulvey, Laura (1975) 'Visual Pleasure and Narrative Cinema', in Bill Nichols (ed.), *Movies and Methods II*, Berkeley: University of California Press [1985], 303–15.

—(1977–8) 'Notes on Sirk and Melodrama', reprinted in Christine Gledhill (ed.), *Home Is Where the Heart Is: Studies in Melodrama and the Woman's Film*, London: BFI [1987].

Naremore, James (1993) *The Films of Vincente Minnelli*, Cambridge: Cambridge University Press.

Neale, Steve (1983) 'Masculinity as Spectacle', in Steven Cohan and Ina Rae Hark (eds), (1993) 'Introduction', eds Cohan and Hark *Screening the Male: Exploring Masculinities in Hollywood Cinema*, London and New York: Routledge: 9–20.

—(1992) 'The Big Romance or Something Wild?: Romantic Comedy Today', *Screen*, 33: 3, Autumn: 284–98.

Neve, Brian (1992) *Films and Politics in America: A Social Tradition*, London and New York: Routledge.

New York Times (1968) Barbara and Peter Wyden, 'Growing up Straight: The Father's Role', *Magazine*, 26 May: 69–72.

—(1969) John Leo 'Irrational Pattern Discerned in Student Revolts', 14 February: 24.

—(1971a) Jane E. Brody 'Homosexuality: Parents Aren't Always to Blame', 10 February: 48.

—(1971b) Ann Richardson Roiphe 'The Family Is out of Fashion', *Magazine*, 15 August: 10, 29–30, 34,

—(1972) 'Hippie Family Life: Rooted in the Past?', 12 January: 325.

—(1973a) Enid Nemy 'Dropout Wives – Their Number Is Growing', 16 February: 44.

—(1973b) 'Divorce Fathers Seeking Reforms', 29 July.

—(1974a) C. Christian Beels 'Whatever Happened to Father?', *Magazine*, 25 August:
    10–11, 52–6, 64, 68.
—(1974b) Lisa Hammel 'A Scholarly "Home-Maker-Father" Studies Others Like Himself',
    14 December: 18.
—(1975a) Perry A. Shoemaker 'A Father's Lament', 15 June: 17.
—(1975b) Herbert Hendin 'Homosexuality and the Family', 22 August: 31.
—(1976) Judith Weinraub 'Behind School Success Is a Father Who Cares', 20 September
    (Family Style section).
—(1977) 'Carter Says Plans of Government Should Keep Families Together', 19 June.
—(1979) Betty Friedan 'Feminism Takes a New Turn', *Magazine*, 18 November:
    40, 92–102, 106.
—(1983) 'Briefing' by James F. Clarity and Phil Gailey, Section B, 16 June: 12.
—(1984a) 'Father's Day 1984, A Time of Activism', Section I, 16 June: 48.
—(1984b) Brock Brower 'A Dad Diminished', Section VI, 26 August: 58.
—(1986) 'The Selling of Father's Day', 14 June: 33–4.
Nichols, Bill (1989) 'Sons at the Brink of Manhood', *East–West Film Journal*, 4: 1,
    December: 27–43.
O'Brien, Margaret (1982) 'Becoming a Lone Father: Differential Patterns and Experiences',
    in Lorna McKee and Margaret O'Brien (eds), *The Father Figure*, London and New York:
    Tavistock.
—(1995) 'Changing Places? Men and Women in Oliver Stone's Vietnam Films', in Pat
    Kirkham and Janey Thumim (eds), *Me Jane: Masculinity, Movies and Women*, London:
    Lawrence and Wishart: 263–72.
O'Brien, Thomas W. (1981) 'Perspectives: Love and Death in the American Movie', *Journal
    of Popular Film and Television*, 9: 2, Summer: 91–3.
Opt, Susan K. (1996) 'American Frontier Myth and the Flight of Apollo 13', *Film and
    History*, 26: 1–4. 40–51.
Parsons, Talcott (1949) 'The Social Structure of the Family', in Ruth Nanda Anshen (ed.),
    The Family: Its Function and Destiny, New York: Harper.
—(1955) 'The American Family: Its Relations to Personality and Social Structure', in Talcott
    Parsons and Robert F. Bales (eds), *Family, Socialization and Interaction Process*, New
    York: Free Press.
Perkins, V. F. (1972a) 'The Cinema of Nicholas Ray', in Ian Cameron (ed.), *The Movie
    Reader*, London: November Books.
—(1972b) *Film as Film: Understanding and Judging Movies*, Harmondsworth: Penguin.
Pleck, Joseph H. (1988) 'American Fathering in Historical Perspective', in Michael S. Kimmel
    (ed.), *Changing Men: New Directions in Research on Men and Masculinity*, London and
    New York: Sage.
Pleck, Elizabeth H. and Pleck, Joseph H. (1997) 'Fatherhood Ideals in the United States:

Historical Dimensions', Michael Lamb (ed.), *The Role of the Father in Child Development* (3rd edn), New York: John Wiley.

Prince, Stephen (2000) *A New Pot of Gold: Hollywood under the Electronic Rainbow, 1980–1989*, New York: Charles Scribner's Sons.

Pumphrey, Martin (1996) 'Why Do Cowboys Wear Hats in the Bath?: Style Politics For the Older Man', in Ian Cameron and Douglas Pye (eds), *The Movie Book of the Western*, London: Studio Vista.

Quart, Leonard (1998) 'These Are Very Uncertain Times: An Interview with Paul Schrader', *Cinéaste*, 24: 1: 12–14.

Quart, Leonard and Barbara (1981) '*Kramer vs. Kramer*', *Cinéaste*, 10: 2, Spring, 37–9.

Quart, Leonard and Auster, Albert (2002) *American Film and Society since 1945* (3rd edn), Westport, CT: Praegar.

Rainwater, Lee and Yancey, William L. (eds) (1967) *The Moynihan Report and the Politics of Controversy*, Cambridge, MA: MIT Press.

Rapoport, Rhona, Rapoport, Robert N., Strelitz, Ziona, Kew, Stephen (eds) (1977) *Fathers, Mothers and Others: Towards New Alliances*, London and Henley: Routledge and Kegan Paul.

Rattigan, Neil and McManus, Thomas P. (1992) 'Fathers, Sons and Brothers: Patriarchy and Guilt in 1980s' American Cinema', *Journal of Popular Film and Television*, 20: 1, Spring: 15–23.

Ray, Robert B. (1985) *A Certain Tendency of the Hollywood Cinema, 1930–1980*, Princeton, NJ: Princeton University Press.

Reeves, Grace (1945) 'The New Family in the Postwar World', *Marriage and Family Living*, 7: 4, Autumn: 73–6; 89–90.

Robertson, James C. (2000) 'Unspeakable Acts: the BBFC and *Cape Fear*', *Journal of Popular British Cinema*, 3: 69–76.

Rosenbaum, Jonathan (1973) 'Circle of Pain: The Cinema of Nicholas Ray', *Sight and Sound*, 42: 4, Autumn: 217–21.

Ross, Steven J. (ed.) (2002) *Movies and American Society*, Oxford: Blackwell: 336–7.

Rotundo, E. Anthony (1987) 'Patriarchs and Participants: A Historical Perspective on Fatherhood in the United States', in Michael Kaufman (ed.), *Beyond Patriarchy: Essays by Men on Pleasure, Power and Change*, Oxford and New York: Oxford University Press.

Roudinesco, Elizabeth (1997) *Jacques Lacan*, Cambridge: Polity Press.

Rowbotham, Sheila (1973) *Women's Consciousness, Man's World*, Harmondsworth: Penguin.

—(1999) *A Century of Women: The History of Women in Britain and the United States*, London: Penguin.

Rubey, Dan (1976) '*Jaws*: The Jaws in the Mirror', *Jump Cut*, 10/11, Summer: 20–3.

Rutherford, Jonathan (1988) 'Who's That Man?', in Rowena Chapman and Jonathan Rutherford (eds), *Male Order: Unwrapping Masculinity*, London: Lawrence and Wishart: 21–67.

—(1992) *Men's Silences*, London: Routledge.

Saturday Review (1951) 14 April.

Sayers, Janet (1992) *Mothering Psychoanalysis: Helene Deutsch, Karen Horney, Anna Freud, Melanie Klein*, London: Penguin.

Schatz, Thomas (1997) *Boom and Bust: American Cinema in the 1940s*, Berkeley and Los Angeles: University of California Press.

Segal, Lynn (1997) *Slow Motion: Changing Masculinities, Changing Men* (rev. edn), London: Virago.

—(1999) *Why Feminism?*, Cambridge: Polity.

Seidler, Victor J. (1985) 'Fear and Intimacy', in Andy Metcalf and Martin Humphries (eds), *The Sexuality of Men*, London: Pluto Press: 150–80.

—(1988) 'Fathering, Authority and Masculinity', in Jonathan Rutherford and Rowena Chapman (eds), *Male Order: Unwrapping Masculinity*, London: Lawrence and Wishart: 272–302.

Seltzer, Judith A. (1991) 'Relationships between Fathers and Children Who Live Apart: The Father's Role after Separation', *Journal of Marriage and the Family*, 53: 1, February: 79–101.

Siegel, David and McGehee, Scott (1994) 'Hysteria', *Sight and Sound*, 4: 10, October: 33.

Silverman, Kaja (1988) *The Acoustic Mirror: The Female Voice in Psychoanalysis and Cinema*, Bloomington and Indianapolis: Indiana University Press.

Silverstein, Louise B. (1996) 'Fathering Is a Feminist Issue', *Psychology of Women Quarterly*, 20: 3–37.

Simpson, Mark (1994) 'When Did You Last See Your Father?', *Independent*, 18 March.

Singleton, John (1991) 'John Singleton, director of *Boyz n the Hood*, talks with Peter Brunette', *Sight and Sound*, 1: 4, April: 13.

Snyder, Stephen (1982) 'Family Life and Leisure Culture in *The Shining*', *Film Criticism*, 7: 1, Fall: 4–13.

Sobchack, Vivian (1996) 'Bringing It All Back Home: Family Economy and Generic Exchange', in Barry Keith Grant (ed.), *The Dread of Difference: Gender and the Horror Film*, Austin: University of Texas Press: 143–63.

Solanas, Valerie (1967) *SCUM Manifesto*, Edinburgh and San Francisco: AK Press [1996].

Spender, Dale (1985) *For the Record: The Making and Meaning of Feminist Knowledge*, London: Women's Press.

Spock, Dr Benjamin (1958) *Baby and Child Care* (new and enlarged edn), London: Bodley Head.

Star (1949) Review of *The Search*, 25 October.

Stearns, Peter N. (1990) *Be a Man! Males in Modern Society* (2nd edn), New York and London: Holmes and Meier.

Steinem, Gloria (1974) 'The Myth of Masculine Mystique', in Joseph H. Pleck and Jack Sawyer (eds), *Men and Masculinity*, NJ: Prentice-Hall, 134–9.

Sternberg, Claudia (1994) 'Real-life References in Four Fred Zinnemann Films', *Film Criticism*, 18–19: 3–1, Spring–Fall: 108–26.

Stone, John (2000) '*Platoon* and *Wall Street* as Modern Morality Plays', *Journal of Popular Film and Television*, 28: 2, Summer: 80–7.

Strecker, Edward A. (1946) *Their Mothers' Sons: The Psychiatrist Examines an American Problem*, Philadelphia, PA and New York: J. B. Libbincott Company.

Sunday Times, The (1949) Review by Dilys Powell of *The Search*, 6 November.

Sutton, Jo and Friedman, Scarlet (1982) 'Fatherhood: Bringing It All Back Home', in Scarlet Friedman and Elizabeth Sarah (eds), *On the Problem of Men: Two Feminist Conferences*, London: Women's Press: 117–27.

Tacey, David J. (1997) *Remaking Men: Jung, Spirituality and Social Change*, London: Routledge.

Tasker, Yvonne (1993a) 'Dumb Movies for Dumb People: Masculinity, the Body, and the Voice in Contemporary Action Cinema', in Steven Cohan and Ina Rae Hark (eds), *Screening the Male: Exploring Masculinities in Hollywood Cinema*, London and New York: Routledge: 230–44.

—(1993b) *Spectacular Bodies: Gender, Genre and the Action Cinema*, London and New York: Routledge.

Thomas, David (1993) *Not Guilty: In Defence of the Modern Man*, London: Weidenfeld and Nicolson.

Thomas, Deborah (2000) *Beyond Genre: Melodrama, Comedy and Romance in Hollywood Films*, Dumfriesshire: Cameron and Hollis.

Thompson, Dorothy 'Is Morality "Normal"?', *Ladies' Home Journal*, March 1958: 11, 20, 169.

Torry, Robert (1993) 'Therapeutic Narrative: *The Wild Bunch, Jaws*, and Vietnam', *The Velvet Light Trap*, 31, Spring: 27–38.

Traube, Elizabeth G. (1992) *Dreaming Identities: Class, Gender and Generation in 1980s Hollywood Movies*, San Francisco and Oxford: Westview Press.

Tuttle, William M. Jr (1993) *'Daddy's Gone to War': The Second World War in the Lives of Children*, Oxford and New York: Oxford University Press.

Verhaeghe, Paul (2000) 'The Collapse of the Function of the Father and its Effect on Gender Roles', in Renata Saleci (ed.), *Sexuation*, Durham, NC and London: Duke University Press: 131–54.

Volling, Brenda L. and Belsky, Jay (1991) 'Multiple Determinants of Father Involvement During Infancy in Dual-earner and Single-earner Families', *Journal of Marriage and the Family*, 53: 2, May: 461–74.

Walcott, Rinaldo (1992) 'Keeping the Black Phallus Erect: Gender and the Construction of Black Masculinity in *Boyz N T H*', *CineAction!*, 30, Winter: 68–74.

Walker, Martin (1995) 'Apollo and Newt', *Sight and Sound*, 5: 9, September: 6–8.

Walker, Michael (1982) 'Ophuls in Hollywood', *Movie* 29/30, Summer: 39–60.

—(1991) 'Robert Mulligan', *Film Dope*, 46, March: 4–6.

—(2004) '*Home from the Hill*', *Cinéaction!*, 63: 22–34.

Wallace, Michele (1992) '*Boyz N the Hood* and *Jungle Fever*', in Gina Dent (ed.), *Black Popular Culture (A Project by Michelle Wallace)*, Seattle, WA: Bay Press: 123–31.

Walsh, Andrea S. (1984) *Women's Film and Female Experience, 1940–1950*, New York: Praeger.

Weiss, Julie (1992) 'Feminist Film Theory and Women's History: *Mildred Pierce* and the Twentieth Century', *Film and History*, 22: 3, September: 75–87.

Wexman, Virginia Wright (1993) *Creating the Couple: Love, Marriage, and Hollywood Performance*, Princeton, NJ: Princeton University Press.

Williams, Linda (1988) 'Feminist Film Theory: *Mildred Pierce* and the Second World War', in Deirdre Pribham (ed.), *Female Spectators: Looking at Film and Television*, London and New York: Verso: 12–30.

Williams, Tony (1996) 'Trying to Survive on the Darker Side: 1980s' Family Horror', in Barry Keith Grant (ed.), *The Dread of Difference: Gender and the Horror Film*, Austin: University of Texas Press: 164–80.

Wilson, Sloan (1955) *The Man in the Gray Flannel Suit*, New York: Four Walls Eight Windows, 2002.

Winnicott, D. W. (1964) *The Child, the Family and the Outside World*, Harmondsworth: Penguin.

Wolfenstein, Martha and Leites, Nathan (1950) *Movies: A Psychological Study*, Glencoe, IL: The Free Press.

Wood, Robin (1979) 'The American Family Comedy: From *Meet Me in St. Louis* to *The Texas Chainsaw Massacre*', *Wide Angle*, 3: 2: 5–11.

—(1985) 'An Introduction to the American Horror Film', in Bill Nichols (ed.), *Movies and Methods II*, Berkeley and Los Angeles: University of California Press: 195–219.

—(1986) *Hollywood from Vietnam to Reagan*, New York: Columbia University Press.

Wylie, Philip (1942) *Generation of Vipers*, New York and Toronto: Farrar and Rinehart Inc.

Yalom, Marilyn (2001) *A History of the Wife*, London: Pandora.

Zinnemann, Frederic (1992) *Fred Zinnemann, An Autobiography*, London: Bloomsbury.

Index

Page numbers in **bold** indicate detailed analysis

List of Illustrations

Since You Went Away, © Vanguard Films; *The Best Years of Our Lives*, Samuel Goldwyn Inc.; *Tomorrow Is Forever*, International Pictures/RKO Radio Pictures; *House of Strangers*, Twentieth Century-Fox Film Corporation; *The Search*, Loew's International Corporation/Metro-Goldwyn-Mayer/Praesens-Film AG; *Teresa*, Loew's Incorporated/Metro-Goldwyn-Mayer; *There's Always Tomorrow*, Universal Pictures Company/Universal-International; *Bigger than Life*, © Twentieth Century-Fox Film Corporation; *Rebel Without a Cause*, Warner Bros.; *Giant*, © Giant Productions; *The Halliday Brand*, Collier Young Associates; *The Big Country*, © Anthony Productions/© Worldwide Productions; *Home from the Hill*, © Loew's Incorporated/© Sol C. Siegel Productions; *Cape Fear*, © Melville Productions/© Talbot Productions; *To Kill a Mockingbird*, Pakula-Mulligan Productions/Brentwood Productions/Universal Pictures; *The Courtship of Eddie's Father*, Euterpe Productions/Venice Productions/Metro-Goldwyn-Mayer; *Jaws*, © Universal Pictures; *The Great Santini*, Bing Crosby Productions/Orion Pictures Corporation; *Kramer vs. Kramer*, Stanley Jaffe Productions/Columbia Pictures Corporation; *Ordinary People*, Wildwood Enterprises/Paramount Pictures Corporation; *Fatal Attraction*, Paramount Pictures Corporation; *Die Hard*, Twentieth Century Fox Film Corporation/Gordon Company/Silver Pictures; *Rain Man*, United Artists/Guber-Peters Company; *Three Men and a Baby*, Touchstone Pictures/Silver Screen Partners III/Interscope Communications; *Gladiator*, © DreamWorks LLC/© Universal Studios; *Boyz n the Hood*, Both Inc./Columbia Pictures Corporation; *Sleepless in Seattle*, TriStar Pictures; *The Object of My Affection*, Twentieth Century-Fox Film Corporation; *Happiness*, © Livingston Pictures, Inc.; *Magnolia*, © New Line Productions, Inc.